Heidegger's Ontology of Events

Heidegger's Ontology of Events

JAMES BAHOH

EDINBURGH
University Press

Edinburgh University Press is one of the leading university presses in the UK. We publish academic books and journals in our selected subject areas across the humanities and social sciences, combining cutting-edge scholarship with high editorial and production values to produce academic works of lasting importance. For more information visit our website: edinburghuniversitypress.com

© James Bahoh, 2020, 2021

Edinburgh University Press Ltd
The Tun – Holyrood Road
12(2f) Jackson's Entry
Edinburgh EH8 8PJ

First published in hardback by Edinburgh University Press 2020

Typeset in 11/13 Adobe Garamond by
Servis Filmsetting Ltd, Stockport, Cheshire, and
printed and bound by CPI Group (UK) Ltd,
Croydon, CR0 4YY

A CIP record for this book is available from the British Library

ISBN 978 1 4744 4368 5 (hardback)
ISBN 978 1 4744 4369 2 (paperback)
ISBN 978 1 4744 4370 8 (webready PDF)
ISBN 978 1 4744 4371 5 (epub)

The right of James Bahoh to be identified as the author of this work has been asserted in accordance with the Copyright, Designs and Patents Act 1988, and the Copyright and Related Rights Regulations 2003 (SI No. 2498).

Contents

Acknowledgements

I'd like to acknowledge several people, communities, and institutions that have supported my work on this project. My interest in Heidegger's ontology of events goes back to a set of graduate seminars led by William Richardson that I attended at Boston College several years ago. From that time until his health declined too far, he offered warm support and sharp feedback on my efforts to make sense of this subject, efforts that would eventually lead to this book. I am deeply appreciative of his mentorship over those years. Fred Evans and Andrew Mitchell both served as readers for my dissertation, and I am thankful for their careful notes on earlier versions of a great deal of material that, after reshaping and rewriting and expanding, ultimately made its way into this book. In 2013, I attended the Collegium Phaenomenologicum on *Heidegger: Gelassenheit, Ethical Life, Ereignis, 1933–1946*. I learned a great deal from the speakers and other participants, and I am grateful for having had the chance to test out some ideas in this book during our conversations there. I thank Jeff McCurry, Director of Duquesne University's Simon Silverman Phenomenology Center, for his support, particularly during my tenure as a scholar-in-residence at the SSPC during academic year 2016–17. I am also grateful to Richard Rojcewicz for making available to me early draft translations of some of Heidegger's relevant work. During 2017–18, the VolkswagenStiftung, in partnership with the Andrew W. Mellon Foundation, provided me a postdoctoral fellowship to work at the University of Bonn's International Centre for Philosophy NRW (IZPH). Though my focus there was on a subsequent project, I was able to wrap up many loose ends in this book during that time. Markus Gabriel and Jens Rometsch warmly welcomed me and supported my research at the IZPH. Their hospitality and intellectual support, as well as the vibrant intellectual culture of the IZPH, made for an extraordinarily stimulating and productive time. This book benefited greatly from conversations during a week-long summer symposium on the philosophy of events that I organised at the IZPH in 2018 (funded largely by the VolkswagenStiftung). I thank the participants, my co-organisers – Sergio Genovesi and Marta Cassina – and the keynote speakers – Markus Gabriel, Anna Longo, Sean Bowden, James Williams, and Jean-Luc Nancy – for their contributions. Over the past few years, more people than I can list have provided an additional helping hand or an open ear as I've tried to work out the ideas in this book. In addition to those already mentioned, I'd like to thank Christopher Heijnen, Marco Altamirano, Travis Holloway, Tianna Lind, Boram Jeong, Martin Krahn, Dave Mesing, Jacob Greenstine, Anton Friedrich Koch, Christopher Merwin, Mehdi Parsa, Joan Thompson, Ron Polansky, and James Swindal. I am grateful to my colleagues here at Marquette University for their camaraderie and stimulating philosophical conversation. I would like to express special appreciation to two people. Dan Selcer, my dissertation director at Duquesne University, the greatest of all possible mentors, has given unwavering support and friendship, not to mention an inclination towards early modern philosophy that has led to my conviction that Heidegger utterly failed to understand that era. Sıla Özkara has been a near-constant interlocutor on all things philosophical (and musical, and artistic, and . . . and . . .). She has sustained me in more ways than I can express.

I'd also like to thank Carol Macdonald and Kirsty Woods at Edinburgh University Press for their support and guidance during the publication process. Finally, an earlier version of material that has gone into Chapters 4 and 5 was published as 'Heidegger's Differential Concept of Truth in *Beiträge*' in *Gatherings: The Heidegger Circle Annual* 4 (2014), 39–69. I thank the editor, Richard Polt, for permission to use that material here.

Frequently Cited Works

Citations referencing both original and translated editions of a text indicate page numbers in the following format: original/translation. With the exception of *Sein und Zeit* and irregular volumes in English translation, my endnotes citing Heidegger refer to his texts according to their *Gesamtausgabe* number.

All 'GA' designations shall refer to Heidegger's *Gesamtausgabe* volumes.

EB   Polt, Richard, *The Emergency of Being: On Heidegger's Contributions to Philosophy* (Ithaca, NY: Cornell University Press, 2006).

EH   Capobianco, Richard, *Engaging Heidegger* (Toronto: University of Toronto Press, 2011).

FE   Sheehan, Thomas, 'Facticity and *Ereignis*', in *Interpreting Heidegger*, ed. Daniel Dahlstrom (Cambridge: Cambridge University Press, 2011), 42–68.

GA65 Heidegger, Martin, *Beiträge zur Philosophie (Vom Ereignis)* (Frankfurt am Main: Klostermann, 2003), GA65. English: *Contributions to Philosophy: Of the Event*, trans. Richard Rojcewicz and Daniela Vallega-Neu (Bloomington: Indiana University Press, 2012). I abbreviate this text as GA65 in endnote citations and as *Beiträge* in in-text mentions.

GA71 Heidegger, Martin, *Das Ereignis* (Frankfurt am Main: Klostermann, 2009). English: *The Event*, trans. Richard Rojcewicz (Bloomington: Indiana University Press, 2013).

HCP Vallega-Neu, Daniela, *Heidegger's Contributions to Philosophy* (Bloomington: Indiana University Press, 2003).

HWB Capobianco, Richard, *Heidegger's Way of Being* (Toronto: University of Toronto Press, 2014).

SZ Heidegger, Martin, *Sein und Zeit* (Tübingen: Max Niemeyer Verlag, 2006). English: *Being and Time*, trans. John Macquarrie and Edward Robinson (New York: Harper and Row, 1962).

WW Heidegger, Martin, 'Vom Wesen der Wahrheit', in [GA9] *Wegmarken* (Frankfurt am Main: Klostermann, 1976), 177–202. English: 'On the Essence of Truth', trans. John Sallis, in *Pathmarks*, ed. William McNeill (Cambridge: Cambridge University Press, 1998), 136–54.

Throughout, within quotations I shall use square brackets for my own insertions or to include original language terms. Parentheses within quotations are those present in the source text.

For my wonderful mother, Arlette

Introduction

The task of ontology is to explain being itself and to make the being of beings stand out in full relief.[1]

1 Thematic focus

A major problem in contemporary ontology is explaining the nature of events and their place in reality. Traditionally, events have most often been assigned a secondary or derivative status with respect to substances or subjects, which are taken to underpin them. An event, for instance, is understood to be an alteration in the attributes of a substance. Linguistically, this framework is replicated in our grammar: a sentence begins with a subject and a predicate, while an event is represented as a change in predicate ('tyranny' was predicated of Athens one day, then 'democracy' another). However, over the past century an increasing number of philosophers have argued that no ontology can be sufficient without assigning events a primary, fundamental, or ontologically distinctive status in their own right (for example, Donald Davidson and Alain Badiou).[2]

At least three varieties of such events should be distinguished. In the first, events are occurrences or things that happen within the regular functioning of a world: a leaf falling to the ground, a decision made, an action performed, a meeting between friends. A second variety of events are irregular transformative ruptures or shifts inaugurating new horizons of possibility. These events might occur in social, political, artistic, linguistic, psychological, conceptual, amorous, literary, and so on, contexts, producing genuinely new forms of thinking, acting, and existing. A third variety of event can be found in the work of philosophers like Martin Heidegger and Gilles Deleuze, who argued that no ontology can be sufficient without assigning *being* an evental nature itself.[3] In other words, they make 'event' the most fundamental term of their ontologies. In this picture, the ruptural form of an event comes to play a central part in the ontological structures of time, ground, truth, language, history, community, the psyche, and so on.

If in one manner or another events are ontologically prior to subjects, the cognitive apparatuses of representation, well-constituted beings populating worlds, and the quasi-stable identities of such beings, then an important consequence has been argued to follow: these sorts of things must be generated by ontological processes involved in events, not the other way around as our ordinary experience might suggest. Many of the central texts arguing for such a view are exceptionally difficult to interpret, and this is often a result of the way their arguments undermine the technical vocabulary of the tradition and its grammar built around subject predication. As a consequence, the reasons for taking such a position are often glossed over in relevant scholarship, which opts for either uncritically adopting the terminology of ontologies of events or dismissing them on the grounds of their conceptual obscurity.

In the following chapters, I aim to help remedy this by developing a critical reconstruction of the ontology of events proposed by Heidegger. Along with Whitehead and Bergson, Heidegger initiated what could be called the 'evental turn' of the twentieth century. His work, though far from the last word on the matter, has both fundamentally shaped the terms of the subsequent conversation and been treated in only fragmentary and often inaccurate ways. Because of what I take to be a poor state of scholarship on his concept of event, several of the advances made by Heidegger – and even the positions his work maintained – have remained the subject of rather flailing debate or have gone altogether unrecognised. One result is that the philosophical consonances and dissonances of his work with that of more recent theorists of events like Deleuze or Badiou have been poorly understood.

Nonetheless, Heidegger's use of the concept of event has had a widespread impact (though mapping it will not be my goal). The main points have of course been in so-called 'Continental' philosophy, beginning especially in the post-phenomenological discourse of 1960s France, which often melded elements of Heideggerian philosophy with structuralism and varieties of formalism generated by early-century French philosophy of science, mathematics, psychoanalysis, and Marxist thought. However, many of Heidegger's most detailed texts dealing with the concept of event were not published during his life and have been trickling out only over the past few decades as released by the editors of his *Gesamtausgabe*. This means both that earlier engagements with Heidegger's concept of event had only partial pictures of it and that more recent work engaging his concept in new and interesting ways continues to emerge.

Generally speaking, philosophies of events often share a commitment to the idea that a logic of change, difference, or rupture is ontologically prior to – and often generative of – the logic of identity or stability we find in the world of well-constituted things. Heidegger's concept of event is a major point of reference for this type of position. In 1966, with Heidegger in the air, Derrida employed the concept of event when describing a transformative disruption in the structural foundations of metaphysics: the 'event' of the decentralisation of structure.[4] His later concept of event is prefigured by that of *différance*, which in 1968 he situated (in part) vis à vis Heidegger's notions of difference and event.[5] Other work by Derrida argues that things like concepts and democracies bear an inherent structural openness to a heterogenous 'other'. This mirrors Heidegger's notion of an historical event, according to which metaphysics bears an openness to its non-metaphysical ontological ground claimed to make possible 'another beginning' for thought. In 1968, Deleuze's landmark *Différence et répétition* appeared and included a substantial, but mostly incognito, engagement with Heidegger's philosophy of difference, which was tightly linked to his concept of event. *Différence et répétition* works out its own philosophy of difference and understands events to be fundamental and transformative differential processes. Badiou cites Heidegger as a major programmatic influence (for example in his 1988 *L'être et l'événément*), though he also moves substantially beyond Heidegger, for instance by integrating the ontology of events and set theory. More recently, 'the event' has become a dominant topic in Heidegger scholarship itself. In North American scholarship, for example, it marks a point of disagreement between Richard Capobianco, who uses it as part of an argument that Heideggerian thought supports a certain type of realism, and Thomas Sheehan, who uses it to argue for a version of Heidegger that can be called anti-realist. In Germany, it remains a central topic in the Heidegger crowd, and beyond this sub-field its impact is growing. Claude Romano has developed a new phenomenology of events that engages Heidegger but expands the concept to transformative ruptures in the lives of individual human beings.[6] Catherine Malabou uses the concept extensively in her work on change.[7] Krzysztof Ziarek has incorporated it into his work on the philosophy of language.[8] And in the growing set of philosophers who reject the Analytic-Continental divide as an artefact of the twentieth century, several have found Heidegger's notion of event to be of importance. Markus Gabriel, for instance, engages it in his development of 'transcendental ontology' and Paul Livingston connects it with the work of Alan Turing and Kurt Gödel as part of a discussion of what he calls the 'metaformal dynamics' of sense, truth, and time.[9] This overview could be greatly expanded, but I hope it begins to give a sense of the plurality of ways that Heidegger's concept of event has had an impact in philosophy over the past fifty or sixty years.

My focus in this book is on Heidegger's account of being (*Sein*) – or rather what he comes to call 'beyng' ('Seyn') – as event ('als Ereignis') or as the event ('das Ereignis') in relation to a set of key topics: history, truth, difference, ground, and time-space. I discuss the distinction between his terms 'being' and 'beyng' later, but beginning now I use them in a way that preserves consistency with their technical senses. The reader who is unfamiliar with this distinction should not worry much about it until Chapter 4. As a general rule, in instances where the distinction is not essential to some point that I make, I use the more conventional 'being'.

In 1927 Heidegger published *Sein und Zeit*, the central text of his early thought. There, he argued that Western philosophy requires drastic revision insofar as its tradition of metaphysics has distorted, or even eclipsed, the problem of the nature of being.[10] The issue is not simply that metaphysics has got it wrong and needs to get its accounts straight. Rather, when it comes to the question of being, metaphysics is a flawed mode of enquiry. In Heidegger's definition metaphysics represents reality as a totalisable collection of objectively present beings (for instance, God, the self, and the world) and enquires into the nature of those beings *as beings*, that is, into their 'Seiendheit' or 'beingness'. It is unable to account for pre-representational, temporally distended features of things that are irreducible to substantial identities persisting through time. More detrimentally, metaphysics is unable to account for the ontological ground making *Seiendheit* possible and, as an extension of this, it is unable to account sufficiently for its own ground. Heidegger recasts this ground in terms of the being (*Sein*) of beings, which is distinguished from their *Seiendheit*. To be sure, this is not to posit being as a transcendent ground separable from the ontic characteristics of beings, but to understand it as the finite, concrete, and temporally dynamic structure of beings that enables those very characteristics. In this view, doing ontology in the framework of metaphysics fatally distorts our accounts of being and, in turn, of the nature and relations of beings. *Sein und Zeit* works to fix this by problematising the foundations of metaphysics and recasting the project of ontology as a whole – a project Heidegger thus calls 'fundamental ontology'. There, he develops the phenomenological, existential analysis of Dasein as the method for doing this. Because the language and conceptual framework of metaphysics are deeply inscribed into our intellectual traditions, the ways we understand the nature of ourselves and the world, and our everyday practices, fundamental ontology entails a *Destruktion* (destruction or deconstruction) of metaphysics and its history with respect to both its theoretical and existential manifestations.[11] Overall, this enterprise is geared towards developing a better understanding of being.

In the early 1930s, Heidegger becomes convinced that *Sein und Zeit* did not accomplish a sufficient overhaul of ontology. This is not a disavowal: he thinks it did establish necessary and far-reaching transformations of philosophy and, importantly, of the existential state of the person who *does* philosophy. In fact, following his argument, the conceptual and methodological position from which his later work critiques *Sein und Zeit* can be properly accessed only by working through the ontological problematic developed in 1927.[12] Yet, for reasons I address later, he argues that *Sein und Zeit* remains metaphysical. Beginning in the 1930s, he aims to remedy this by rethinking being in terms of *Ereignis*.[13] Being – or now beyng – is described as evental in nature. To be sure, Heidegger's claim is not that beyng is like an occurrence within time (as in the first variety of events indicated above), and for this reason he warns against translating 'Ereignis' as 'event'. Nonetheless, I will argue that 'event' is in fact the best translation to use. To understand beyng as event will rather be something like understanding it as a differential logic according to which anything that can occur can occur at all. Working out the nature of beyng as event and unpacking the philosophical implications of this new position become central to Heidegger's post-*Kehre* project. As he notes in the margin of 'Brief über den "Humanismus"' in his personal copy of the 1949 first edition of *Wegmarken*: 'For "event" [Ereignis] has been the guiding word of my thinking since 1936'.[14]

I will argue that there are in fact two main senses of 'event' for Heidegger. One is of a transformative rupture in the history of Western thought that opens the possibility for new, non-metaphysical approaches to our theoretical and practical endeavours. This involves a re-appropriation of the ontological ground from which human existence has become alienated: beyng. The other sense is that indicated a moment ago pertaining to the nature of beyng itself. Beyng, Heidegger argues, is evental. The second sense will be my focus, though I will argue that understanding Heidegger's approach to it and its stakes requires first addressing elements of the first, which I do in Chapter 2.

For Heidegger, the heart of beyng as event is difference. It is well known that the ontological difference between being and beings plays a major role in his early work. Yet, in the 1930s he problematises the ontological difference by enquiring into the ground that enables it to be determined at all. This forms a key moment in his methodological path, one by which he generates a new, more fundamental concept of difference. I suggest that this difference can be called 'pure' in the sense that it is ontologically prior to determinate beings, not derived from any *a posteriori* relations between them. It forms the ground making worlds of beings possible (so in this sense it can be called transcendental), but it in no way constitutes a metaphysically transcendent domain of reality. Heidegger does not clarify the details very well, but I argue that the structure of the event can be worked out in terms of the logic of this difference, which I maintain is expressed in or underwrites the ontology presented in his most important work on the event, *Beiträge zur Philosophie (Vom Ereignis)* (written 1936–8, published 1989). In this picture beyng as event is a self-differentiation of pure difference, together with what I call a 'logic of determinateness' thereby generated. The logic of determinateness composes the ontological structure of the Da expressed in the term 'Da-sein', that is, the logic of the world. Truth, ground, and time-space are interrelated registers in which the logic of the event is elaborated in the Da. The decisive role of difference here is often neglected in the scholarship, resulting in readings that in my mind incorrectly attribute to beyng a character of originary oneness (cf. *hen*) or identity and, consequently, a theological content. On this count, Heidegger is much closer to someone like Deleuze who argues that being or the event is difference and that difference differentiates by way of 'smaller' immanent events.

Heidegger's work dealing with the concept of event is complex and ranges through several texts, including a variety made public during his life and a distinctive cluster of private works written during the 1930s and early 1940s.[15] The latter are often referred to as the 'seynsgeschichtliche Denken' ('beyng-historical thinking') treatises or the private manuscripts and they did not begin to appear in publication until the 1989 release of *Beiträge*, several years after the author's death.[16] *Beiträge* forms the core of these private manuscripts, which I believe offer Heidegger's most developed account of the event despite their fractured composition. Later texts like 'Zeit und Sein' (1962) had the advantage of being polished for a public audience, but they offer a far narrower scope on the concept and, I argue, treat it at a more derivative level. Consequently, my focus will be on *Beiträge* (I go into greater detail about my reasons for this in Chapter 1). I also include fairly lengthy engagements with *Sein und Zeit* (1927) and 'Vom Wesen der Wahrheit' (lecture 1930, print 1943), which provide important context, and I touch on a number of other texts, including *Das Ereignis* (written 1941–2, published 2009), which offers an important bit of elaboration on the connection between event and difference.

The timeline on which the private manuscripts have been released has had a significant impact on the treatment of Heidegger's concept of event by other philosophers. As noted, the work the manuscripts contain was simply unavailable when many of the important texts by 'post-Heideggerian' authors dealing with the theory of events were written. This together with the inconsistent state of scholarship on those manuscripts has meant that many of the ideas they present have only recently begun to be integrated into the broader discourse on events. By extension, the philosophical encounter between Heidegger's fuller ontology of events and the ontologies presented by many more recent thinkers is still in a relatively nascent stage. I have a particular interest in Deleuze, so I will occasionally highlight points of intersection with his work throughout this book.

The compositional character of Heidegger's private manuscripts makes them extraordinarily difficult to work on. I am greatly indebted to several interpreters who – to use Richardson's image – have left a trail of blood on the rocks that I have tried to follow. Yet, it is my view that most scholarship on these texts has botched the ontology presented in them. I think that several of the moves Heidegger made have gone largely unrecognised or unexplored in a systematic manner and this has led to flawed interpretations of his texts.

One of the results is a misconception of the proper philosophical grounds on which Heidegger's later work should be put into contact with other philosophers. Gavin Rae, for example, offers one of the very few book-length comparative analyses of the relation between Heidegger and Deleuze. Rae's approach is correct in its guiding assertion that a comparison of the two on any topic must be grounded in an analysis of their ontologies. But for all his book's merits, he frames the Heidegger-Deleuze encounter by defining ontology as the project 'trying to answer the question: what does it mean to say that something *is*?'[17] This is plausible when it comes to Heidegger's early philosophy, but it overlooks one of his project's defining arguments in the late 1930s, early 1940s, and beyond. Namely, according to Heidegger the attempt to break out of metaphysics by thinking beyng as event in *Beiträge* requires that we do not conceptualise beyng in terms of the being of beings. Ontology must render an account of beyng in beyng's own terms: 'beyng can no longer be thought on the basis of beings but must be inventively thought from itself'.[18] Without registering this move, any account of Heidegger's ontology of events remains fundamentally misconstrued and, given the centrality of the event to his later work, consequently misrepresents his overall project. The proper ground for comparing and evaluating Heidegger's ontology in relation to those of other philosophers is simply not attained.

I will argue that a similar problem arises when it comes to making sense of many of the unusual terms introduced in Heidegger's post-*Kehre* philosophy. Given the fundamentality of the concept of event, clarifying these more derivative terms requires grounding them in the formulation of the problematic of the event. Failure in this regard results, as Spinoza said, in thinking of conclusions as if divorced from their premises.

At this point, I'd like to make a brief remark on an important issue: the recent publication of Heidegger's *Black Notebooks*, some of which were written contemporaneously with *Beiträge* and the related private manuscripts. The release of the *Black Notebooks* has generated a great deal of scholarship on the issue of Heidegger's anti-Semitism and involvement with the Nazi Party. They contain both new instances of overtly anti-Semitic comments by Heidegger and examples in which he tied anti-Semitic views to certain of his philosophical concepts. Many of the specifics of these comments have been well documented and there are a number of analyses available (for example, the volumes, *Heidegger's* Black Notebooks: *Responses to Anti-Semitism*, edited by Andrew Mitchell and Peter Trawny and *Reading Heidegger's* Black Notebooks *1931–1941*, edited by Ingo Farin and Jeff Malpas). Such facts about Heidegger are deeply disturbing but are by no means new news. They have been addressed extensively by commentators over the years (for example, Tom Rockmore's 1992 *On Heidegger's Nazism and Philosophy*). Nonetheless, the main issue revisited after the publication of the *Black Notebooks* is the extent of his anti-Semitism and whether it ought to disqualify Heidegger's work from contemporary philosophical discourse. Within that larger frame of this issue, some have speculated more narrowly that since Heidegger developed his concept of an historical event especially during the 1930s, it must really be nothing more than a philosophical concept for the intended cultural transformation of the German people by the Nazis and, eventually, the (catastrophic) other beginning for history intended by a German victory in the war.

In the introduction to their volume, Mitchell and Trawny highlight two problematic, but common, approaches to the issue of Heidegger's anti-Semitism. The first approach attempts to exonerate Heidegger either because of the quantitatively small number of anti-Semitic remarks relative to his vast corpus or by distinguishing between Heidegger the man and Heidegger the philosopher.[19] For those who take this position, 'the limited number of remarks regarding the Jews are attributed to the personal opinions of Heidegger the man; they are independent of Heidegger the philosopher. They are the lamentable, though understandable, failings of a man to escape the prejudices of his time'.[20] The second approach is to condemn Heidegger as an anti-Semite *in toto* and to conclude that this compels the disqualification of his philosophy. Though I will keep my commentary here very brief, I take both of these approaches to be misguided. The first tends to minimise truly reprehensible things that Heidegger said and did. The second fails to contend with the actual philosophical accounts and arguments that Heidegger produced, amounting to an *ad hominem* fallacy. I agree with Mitchell and Trawny that 'this condemnatory stance is as much of a failure to read Heidegger as that of his exonerators'.[21] My approach is a bit different from both.

Martin Heidegger was without a doubt anti-Semitic (at minimum, through the duration of World War II), and this should be condemned in the strongest way. I am interested in defending neither Martin Heidegger the man *nor* Martin Heidegger the philosopher, that is, the man insofar as he did philosophy. I find that the latter approach implicitly reduces philosophy to a sort of author-centred relativism and work done on the history of philosophy to competitive biography. In contrast, I find that in addition to the creative or productive work done by an author, concepts, arguments, accounts, and ideas have a life of their own, and part of that life is their ability to get it right or get it wrong when it comes to their subject matter. The subject matter addressed in Heidegger's work is being (*Sein*), and only a remarkably anthropocentric interpretive strategy could reduce a well-considered account of the nature of being (like his) to a narration of its author's intellectual life – the man insofar as he did philosophy. In this book I am interested in the ontology itself that Heidegger developed. I do not find convincing the idea that that ontology is itself essentially anti-Semitic or fascistic. To be clear, I think it is rather evident that during a certain period Heidegger *wanted* to align his philosophy with elements of the Nazi programme and even *understood* (or perhaps better, fantasised about) his work as a philosophical foundation for it. He sometimes mobilised Nazi rhetorical tropes and expressed anti-Semitic views within his work during that time (though it should be pointed out that in work of the same period he also sometimes wrote things quite critical of the Nazi Party and its movement). However, I have little faith in the authority of an author over their work. When I say this, I am not making a claim about some strange postmodern death of the author. Rather, I hold that the meaning of a work is not indexed to its author's intentions, but categorically exceeds them, and that the interpretations one has of their own work have no special authority over it. An account produced is not under the authority of the author who produces it – children are rebellious and have a way of making their own world, even if the parent narrates it in the terms of theirs. Thus, in most cases when I refer to 'Heidegger' in this book, what I really mean is the textual corpus he produced and the accounts and concepts it contains, unless I indicate some specific biographical consideration in relation to them. This being said, the vast majority of the concepts Heidegger develops are not directly related to political discourse; they deal with fundamental metaphysical or ontological issues. In fact, Heidegger has often been criticised for *not* having a substantial ethical or political theory. In the cases in which Heidegger did adopt anti-Semitic or Nazi rhetoric in his philosophical discourse, that rhetoric was parasitical on – but not defining for – the account of being and of beings he produced. When it comes to the theory of events, the case is no different. An analysis of the actual functioning of Heidegger's concept within the account it is a part of, and of the relation of this concept to the others proximate to it in the problematic field they define, shows clearly that his concept of an historical event is (contextually) defined in relation to the technical historical framework of metaphysics. Moreover, as I shall argue, the historical concept of event in Heidegger's work is derivative in relation to his ontological concept of event and, consequently, *systematically* speaking, is properly defined in relation to that ontological concept and its relation to the undoing of metaphysical alienation, not in relation to his Nazism or anti-Semitism.

2 Translating 'Ereignis'

Heidegger's 'Ereignis' has been translated in a number of different and sometimes confounding ways: the major translations are 'event' (Rojcewicz and Vallega-Neu), 'appropriation' (Sheehan), 'event of appropriation' (Stambaugh), and 'enowning' (Emad and Maly). Adding to the complication, Heidegger stated that his term should not be translated in terms of the regular meaning of 'event', that is, in the sense of an intra-temporal occurrence or incident.[22] Nonetheless, I am convinced that 'event' is indeed the best option.

As I shall continue to argue, I find an author's interpretive claims about their own work to be of limited significance. The richness and meaning of a text surpasses that which its author intended or comprehended. Moreover, Heidegger's warnings regarding the term 'Ereignis' fail to recognise the possibility of translating it with a regular word and building a technical definition for that word that goes beyond its regular use. This is my approach, which is consistent with the precedent set by Rojcewicz and Vallega-Neu's translation of Heidegger's *Beiträge*.

Their translation marks a vast improvement over Emad and Maly's, which rendered 'Ereignis' as 'enowning'. 'Enowning' is a bad translation for at least two reasons. First, it is meant to capture the sense of 'propriety' or 'ownership' carried by the German 'eigen'. While this is indeed an important sense of Heidegger's term, it is not the only one. Sheehan effectively demolishes translation choices like Emad and Maly's through the etymology of the term 'Ereignis'.[23] Etymologically, its meaning is rooted in the Old High German word for 'eye' – 'ouga' – and only more recently gained the sense of 'ownership'. With this origin, 'Ereignis' includes a connotation of *sight*. 'Enowning' excludes this connotation. The second reason 'enowning' is a bad choice is that it is barely a translation at all. 'Enowning' is not an ordinary English word and whatever meaning it has is quite opaque. To make sense of it, it must be translated as well. But this defeats the purpose of translating the word in the first place.

Sheehan translates 'Ereignis' with 'appropriation' and justifies this by arguing that 'appropriation' captures the senses of both ownership and sight.[24] It carries the meaning of ownership in the sense of the Latin 'proprietas', which refers especially to the essential qualities belonging to something and making it be what it is. He attempts to connect 'appropriation' with sight by focusing on Heidegger's suggestion that in *Ereignis*, something comes into view. What comes into view is purportedly Dasein or human existence, specifically with respect to the way that Dasein constitutes a cleared or open space that enables its meaning-making activities in the world. In Sheehan's interpretation, this dimension of Dasein is what is most proper to it, that is, it makes Dasein be what it is. Thus, ownership (as propriety) and sight are melded together in the word 'appropriation'. Though this translation is an improvement over 'enowning', it also has a fatal flaw. The term is distinctly theory-laden, particularly insofar as Sheehan's account of the sight involved here rests upon his broader – very much controversial – interpretation of Heidegger (which I engage in Chapter 4). I argue that his interpretation is flawed insofar as it fundamentally misconstrues Heidegger's ontology as a theory of the meaning-making activities of Dasein. Consequently, the basis for Sheehan's translation choice is undermined. Similar problems arise for Stambaugh's 'event of appropriation', which loads the translation with theoretical content that artificially limits the sense it carries in Heidegger's own usage.

My approach, on the other hand, is quite simple. My view is that it is best to translate 'Ereignis' with its ordinary English counterpart, 'event'. Heeding the substance of Heidegger's warning, this choice does not fall into the trap of confusing *Ereignis* with the ordinary sense of an intratemporal occurrence for a simple reason: any serious reader of Heidegger will be able to keep in mind that this is not Heidegger's meaning. 'Event' is a standard translation, a recognisable and ordinary term, and does not carry the excessive theory-ladenness of the other options. Instead, this straightforward translation allows the content of the concept to be built through analysis of the actual use of it within Heidegger's system. It is no doubt true that the term 'Ereignis' carries both the sense of appropriation and of sight that Sheehan emphasises. Yet, we should not forget that Heidegger did select this term and that it also carries another important sense: that of *event*!

3 Overview of Chapters 1 to 6

Chapter 1 focuses on a set of methodological problems that I argue must be addressed if Heidegger's concept of event is to be coherently reconstructed. These problems have stymied previous approaches to his difficult later work and led to substantial inconsistencies in the available scholarship. I argue that solving them requires a revised interpretive approach to Heidegger. I propose a reconstructive methodology that I call 'diagenic analysis', which is based on an examination of the role of the concept of 'ground' in his ontology and in the methodological evolution of his work. This approach aims to clarify Heidegger's ontology by clarifying the relations between ground*ing* and ground*ed* terms within it. If one term is grounded by another, which is in turn grounded by another, I call this chain a 'diagenic axis'. One of this book's central theses is that the evolution Heidegger's philosophy undergoes throughout his career progresses along a diagenic axis. I argue that his ontological concept of 'event' marks the apex of this progression. In Chapter 1, I also clarify how the diagenic methodology operates through an analysis of what Heidegger calls a 'productive logic' of 'ground-laying' (*Grundlegung*) that drives the evolution of his ontology. Contrary to some Derridean readings, this productive logic shows that Heidegger's methodology included both conceptual deconstruction *and* a rigorous and constructive conceptual experimentalism. I argue that diagenic analysis not only solves the problems highlighted at the beginning of this chapter but allows a precise explanation of some of the essential characteristics of Heidegger's concept of event itself. It does this because of the simultaneously methodological and ontological status of the concept of ground in his work, and the distinctive relation of this concept to that of event.

The subsequent chapters of this book use a diagenic interpretive approach to reconstruct the transformation of Heidegger's ontology from the time of *Sein und Zeit* (1927) to that of *Beiträge* (1936–8) and, on the basis of the methodologically immanent definition of his concepts that this generates, to reconstruct his accounts of both the historical and ontological senses of event.

In Chapter 2, I go into detail about the distinction between what I call the historical and ontological senses of 'event' in Heidegger's work. Most commentators have not registered this distinction and I maintain that this has led to a conflation of many of his terms.

According to Heidegger, Western history over the past 2,500 years has been defined by a transmission and transformation of errors set in place by the ancient Greeks. These errors define both (1) the scope and nature of the philosophical science we now call 'metaphysics' and (2) the form of the lengthy historical 'epoch' in which we live. Since these formative errors eclipse our exposure to the question of being, Heidegger calls the history of metaphysics the history of the 'forgetting' of being. A central and well-known concern of his work, then, is to deconstruct the foundations of metaphysics in order to bring the question of being into focus and not lose sight of it again. His concept of an historical event provides his most far-reaching attempt to do this. In its historical sense, often referred to in the terminology of 'seynsgeschichtliche Denken' or 'beyng-historical thinking', 'event' names a fundamental rupture within the history of metaphysics that has the potential to generate what Heidegger calls 'another beginning' – a radically different framework for the intellectual and practical lives of human beings. To be clear, the historical sense of event also has an ontological dimension in a precise sense: it has to do with the ontological constitution and transformation of history. However, this is not to be confused with the second and properly ontological sense of 'event', which articulates the very nature of beyng.

After establishing the distinction between the historical and ontological senses of event, the chapter turns to their relation. This relation determines the structure for the rest of the book. Because, according to Heidegger, we necessarily approach the project of ontology from within the framework of metaphysics, the historical sense of event has a *methodological* priority over the ontological one. Yet because the historical rupture with metaphysics that he aims to accomplish would be impossible if being did not exceed the domain of metaphysics, I argue that the ontological sense of 'event' has an *ontological* priority over the historical one, which is dependent on it. No rupture with the history of metaphysics would be possible if metaphysics did in fact provide a sufficient science of being. Chapters 2 to 6 are arranged according to this relation: the remainder of Chapter 2 focuses on the historical sense of event, Chapters 3 and 4 focus on the transition from the historical to the ontological sense of event by way of the problematic of truth, and Chapters 5 and 6 focus on the properly ontological sense of event.

My analysis of the historical sense of event in the rest of Chapter 2 works in the context of Heidegger's philosophy of historical alienation in *Sein und Zeit* and *Beiträge*. As is evident, in his account the theme of history is directly related to that of metaphysics. Indeed, what it would mean for the historical event to be accomplished is that a transformative rupture in the historical framework of metaphysics has occurred. A central task of this chapter, then, is to explain the form of such a rupture by explaining the relation between metaphysics and historical alienation. I argue that the account of these topics in *Beiträge* can be properly understood only as the product of a conceptual evolution begun in *Sein und Zeit*.

It is one thing to say that an historical event of this sort could happen; it is another to explain how. Heidegger scholarship has had only a vague grasp on this. I close this chapter by arguing against what I call the 'fatalist' interpretation of Heidegger according to which the historical event in question is accomplished only by a mysterious quasi-agency of being, while human beings can do little more than sit around and wait. I argue that the explanation of how an historical event might occur is found in *Beiträge* in terms of Heidegger's recalibration of the task alienated Dasein is posed with: to re-ground itself. This presents a distinctly human role in the historical event. Heidegger now uses the term 'Er-gründung' or 'fathoming the ground' to describe this diagenic process of regrounding that generates another historical beginning, that is, an historical event. I argue that explaining how he tries to accomplish this event requires engaging his ontology of truth, to which I turn in Chapters 3 and 4.

One of my central claims governing Chapters 3 and 4 is that the operation by which fathoming the ground is accomplished is *doing ontology*, since this is the diagenic operation by which Dasein undergoes existential transformation such that it becomes realigned with being. It is true that the historical sense of event has methodological priority over the ontological sense because we pursue the problematic of being (and live our lives) from within the historical framework of metaphysics. However, I argue that bringing about the historical event is made possible precisely by generating a properly grounded account of beyng as event, that is, of the ontological sense of event.

According to Heidegger, the track of ontological enquiry best suited to do this focuses on the 'essence' of truth. Beginning around 1930, 'truth' becomes one of the main terms he uses to articulate the nature of being. Plenty of scholars have discussed Heidegger's association of the concepts of truth and event. Some, like Capobianco, have more or less equated the two, a position that I argue against in Chapter 4. To my knowledge, however, none has sufficiently explained the specific methodological relation of truth to event that Heidegger makes a centrepiece of his work in *Beiträge*. Namely, the question of truth is the 'precursory question' to that of beyng as event. Thus, I argue that it is by working through the ontology of truth that access to the evental structure of beyng is secured.

Chapter 3 begins with a look at Heidegger's critique of representational models of truth. It then reconstructs the diagenic development of his ontology of truth from the pre-*Kehre* model advanced in *Sein und Zeit* to the model produced during the *Kehre* or 'turn' in his 1930 lecture 'Vom Wesen der Wahrheit'. This establishes methodological and conceptual continuity between Heidegger's early grounding of the problematic of being and his later work, and it defines the context in which he addresses truth a few years later in *Beiträge* (I turn to this in Chapter 4). My intention here is not to reproduce existing research on Heidegger's theory of truth (for example, Daniel Dahlstrom's excellent *Heidegger's Concept of Truth*), but to explain the elements of the ontology of truth necessary for accessing the structure of the event.

The touchstones of the diagenic evolution that I trace are as follows. Throughout the late 1920s and early 1930s Heidegger maintains what I call an *a-lēthic* account of the essence of truth. That is, he casts truth and untruth in terms of the Greek ἀλήθεια and λήθη. Following Richardson's *Heidegger: Through Phenomenology to Thought* and other commentators to a degree, I identify two main stages of Heidegger's *a-lēthic* account of truth. The first is expressed in *Sein und Zeit*'s phenomenological account of truth. The second, more originary stage, emerges in 'Vom Wesen der Wahrheit' where the elements of the essence of truth shift to become structures of being that ground human existence. In Chapter 4, I argue that Heidegger's ontology of truth in *Beiträge* takes a step farther to a third stage.

Heidegger's account of being as event is philosophically dependent on the lines of thought that lead up to it, that is, on the evolution of his ontology. I argue that truth is important because it has to do not merely with defining criteria for what is true and what is false, or what can be described phenomenologically and what cannot, but with what makes possible the very domain of truth and falsity, or, in other words, what makes possible the domain of phenomena. Heidegger's question about truth enquires into the ground enabling such things to occur at all. In this way, truth is not primarily an epistemological term, but an ontological one. Moreover, it is an ontological term with a unique characteristic: at its more derivative levels, 'truth' designates being insofar as being is disclosed in a meaningful way to Dasein, in other words, insofar as it is *thought*. I argue that in Heidegger's ontology, the logic of thought, that is, the logic of the being of thought, is continuous with the logic of being. Thus, by tracking the former it is possible to gain access to the latter. This proceeds via the question of truth, which in the 1930s moves well beyond the existential analysis of Dasein. Yet in the version of truth presented in 'Vom Wesen der Wahrheit', the historical framework of metaphysics still lingers.

In *Beiträge* Heidegger argues that to eliminate the vestiges of metaphysics still present in his prior work certain rather dramatic shifts in his approach are needed. Chapter 4 begins by arguing that registering the methodological role of these shifts is crucial for making sense of the further transformed account of truth he gives in this text and, in turn, of his concept of event. These shifts centre around:

1. a distinction between what Heidegger calls the 'Leitfrage' or 'guiding question' that has defined the scope of philosophy as metaphysics and the 'Grundfrage' or 'basic question', with which he now aligns his project. The *Leitfrage* asks about beings as beings (ὂν ᾗ ὄv) and is rendered in its most general form by Aristotle's 'τί τὸ ὄv' ('What are beings?'). The *Grundfrage* does not enquire into beings, but into the essence of truth – as a feature of the event – in its own terms, that is, independently of beings.

2. the counterintuitive claim that being must be rethought as independent of beings. I argue that Heidegger's claim is not a move to a metaphysics of transcendence, but rather to a deeper methodological immanence within the question of beyng (that is, the event).

3. the terminological distinction between 'Sein' or 'being' and 'Seyn' or 'beyng'. These terms are frequently conflated by some commentators. I argue that Heidegger uses them to draw a technical distinction between approaches to his central topic that operate within the rubric of the *Leitfrage* (as *Sein und Zeit*'s analysis of Dasein did) and his new approach within the rubric of the *Grundfrage*.

Heidegger's approach to the essence of truth in *Beiträge* must be read in light of these shifts. In the rest of this chapter, I argue that doing so reveals a profoundly transformed account of truth, which opens the possibility to develop a properly grounded definition of the concept of beyng as event.

Nearly all available scholarship addressing Heidegger's account of truth in *Beiträge* takes it to remain within the basic framework of the second stage of the *a-lēthic* account in which the ἀλήθεια-λήθη dynamic is used to articulate the fundamental nature of beyng. This is a product of overlooking the shifts noted and certain structural developments taking place in his conception of truth. I argue that in *Beiträge* Heidegger moves to a third stage, which cannot be properly accounted for in terms of the *a-lēthic* framework. I show that he does this by enquiring into the ontological ground generating the very structures of ἀλήθεια and λήθη, thereby moving to a philosophical position more originary on the diagenic axis. Ἀλήθεια and λήθη are originated in a primal process of differentiation, which constitutes not only the essence of truth but a key operation of the evental dynamic of beyng. Thus, I claim that in this third stage Heidegger's ontology offers a *differential* concept of truth, which is more originary than the earlier *a-lēthic* concepts. The essence of truth, which Heidegger now designates 'the clearing for/of self-concealing' ('die Lichtung für das Sichverbergen' or 'Lichtung des Sichverbergens'), is the differential logic of beyng as event insofar as this constitutes ontological structures that enable beings to be, structures like ἀλήθεια and λήθη. Or, more precisely, truth is one of *three* overlapping registers in terms of which Heidegger articulates these evental structures. The other two are ground and time-space.

The arguments I make in this chapter allow me to develop critiques of two interpretive positions that have been dominant in recent work on Heidegger's concept of 'event'. The first is the 'correlationist' interpretation maintained positively by Sheehan and negatively by Quentin Meillassoux. According to this position, Heidegger's concept of event names a mutual appropriation or correlation of human existence to being and being to human existence, such that neither would 'be' at all without the other. I argue that Heidegger's claim that beyng is independent of beings – most notably of human beings – invalidates Sheehan and Meillassoux's correlationist interpretation of Heidegger's concept of event. Said differently, Heidegger maintains a fascinating form of ontological realism. The second position I critique claims that 'event' is simply an alternative name for the characteristics of being that Heidegger elsewhere describes in terms of 'anwesen' (presencing) or 'das Anwesen des Anwesenden' (the presencing of what is present), 'ἀλήθεια', 'φύσις', and several other terms. This is the position maintained by Capobianco. I argue that such a position is incomplete, since it does not recognise the major shift in *Beiträge* according to which 'event' is posited as the ground *enabling* presencing, 'ἀλήθεια', and 'φύσις', and therefore cannot be just another name for the same thing.

Chapters 3 and 4 offer a diagenic reconstruction of Heidegger's philosophy of truth, which serves as the methodological means of access to the concept of event in its ontological sense. More precisely, the analysis of truth provides a foothold in the differential logic of beyng as event. Focusing again on *Beiträge*, Chapter 5 elaborates the concept of event via that foothold.

A major line of argument in this book comes to a head in Chapter 5; namely, the argument begun in Chapter 1 where I claimed that a diagenic methodology alleviates the remarkable confusion that has surrounded Heidegger's ontology of events, especially as presented in *Beiträge*. I attribute much of this confusion to a failure in the scholarship to adequately clarify the structural relations defining many of Heidegger's idiosyncratic concepts. I attribute *that* to a failure to register Heidegger's diagenic shift to a differential concept of truth, since this provides access to the logic of the ground that articulates these relations, that is, to the logic of the event. If the problematic of truth is the problematic preliminary to that of beyng as event, then how one understands Heidegger's account of the essence of truth directly impacts how one understands his account of the event. Understanding the essence of truth to be most fundamentally *a-lēthic*, leads to an account of the evental nature of beyng in terms of the *a-lēthic* framework (for example, Capobianco in *Engaging Heidegger*). However, this account leads to confusion about many concepts related to the event, which appear out of joint, disconnected, or connected only extrinsically by Heidegger's fiat. Treatments of Heidegger's evental concepts within the *a-lēthic* framework, then, are unable to make sense of important parts of the text without reducing them to mysticism, arbitrariness, or appeals to authority. I argue that this is because the *a-lēthic* framework falls short of the most originary level of grounding active in the text. In contrast, registering *Beiträge's* differential conception of truth enables a better-grounded explanation of the event, on the basis of which those concepts snap into place. This allows for rigorous analysis of those concepts and their intrinsic, essential relations and, in turn, a reconstruction of his broader ontology of events in a unified, consistent fashion. This chapter establishes the basis for doing just this.

It is built around:

1. an analysis of Heidegger's ontology of difference in *Beiträge*, focusing on his rarely discussed shift from the concept of the ontological difference between being and beings (prevalent in his early work) to the concept of originary difference or the ground that enables the difference between being and beings to arise at all. This forms a key diagenic moment in his methodological path and places Heidegger closer to thinkers like Deleuze and Badiou than has been widely acknowledged in related scholarship.
2. an expansion of Chapter 4's concluding thesis, that Heidegger shifts to a differential concept of truth, by detailing the differential logic of the essence of truth and its onto-genesis of the *a-lēthic* structures.
3. a recasting of the differential logic of truth in Heidegger's core *evental* terms: 'appropriation' (*Er-eignis*) and 'expropriation' (*Enteignis*). By doing this, the chapter establishes the differential logic of beyng as event that is expressed in or underwrites the rest of this text.
4. an analysis of an ineliminable form of ontological distortion that Heidegger calls the 'distorted essence' or 'Un-wesen' of beyng and the distorted essence of truth or 'Un-wahrheit' (un-truth).

This chapter allows a definition of Heidegger's ontological concept of event according to which beyng as event is a differentiation of 'pure' difference from itself, together with the logic of determinateness that this originates and an 'abyss' of difference that exceeds that determinateness. The logic of determinateness is the logic of the Da expressed in the term 'Da-sein', that is, it is the logic of the world. This is articulated in terms of the correlative evental problematics of truth, ground, and time-space.

While this chapter addresses the connection of truth and event, it does not address ground or time-space.

Chapter 6 completes the partial explanation of the structure of the event given in Chapter 5. There, I defined beyng as event in relation to the differential logic of truth. Truth, ground, and time-space are the three central registers in terms of which Heidegger addresses the structures of the event having to do with the genesis of determinate worlds of beings. Chapter 6 fills out the picture by reconstructing his concepts of ground and time-space as components of the logic of the event. This focuses on the notoriously difficult §§238–42 of *Beiträge*.

4 The question of poetic (or poietic) language and art

One further point should be made here. Over the past decades many scholars have focused on the idea that the transition from Heidegger's pre- to post-*Kehre* work is essentially a turn to language and to a poetic (or poietic) mode of thinking. The poietic operation at stake applies not just to the 'bringing forth' that happens in what we ordinarily consider language, it extends to the creative enterprise of great art. Thus, the focus on the former often goes hand in hand with a focus on the latter. This view is built on the idea that both are grounded in a poietic way in which human beings can engage with being – a way that channels the manner in which being brings forth beings (all the while withdrawing from them) and preserves it in poetic language or works of art. As a result, it is suggested that Heidegger's concept of event must be understood in terms of the problematic of poietic language and art. Daniela Vallega-Neu and Krzysztof Ziarek give two of the best-argued and most recent versions of this position. Vallega-Neu, for instance, writes that

> with Heidegger's failure to complete the project of *Being and Time* and the subsequent turn in his thinking began a relentless quest for words and ways of thinking and speaking that brought the issue of language to the forefront of his concerns.[25]

She thus makes language – specifically poietic language – the cornerstone of her interpretation of *Ereignis*, going so far as to call the set of private manuscripts of which *Beiträge* forms the heart 'Heidegger's poietic writings'.[26] While this leads to a rich interpretation, I think its prioritisation of the question of language is detrimental to other, more fundamental elements of Heidegger's ontology of *Ereignis*. To be fair, Vallega-Neu does seem to leave some space for alternative approaches. Ziarek puts the emphasis on language perhaps a bit more starkly:

one cannot hear what is at issue in Heidegger's thought – let alone how and from where this thinking itself issues – nor determine its stakes, without primary attentiveness to language: both Heidegger's language and the way it issues from the problematic of language understood as being's event.[27]

Without a doubt, the questions of poietic language and art are important elements in Heidegger's work on the concept of event. Careful reflection on them will substantially enrich one's understanding of it. One might, therefore, expect this book to follow course and give these topics a central role. This is not the case, although I do return to limited discussions of them at different points. The issue has been covered at length both by Vallega-Neu's *Heidegger's Poietic Writings* and Ziarek's *Language after Heidegger*, and I will not repeat that work here. More to the point, though, I hold that while the questions of poietic language and art are important for understanding the relation of the human being to Heidegger's historical event, they form neither the conceptual nor the methodological core of his treatment of the ontology of events overall. There are four immediate reasons for this.

First, the focus on defining Heidegger's concept of event in terms of poietic language and art has resulted from an exclusive focus on the historical sense of event in his work. However, this rests upon a conflation of the historical and ontological senses of that concept. By marking the difference between the two senses, I hold that the issues of poietic language and art take a derivative position in relation to the problematics of truth, difference, ground, and time-space, which define the event in its properly ontological sense. Thus, my focus will be on these instead.

Second, and more specifically: although Heidegger certainly emphasises the connection of poietic language and art to the event, it is the problematic of truth through which he actually *does* the ontology of events in *Beiträge* (which is then elaborated in terms of ground and time-space). For Heidegger, the question of the essence of truth, not language, is the preliminary question (*Vorfrage*) via which we come to articulate the nature of beyng as event.[28] For evidence of this, see *Beiträge* §§204–37, which form the path of access to the heart of the text's account of beyng as event in §§238–42.

Third, Heidegger explicitly claims that to break with the errancy of metaphysics, the nature of beyng as event must be thought in a way not based on the relation of beyng to beings (since this taints the account of beyng with traces of *Seiendheit*), but in its own independent terms. Explaining what exactly this means and how it does not establish a new metaphysics of transcendence will have to wait until later. The point for now is that language and art are decisively wrapped up in the lives of discursive beings, so to think beyng as event on such a basis is to think it in terms of its relation to beings. It is to repeat the metaphysical error in which the nature of beyng is traced off *Seiendheit*. Moreover, it is to fall into the trap of the untenable correlationism that I address in Chapter 4.

My final point has to do with the relation of truth and language. The topic of truth is clearly linked to that of language: in the traditional view, the adequation defining truth takes the form of a representational proposition in which a predicate is attributed to a subject. I deal with this at length in terms of truth. Nonetheless, we must be careful not to reduce truth to language or vice versa. In Heidegger's ontology, the essence of truth is a structural function of beyng that must be articulated in terms of the logic of the event, independently of the relation of that logic to 'what is true' (that is, to beings). The essence of truth is part of the structure of beyng; poietic language in the context of ontology is a register of beyng's relation to beings endowed with language. It is therefore the question of truth that gets at the nature of beyng as event itself (the ontological sense of event), not language. I anticipate that one might object by arguing that the logic I've named (the *logos* of the event) is just what the question of language aims to address at the ontological level. In this case, my response is: wonderful, then that is exactly what this book is about . . . except it approaches this in the register of truth, which is precisely what Heidegger's text does. If, on the other hand, one maintains that the logic of the event is not what Heidegger's question of language is ultimately about, then language cannot be the central term in which his ontology of events can be treated.

Notes

1. *SZ* 27/49.
2. For instance, Davidson writes, 'I do not believe we can give a cogent account of action, of explanation, of causality, or of the relation between the mental and the physical, unless we accept events as individuals' and that we require 'an explicit ontology of events' (Davidson, *Essays* 165).
3. Heidegger writes, 'Beyng essentially occurs as the event' ('Das Seyn west als das Ereignis') (GA65 30/25). Deleuze writes, 'Being is the unique event in which all events communicate with one another' (Deleuze, *Logique du sens* 211/180).
4. Derrida, 'La structure, le signe et le jeu dans le discours des sciences humaines', in *L'écriture et la différence*.
5. Derrida, 'La différance' and 'Ousia et Grammè', in *Marges de la philosophie*.
6. Romano, *Event and World*.
7. Malabou, *The Heidegger Change*.
8. Ziarek, *Language after Heidegger*.
9. Gabriel, *Transcendental Ontology* and Livingston, *The Logic of Being*.
10. I replace Macquarrie and Robinson's translation of *Sein* as 'Being' with 'being' throughout.
11. *SZ* 19/41. As Richardson emphasises, Heidegger's 'destruction' is not to be an annihilation of the edifice of metaphysics altogether. Problematising the grounds of

metaphysics and carrying out fundamental ontology entails working out the non-metaphysical grounds of metaphysics in a more originary ontology, consequently establishing the possibility to reground metaphysics such that it might eventually be recuperated (Richardson, *Through Phenomenology to Thought* passim).

12. 'Only by way of what [Heidegger] I has thought does one gain access to what is to-be-thought by [Heidegger] II. But the thought of [Heidegger] I becomes possible only if it is contained in [Heidegger] II' (Heidegger, 'Preface', in Richardson, *Through Phenomenology to Thought* xxii). Richardson's distinction between Heidegger I and II demarcates Heidegger's work prior to 1930 and from 1930 until his death in 1976, respectively (see ibid. 22, 230, 476, 623–8, 632–3). For more, see Richardson's index entries 'Heidegger I', 'Heidegger II', and 'Heidegger I and II' (ibid. 756). Richardson takes Heidegger's 1930 lecture 'Vom Wesen der Wahrheit' to mark the inauguration of Heidegger II (ibid. 624).

13. Herrmann points out that there is evidence this problematic of the event is active in Heidegger's work beginning as early as 1932 (Herrmann, *Wege ins Ereignis* 1).

14. GA9 316nA/241nB, translation modified.

15. For discussion of Heidegger's early uses of 'Ereignis', see Polt, 'Ereignis' 376–80 and *EB* 33–7. Polt also emphasises that Heidegger's January–April 1919 lecture course (published as *The Idea of Philosophy and the Problem of Worldview* in GA 56/57) is noteworthy because in it 'the word plays a central part' (Polt, 'Ereignis' 375).

16. Though there are a number of closely related texts, Herrmann defines the core group of private manuscripts to include GA65 *Beiträge zur Philosophie (Vom Ereignis)*, GA66 *Besinnung* (written 1938–9, published 1997), GA70 *Über den Anfang* (written 1941, published 2005), GA71 *Das Ereignis* (written 1941–2, published 2009), and GA72 *Die Stege des Anfangs* (written 1944, still unpublished). He highlights two additional texts that are 'in thematic proximity' to these: 'Die Überwindung der Metaphysik' in GA67 *Metaphysik und Nihilismus* and GA69 *Die Geschichte des Seyns* (1938–40). For this and other information on the provenance and preparation of these manuscripts, see Herrmann, 'Nachwort des Herausgebers', in GA66 429–37/379–85.

17. Rae, *Ontology in Heidegger and Deleuze* vii.

18. GA65 7/8.

19. Mitchell and Trawny, *Heidegger's* Black Notebooks XX–XXI. It is important to be clear about the biographical limits of Heidegger's racism: to the best of our knowledge, as Mitchell and Trawny point out, 'there are no records of anti-Semitic views expressed by Heidegger after the war, in the subsequent *Black Notebooks* or elsewhere' (ibid. XXII).

20. Ibid. XXI.

21. Ibid. XXII.

22. For instance: 'Wir können das mit dem Namen "das Ereignis" Genannte nicht mehr am Leitfaden der geläufigen Wortbedeutung vorstellen; denn sie versteht "Ereignis" im Sinne von Vorkommnis und Geschehnis' (in Stambaugh's translation: 'What the name "event of Appropriation" names can no longer be represented by means of the current meaning of the word; for in that meaning "event of Appropriation" is understood in the sense of occurrence and happening' (GA14 25–6/*On Time and Being* 20). Note that Sheehan references this passage as evidence that 'event' should not be used to translate 'Ereignis' (Sheehan, *Making Sense of Heidegger* 232). However, to do so he translates 'Vorkommnis' as 'event' and then uses the resulting statement as the evidence that 'Ereignis' ought not to be translated as 'event'. In other words, he frontloads his claim into a translation choice and then uses that translation choice as evidence for his claim. But that is straightforwardly begging the question.

23. See Sheehan, *Making Sense of Heidegger* 232–6.

24. Ibid. 232–8.

25. Vallega-Neu, 'Heidegger's Poietic Writings' 101.

26. Vallega-Neu, *Heidegger's Poietic Writings*.

27. Ziarek, 'Giving Its Word' 88. For Ziarek's full view on this, see his *Language after Heidegger*.
28. GA65 387/305.

Chapter 1

The Methodological Ground of Heidegger's Ontology of Events

> The event is the self-eliciting and self-mediating center in which all essential occurrence of the truth of beyng must be thought back in advance. This thinking back in advance to that center is the inventive thinking of beyng. And all concepts of beyng must be uttered from there.[1]

Making clear, philosophically rigorous sense of Heidegger's work after around 1930 is notoriously difficult. This chapter focuses on a set of methodological problems that contribute to this difficulty and that must necessarily be addressed if his concept of event is to be coherently reconstructed. Solving them requires a revised interpretive approach to his philosophical corpus. Based on the role of the concept of 'ground' in Heidegger's ontology and in the methodological evolution of his work, I propose a reconstructive methodology that I call 'diagenic analysis'. This approach aims to clarify Heidegger's ontology by clarifying the relations between ground*ing* and ground*ed* terms within it. I justify its use by examining a number of supporting examples and responding to objections that might be raised on the basis of texts like 'Der Lehrer trifft den Türmer' in GA77 *Feldweg-Gespräche* (1944–5), which seems to disavow the notion of ground altogether. I then clarify how the diagenic methodology operates through an analysis of what Heidegger calls a 'produktive Logik' of 'Grundlegung' that drives the evolution of his ontology.[2] I hold that diagenic analysis not only solves the problems I highlight, but allows a precise explanation of some of the essential characteristics of Heidegger's concept of event itself. It is able to do this because of the simultaneously methodological and ontological status of the concept of ground in his work, and the distinctive relation of this concept to that of event. The remaining chapters of this book use this interpretive approach to reconstruct the transformation of Heidegger's ontology from the time of *Sein und Zeit* (1927) to that of *Beiträge zur Philosophie (Vom Ereignis)* (1936–8) and, on the basis of the methodologically immanent definition of his concepts that this generates, to reconstruct his account of beyng (*Seyn*) as event (*Ereignis*).[3]

I Problems

The main reasons for the difficulty in making good sense of Heidegger's later work revolve around ongoing transformations in the ontology he produced. His project in the late 1920s famously turned around the ontological difference, that is, the difference between being and beings. In *Sein und Zeit*, he argues that being is neither *a* being nor the totality of beings.[4] Rather, his question is about 'the being of beings'.[5] The project he terms 'fundamental ontology' proceeds within the methodological horizon of the existential analysis of Dasein or human existence, and Heidegger develops a series of different renditions of the being of Dasein: being-in-the-world, care, thrown projection, and temporality. After *Sein und Zeit*, he argues that this ontology is insufficient and recasts the problematic of being again and again, extending a series of accounts that I shall argue finds its apex in thinking beyng as event. Notoriously, though, much of the terminology he introduces in this process is very bizarre, and much of it is associated with his concept of event. For instance, in *Beiträge* Heidegger claims that the essence of truth is 'die Lichtung für das Sichverbergen' (the clearing for self-concealing).[6] What on earth could that mean? To be sure, there is no consensus in the scholarship. This problem can lead to outright mystification when such terminology is collected into lengthier statements:

> *Der Zeit-Raum ist der berückend-entrückende sammelnde Umhalt, der so gefügte und entsprechend stimmende Ab-grund, dessen Wesung in der Gründung des 'Da' durch das Da-sein (seine wesentlichen Bahnen der Bergung der Wahrheit) Geschichtlich wird.*

> Time-space is the gathering embrace that captivates and transports at once; it is the abyssal ground which is structured in this way, which disposes accordingly, and whose essential occurrence becomes historical in the grounding of the 'there' by Da-*sein* (by its essential paths of sheltering the truth).[7]

Unusual, indeed nearly unrecognisable, formulations like these have led to confusion in scholarship on both Heidegger's post-*Kehre* work generally and the concept of event specifically. If Heidegger's later work is to be taken seriously, we need a consistent methodology for reconstructing it in a philosophically sensible manner. To state the issue more pointedly, there are at least four related problems that must be solved if a philosophically coherent explanation of Heidegger's account of beyng as event is to be given.

1. The first problem is that of consistency. Heidegger gives different accounts of the same things in different texts. In many cases, these accounts appear to be inconsistent. Take the question of the essence of truth. In *Sein und Zeit*, the essence of propositional truth is the phenomenological ἀλήθεια or uncoveredness (*Entdecktheit/Unverborgenheit*) of beings in the world together with its counterpart, untruth, which is understood to be phenomenological λήθη or coveredness (*Verborgenheit*). Both ἀλήθεια and λήθη are grounded in Dasein's structure of disclosedness (*Erschlossenheit*). A few years later in 'Vom Wesen der Wahrheit' Heidegger continues to maintain that the essence of truth is the ἀλήθεια-λήθη coupling, but now these are the ground enabling Dasein (to be distinguished from Da-sein) to be at all. In other words, there seems to be a reversal of the grounding and grounded term. Then in *Beiträge*, he is no longer satisfied with the *a-lēthic* account of the essence of truth, suggesting that the ἀλήθεια-λήθη coupling must be grounded in something new entirely. So, which is it? Is Heidegger's work internally consistent or not, particularly when comparing different texts or even, as I shall suggest, different parts within a single text? It should not be overlooked that scholarship has dealt with transformations in Heidegger's thought, largely focusing on the macrological *Kehre* or shift from the so-called early period to the later period, and sometimes including a third, 'middle' period. This is helpful to a certain extent, but it does not solve the problem of consistency because, at the very least, it does not explain seeming inconsistencies that appear at micrological levels within any single period of Heidegger's thought or individual texts. My claim is that this is because it does not explain micrological *transformations* of Heidegger's account that are consistent because of the way they are related via his methodology.

2. The second problem, which follows from the first, is that of arrangement. If Heidegger's ontology is indeed consistent and yet transforms through different stages that can *appear* inconsistent, can we systematically make sense of these transformations, such that we can avoid mixing up elements of different stages of his thought and consequently muddling the account he gives? How should different stages, or the ideas presented within them, properly be arranged? This is a problem that has led otherwise good scholarship to fundamental mischaracterisations of Heidegger's work. For instance, a troubling interpretive habit has become prevalent in some scholarship lately: statements about a

theme (like 'truth', 'Dasein', or 'Ereignis') are cherry-picked from far-removed locations in Heidegger's corpus, listed, and then treated as if they provide the rules for defining that topic in an entirely different part of the corpus, or even in the corpus as a whole.[8] If Heidegger's project were simply to clarify analytically one or two static positions that he maintained throughout his life, this would be fine. But if his ontology *develops*, if its terminology and horizons are a product of ongoing evolution, then this approach is essentially flawed.

3. The third problem, which correlates with the first two, is that of terminology and grammar. Especially in his later work, Heidegger employs bizarre terminology and linguistic formulations that violate ordinary grammar and appear more poetical or mystical than philosophically rigorous. This is the problem on the basis of which Rudolph Carnap dismissed Heidegger. Lee Braver captures his position concisely: for Carnap 'Heidegger's ideas are based on a grammatical mirage which vanishes once logical analysis shows what is really going on inside these sentences'.[9] Do Heidegger's unusual linguistic formulations amount to nonsensical or logically vapid statements? Is his philosophy linguistically rigorous? I should point out that my interest relative to this problem is not in Heidegger's philosophy of language, but in his *use* of language. Plenty of scholarship is available on the former, and I will not recount it.

4. The fourth problem is that of textual priority. If, as the problem of consistency indicates, different of Heidegger's texts give seemingly inconsistent accounts of the same subject matter, which one should be given priority? In 'Der Satz der Identität' (1957), the primary sense of the event is an 'owning in which man and being are delivered over to each other' or 'the belonging together of man and being'.[10] However, earlier in *Beiträge* beyng *is* the event, which in its most essential register is claimed to be independent of any relation with beings, notably with human beings. Some scholars take texts like 'Der Satz der Identität' to provide Heidegger's 'real' post-*Kehre* thought because they were honed for publication (*Beiträge* was not) and were written later, thus benefiting from greater refinement. Is this the proper approach? Or, if, as the problem of arrangement indicates, Heidegger's ontology transformed through different philosophical stages, should a priority be given to texts that advance his project the farthest, regardless of compositional character or chronology?

It is my thesis that solving these problems and clarifying Heidegger's account of the event requires clarifying the way his ontology develops, that is, the movement of his thought. In particular, a great deal of the confusion in scholarship stems from a lack of clarity about a dynamic, reflexive relation between the methodology he employed and the subject matter he enquired into. By taking a closer look at this, what I believe is the proper method for reconstructing Heidegger's accounts can be generated (diagenic analysis). Without attention to the development in question, his concepts become disconnected from aspects of the ontology they were built to articulate. They then seem arbitrary or become easily misunderstood, like conclusions divorced from their premises, to paraphrase Spinoza again. I take this to be the root of the dismissive attitudes towards Heidegger's later thought held by many philosophers of the Anglo-American tradition. I also take it to have led to some subsets of the Heideggerian-phenomenological tradition rightly criticised for lacking rigour. Carnap's condemnation of Heidegger exemplifies how this all can go wrong. My view is that when put into the context of the methodological evolution of Heidegger's programme, many of his unusual formulations are in fact rigorous. As others have argued, Richardson most notably, the series of renditions of the ontological problematic that Heidegger develops throughout his career do not correlate with programmatic breaks.[11] They are not the result of the author deciding his earlier work is wrong and developing new positions inconsistent with previous ones. Yet a surpassing of previous renditions in favour of better ones *is* involved. The series of accounts Heidegger generates manifest a dynamic evolution of his ontology, and making sense of the concepts he uses, like that of event, requires clarifying the mechanism of that evolution.

Along with scholarship that addresses the macrological transformation from the pre- to post-*Kehre* periods, a good deal indirectly addresses micrological movements in Heidegger's thought by examining particular topics over different points in his career.[12] Yet, none that I have found sufficiently explains the engine of this movement or what I find to be a clear structural homology through these scales. To do this, I shall focus on a difficulty that characterises his corpus at both macrological and micrological levels and ties together the four problems listed. The difficulty, which I shall call the 'reflexive difficulty', is as follows: throughout Heidegger's texts, the foundations of the methodology and of the conceptual apparatus through which he gives an account of his core problematic are brought into play by the nature of that problematic, according to the very account they enable. In other words, there is a reflexive, transformative relation between the account and what the account is about, a relation that drives forward an immanent evolution of that account and implies the supersession of earlier stages of it. Since this reflexive (therefore, non-linear) relation prompts its own recursion, it involves a further difficulty: its non-linearity is carried over to the relations between different stages.

2 Methodological principles

Diagenic analysis is a realigned methodology for interpreting Heidegger's corpus in a way able to deal consistently with the reflexive difficulty and the problems that arise from it. This methodology takes the relations between ground*ing* and ground*ed* terms to be central to his thought. To clarify these relations, I distinguish between what I shall call diagenic axes (or axes of ground) and syngenic axes (or axes of the grounded). I use the root γένω (*geno*) because according to Heidegger's concept, ground explicitly entails a character of enabling what is grounded to be (for example, as *Grund der Ermöglichung*) and an originary (*ursprüngliche*) character (as in 'Der Ab-grund ist die ursprüngliche Wesung des Grundes').[13] In this sense, ground bears an essential genetic character. To be clear, this genetic character must not be confused with that of metaphysical concepts of cause, which bear presuppositions about the nature of being and of beings that Heidegger rejects. I use the δια and συν prefixes to indicate something similar to Saussure's diachronic/synchronic distinction.[14] Where Saussure's distinction is organised on temporal lines, the one I am attributing to Heidegger is organised on lines of ground.[15] Diagenic axes run into the ground, that is, from that which is grounded into its ground or, inversely, from ground to that which is grounded. In *Beiträge* 'space' and 'time' are situated along a diagenic axis with respect to 'time-space', which is the ground whence they are originated.[16] Such axes can in some cases be carried along farther: from p to its ground q; from q to its ground r; from r to s, and so on. In Chapters 3 and 4, I lay out such a sequence in the transformation of Heidegger's account of truth from *Sein und Zeit* to 'Vom Wesen der Wahrheit' and finally to *Beiträge*. In this sequence, the traditional account of truth as correctness is grounded in truth as the phenomenological uncoveredness and coveredness of beings, which are grounded in truth as *a priori* ontological structures of ἀλήθεια/freedom/openness and λήθη/concealment/closedness/withdrawal, which are grounded in truth as self-differentiation.

In distinction, to a syngenic axis belong a set of entities, processes, or structures all grounded in the same manner, horizontal to or side by side one another. In Heidegger's early work, a good example of this is found in his account of the basic/ground constitution (*Grundverfassung*) of Dasein as being-in-the-world. Various existentialia of being-in-the-world, that is, 'constitutive items in its structure', are arranged on a syngenic axis, each equiprimordial (*gleichursprünglich*) with the others.[17] Among these are being alongside (*Sein bei*) the ready-to-hand, being-with (*Mitsein*), state-of-mind (*Befindlichkeit*), understanding, and discourse (*Rede*). Likewise, at each of the diagenic moments in Heidegger's account of truth, a set of syngenically related terms is developed articulating it. In *Sein und Zeit*, the phenomenological unconcealment and concealment of beings are syngenically related to one another, while diagenically related to Dasein's disclosedness. In *Beiträge*, space and time are on a syngenic axis with respect to each other. Perhaps more recognisably, my pen and my desk are beings related on a syngenic axis within the unconcealment of beings.

Proposing an interpretive methodology in these terms is no doubt controversial, since many Heideggerians believe that the concept of ground is thoroughly metaphysical, so Heidegger's rejection of metaphysics entails that ground is tossed out as well. In fact, some have argued to me that the very notion of ground is offensive to the Heideggerian mode of thinking. Such a position, however, is flatly false. Not only does Heidegger consistently use the terminology of ground as a part of his lexicon, the relation of grounding to grounded terms forms a central organising principle in his thought. Often this relation is made explicit by the language he uses, though sometimes it remains implicit. Indeed, more important than the terminology of ground itself are the relations it describes. Heidegger's programme is oriented by the task of uncovering the originary ground of whichever terms are used in some particular stage of the ontology to articulate the problematic of being. This enacts his *produktive Logik* of *Grundlegung*, to which I shall turn in a moment. Though this movement resembles Kantian and post-Kantian transcendental philosophy, the two are importantly distinguished by the fact that Heidegger's *Grundlegung* is not bound to the investigation of the cognitive apparatus of a representing subject. As a few characteristic examples of Heidegger's use of ground, take the following:

1. GA24 *Die Grundprobleme der Phänomenologie* (1927): Here, Heidegger explains the task and result of the existential analytic of Dasein: 'Exposition of the basic/ground constitution [Grundverfassung] of Dasein, its existential constitution, is the task of the preparatory ontological analytic of Dasein's existential constitution. We call it the existential analytic of Dasein. It must aim at bringing to light the ground [gründen] of the basic/ground structures [Grundstrukturen] of Dasein in their unity and wholeness.'[18] 'In my treatise on *Being and Time*, I set forth what the existential analytic encompasses in its essential results. The outcome of the existential analytic, the exposition of the ontological constitution [Seinsverfassung] of Dasein in its ground [Grunde], is this: *the constitution of Dasein's being is grounded in temporality [gründet in der Zeitlichkeit]*'.[19]

2. 'Der Ursprung des Kunstwerkes' (1935–6): The subject matter of this

text is what its title suggests, the origin of the work of art. 'Origin [Ursprung] means here that from which and through which a thing is what it is and how it is. That which something is, as it is, we call its essence [Wesen]. The origin of something is the source of its essence. The question of the origin of the artwork asks about the source of its essence.'[20] In a way similar to *Sein und Zeit*'s investigation of being in general via the being of Dasein, in this text Heidegger articulates the problematic of being in terms of that of the artwork. He does this by advancing along a diagenic axis from the artwork to the onto-logical origin or being of the artwork, and thereby to a characterisa-tion of being itself.[21] In a familiar Heideggerian move, the essence of the artwork is connected to that of truth. In the author's words, 'the reality [Wirklichkeit] of the work . . . [is] defined in terms of what is at work in the work, in terms, that is, of the happening [Geschehen] of truth. This happening we think of as the contesting of the strife [Bestreitung des Streites] between world and earth. In the intense agita-tion of this conflict presences [west] repose [Ruhe]. It is here that the self-subsistence, the resting-in-itself [insichruhen] of the work finds its ground [gründet].'[22] The artwork is what it is insofar as it is grounded in the strife of world and earth. This strife, moreover, names the logic of the relation of world and earth whereby they are traced to a common ontological origin that constitutes an originary intimacy between them. 'The strife is not rift [Riß], in the sense of a tearing open of a mere cleft; rather it is the intimacy of the mutual dependence [Sichzugehörens] of the contestants. The rift carries the contestants into the source of their unity, their common ground [aus dem einigen Grunde]. It is the fundamental design [Grundriß]. It is their outline sketch [Auf-riß] that marks out the fundamental features [Grundzüge] of the rising up of the clearing [Lichtung] of beings.'[23] Indeed, for Heidegger, the common ontological origin is the event.[24]

3. 'Zeit und Sein' (1962): This text rarely uses the terminology of ground; I include it to emphasise that what is most important in marking out a diagenic axis is not the terminology itself but the relations it describes. In this case, the text enquires into the relation between being (as the 'presencing' of beings) and time. 'Being and time determine each other reciprocally, but in such a manner that neither can the former – being – be addressed as something temporal nor can the latter – time – be addressed as a being.'[25] 'Being' and 'time' cannot simply be collapsed into one term, yet there is an intimate relation between the two. The 'task of thinking' set in this text is to investigate that 'which holds both matters [time and being] toward each other and endures their relation'.[26] The project begins by arranging time and being on a syngenic axis: they

are reciprocally determined, but neither is the originary ground of the other. That which holds time and being together, enduring their relation, is denoted by 'es gibt' (there is/it gives).[27] Structurally speaking, the *es gibt* is not something simple, even if what 'there is' is time or being (that is, if 'es gibt' is taken in the sense of 'there is time' and 'there is being'): it must necessarily involve both the giving dimension and that which does the giving. Additionally, a third dimension is found in what is *given*, the so-called 'gift'. In this case, what is given on the one hand is time and, on the other, being. The task, then, is to think each prong of the problematic – that of being and that of time – in such a way as to discover in each what is concealed, but essential to it: to bring into view the *es gibt*, from whence each respectively is given. Said differently, the task is to take each term and to think into its ontological origin or what would ordinarily be called its ground. Even though there is no precise boundary distinguishing time or being from the giving whereby each is given (both time and being are 'retained in the giving'), there nonetheless is a genetic order of ontological determination at work.[28] That order is precisely a diagenic axis: there is the 'It', the 'giving', and the 'gift' (time, being). Given this arrangement, the question becomes: what is the 'It' that gives time and being? The answer: 'the It that gives in "It gives being," "It gives time," proves to be the event [Ereignis]'.[29] 'What determines both, time and being, in their own, that is, in their belonging together, we shall call: the event.'[30] Thus, time and being, though syngenically related to one another, are diagenically related to the event, which is the ontological ground whence they are originated.

Without a doubt, Heidegger was exceptionally critical of metaphysical concepts of ground taking the form of a substance, absolute foundation, transcendent entity, first principle, or the cognitive apparatus of a representing subject. With the interpretive methodology I am suggesting, then, one must keep in mind that for Heidegger ground is not assimilable to any such metaphysical entity. While his conception of ground developed over time, it never has the sense of something fully present, static, or absolute. In his general use prior to the *Kehre*, the ground of something is simply whatever ontological structure enables it to be. 'Vom Wesen des Grundes' (first edition 1929) offers the most theoretically developed statement on this topic during the early period. It gives a condensed definition of 'the essence of ground' as 'the transcendental springing forth of grounding [entspringende . . . des Gründens], strewn threefold into projection of world [Weltentwurf], absorption within beings [Eingenommenheit im Seinden], and ontological grounding [Begründung] of beings'.[31] After the *Kehre*, Heidegger's work contains an emerging conviction that being should not be understood as the ground *of beings*. His concern, which I shall discuss in detail in Chapter 4, is that this casts being in terms of a relation with beings and by doing so mistakenly characterises the former in terms of the latter. Heidegger's controversial claim in *Beiträge* that beyng is independent of beings is meant to solve this problem. However, it in no way amounts to an overall disavowal of ground, but instead is bound to the important distinction between thinking of being as a ground for beings and thinking of the grounding characteristic belonging to being *itself* (what we just saw in 'Zeit und Sein' addressed as the *es gibt*). *Beiträge* gives a complex account of this latter characteristic in terms of *Ab-grund*, *Ur-grund*, and *Un-grund*. With this, the difference between Heidegger's concept and metaphysical concepts of ground is quite distinct: not only is being not understood as the ground of beings – instead having an essential grounding characteristic itself – but also all grounding operations entail *Ab-grund* or abyssal ground, which both originates and exceeds ground, and this prevents any ground from becoming absolute.

If Heidegger's actual *use* of the concept of ground and the relations it describes were not enough to justify the methodological role I am suggesting, a further point can be emphasised: the problematic of ground itself forms a key register in terms of which he addresses the nature of being. In 'Vom Wesen des Grundes', '"ground" is a transcendental characteristic of the essence of being in general'.[32] In *Beiträge*, *Ab-grund*, *Ur-grund*, and *Un-grund* constitute an essential aspect of beyng as event. The event is characterised by its grounding operations, which are named by these terms. In other words, the structural modalities of ground are used as a way of articulating the evental nature of beyng. In addition to these two exemplary texts, Heidegger directly thematised ground in numerous other instances that bear on his programme in important ways. Adding to those already mentioned, a very abbreviated list might include GA3 *Kant und das Problem der Metaphysik* (1929), GA42 *Schelling: Vom Wesen der Menschlichen Freiheit* (1936), and GA10 *Der Satz vom Grund* (1955–6).

To push back on this interpretive methodology a bit, what about the fact that certain of Heidegger's later texts seem to reject the notion of ground directly? Does it still hold in their light? I believe it does. Let us take one of the counter-examples that most directly critiques ground: 'Der Lehrer trifft den Türmer' in GA77 *Feldweg-Gespräche* (1944–5). Since my task here is to address objections from those who are already familiar with texts like this, I will not unpack the philosophical sense of most of the ideas it presents, but simply use its terms to outline a set of its main moves and show the role of diagenic and syngenic relations. Three main points show why this text does not invalidate diagenic analysis but is in fact consistent with it.

One of the text's central suggestions is that we (yet again) need a full reorientation of the endeavour of thinking, and this requires a critique of 'ground'. In a clear reference to the Aristotelian foundations of thought, we are to give up the 'wondrous' (*Wundersame*), which 'arouses our questioning', 'in favor of the strange' (*Seltsame*), which 'hints back into itself'.[33] Who knows what exactly is meant by the 'strange' here. What is clearly stated, though, is that the 'will of questioning' aroused by the wondrous holds within itself a 'will to fathom [Ergründen] and substantiate [Begründen]'.[34] However, it is also clearly stated that 'to search for grounds, whereby we would once again fall back into questioning as the will-to-a-ground [den Willen zum Grund]' is 'far removed from the way to the strange'.[35] So, that cannot be the proper way for thinking to proceed, according to this text. In contrast, the 'matter for thinking' (*Sache des Denkens*) – the strange – is attained by what Heidegger calls 'a turning-back' (*Rückkehr*).[36] What does that mean? A turning back from where to where? The answer: 'from everywhere we must continually turn back to where we truly already are . . . to *the* inception'.[37] Heidegger calls this other kind of thinking 'inceptual [anfängliche] thinking'.[38] In this manner, inceptual thinking is decisively contrasted with thinking in the form of a will to a ground. So, what of the notion of ground could survive such an attack?

My first point has to do with the distinction between inceptual thinking and the will to a ground. The critique of ground on the basis of which this distinction is made is a critique of the human activity – indeed human *will* – of searching for grounds, not of the ontological status of grounds themselves. This important distinction can be seen prominently in Heidegger's account of beyng as event, in which he lays out two very distinct registers of ground: *gründender Grund* or 'grounding ground' and *Er-gründung* or 'fathoming the ground'. In 'Der Lehrer trifft den Türmer', the critique of the will to ground in the form of *Ergründen* and *Begründen* squarely targets the second – *Er-gründung* – which is derivative of the first. The first, *gründender Grund*, designates not a human will or activity at all, but the operations of beyng as event itself whereby beyng originates and *has* a grounding capacity (*Ab-grund*, *Ur-grund*, and *Un-grund* comprise this register). In *Beiträge*, there are two modes of thinking that correspond with these modes of ground: first is that whereby Dasein – alienated from its being – regrounds itself through *Er-gründung*. The second proceeds not as a search for a ground, but rather *from* the originary, grounding character of the event *to* that which is originated or grounded. This second mode of thinking is precisely the most crucial element of what Heidegger calls 'inceptual thinking', that is, the mode of thought advocated in 'Der Lehrer trifft den Türmer'. Thus, the critique of ground in this text addresses only one dimension of Heidegger's concept and leaves the second, indeed the most ontologically essential dimension, intact.

The second point is that despite this text's critique of the conceptions of ground noted, the diagenic relation is still prominently active in it, even if in an implicit manner. This is seen in a number of contexts. For example, one central theme is the configuration of history that Heidegger argues has given rise to the dominance of 'the essence of modern technology', from which stems 'natural science's manner of representation'.[39] Shortly after bringing up these topics, the discussion turns to asking from whence technological science and representation arise (that is, it takes a methodologically diagenic step). The answer is that they are 'manners of comportment [Verhaltens]' that '*belong* in a sojourn [Aufenthalt] of the human'.[40] Whatever this sojourn happens to be, technological science and representation belong to it, that is, it is that which enables them to be and determines their manner of being. Sojourn has the function of what Heidegger in other texts would refer to as their ontological *ground*. Taking a step farther still, Heidegger claims that 'the domain from out of which we are to think sojourn' is simultaneously the domain 'out of which we are to think . . . the relation between science and technology'.[41] This domain is once again 'the strange'. Thus, the relations of these terms are drawn out on a patently diagenic axis: technological science and representation are grounded in the sojourn, while the sojourn is grounded in the strange.[42]

Third, towards the end of the text, Heidegger asserts a distinction between the question of 'ground' and the question of 'provenance' (*Herkunft*).[43] Unfortunately for us, he does not explain the difference, but suggests that ground is associated with the Greek ἀρχή and αἰτία, terms with lengthy metaphysical legacies. Nonetheless, the provenance of something is its 'whence', its origin, the story of its ontological genesis. In other words, provenance is supposed to give us a way of talking about the ground of something without an admixture of metaphysical content. In a *meta* move that could easily make the reader's eyes roll, the text's discussion leaves off by raising not just the 'question of provenance', but 'the question of the provenance of provenance'.[44] This might be cringe-worthy phrasing, but there is something very interesting going on here, which relates to both the concept of event and of ground. Structurally speaking, the notion of ontological (not simply ontic) provenance requires two elements related in a certain way: the 'thing' whose provenance is in question and that which explains the origination of that thing. Said differently, what is required is the relation between a grounded and a grounding term, in the Heideggerian sense. That which explains the origination of something and the thing itself cannot be simply identical, because then there would be no provenance involved at all. Rather, the relation is between one thing and something *other* from which it is differentiated, and this relation is of a special sort: the latter is what enables the ontological genesis of the former. Consequently, the former bears an inherent, essential, ontologically constitutive reference to the latter and the term 'provenance' encompasses this entire relation. If the question of provenance enquires into the ontological origin of something, the question of the provenance of provenance enquires into the origination of the very relation captured by the term 'provenance'. Whence the differentiation of grounding and grounded terms at all? As I shall argue later, this is answered in Heidegger's ontology of the event, where the question of the genesis of anything that has, as a feature of its being, a constitutive reference to something other than itself is raised. The feature of the event described as 'Ab-grund' originates that described as 'Ur-grund', the most primordial ontological structure able to bear (*tragen*) something else. Because of all this, the further point can be made that the diagenic axis reaches its end in Heidegger's account of beyng as event. That is the apex of his ontology, while related projects like that of thinking *das Geviert* (the fourfold) or *Gelassenheit* (releasement) are extensions of the inceptual thinking grounded therein. Returning to the main question at hand, though, in 'Der Lehrer trifft den Türmer', the grounding relation – in the Heideggerian sense – is alive and well, in fact residing at the core of the text's subject matter.

3 Heidegger's productive logic

Having laid out this preliminary justification for a diagenic reconstruction of Heidegger's ontology, it remains to be explained what exactly the philosophical mechanism is by which this ontology advances along a diagenic axis, that is, to explain the *movement* of Heidegger's thought. It also remains to be demonstrated how this approach solves the four problems listed and allows us to navigate the reflexive difficulty (and subsequent recursive difficulty) in a philosophically rigorous way. I would like to begin by looking at an example of the reflexive difficulty so that it can be more easily identified in Heidegger's puzzling conceptual contexts. This will outline an important 'abyssal' logic that structures his thought, that is, a diagenic axis that finds its end in nothing other than the abyss or *Ab-grund* of beyng. To see how Heidegger navigates this abyssal logic – that is, the mechanism of the movement or evolution of his thought – I will then turn to what he calls the operation of 'Grundlegung' in his 'produktive Logik'.

A clear example of the difficulty that arises from the dynamic, reflexive relation between the methodology Heidegger employed and the subject matter it enquired into is found in the basic terms presented in *Sein und*

Zeit. For Heidegger, the condition for the possibility of doing ontology at all is Dasein's very existence (indeed, in that text Dasein is the ground presupposed by all metaphysics, but which metaphysics is unable to account for). In contrast to the framework of metaphysics, in which the human mind is posited as separated from the object of its enquiry, fundamental ontology recognises that thought *is*. In other words, to do ontology, thinking need not bridge a subject-object gap, it can enquire into its own being and, through that, clarify being in general. 'Dasein', of course, is the name for a being for whom this is the case: a being that is distinguished from others insofar as it has its own being as an issue. But this means that Dasein's enquiry into its own existence is *part of its own existence*, that is, there is a reflexive relation between the matter investigated and the investigation itself. And since the very existence into which Dasein enquires is partially constituted by the operation of questioning, each moment of carrying out that operation modulates its existence. This in turn prompts a recursion of the investigation (also known as the hermeneutical 'circle'). Since a modulation of the subject matter is an ongoing product of the recursive enquiry into it, a dimension of that subject matter is necessarily and perpetually deferred beyond the dimension articulated by the terms of the enquiry, that is, beyond Dasein's discursive understanding of its own being. Dasein's existence always includes an excess over the account developed of that existence.

The issue can be seen clearly insofar as this forms a Heideggerian version of the familiar productive paradox illustrated in the following thought experiment. Imagine I have been tasked with composing a catalogue of every fact about everything that exists. I begin by listing facts about the things I see around me ('The glass is on the table.' 'The table is made of wood.' And so on . . .). Eventually, though, if my list is to be complete, it has to include all the facts about the list itself (for example, 'The list has N entries.'). And this leads to an infinite proliferation. When I add a fact about the list to the list, I have changed it, producing new facts that must in turn be listed. So, I list them. But each time I add another entry, I change the list again, generating new facts, and so on to infinity. In this scenario, there is always a necessary excess of facts over the discursive domain of the list.[45]

For various well-known reasons, Heidegger is not interested in compiling a list of facts like this. Instead, for him the ontology developed by Dasein – the discursive understanding of its own existence and thereby of being – through existential analysis takes the position of the list, while the heart of the subject matter takes that of the excess generated over the list. In Heideggerian terms, suppose that I – Dasein – decide I am going to do fundamental ontology and systematically enquire into my own existence.

As we know from the first division of *Sein und Zeit*, my facticity, under-standing, and the interpretive process itself are important parts of my existence, that is, of the subject matter to be enquired into. For the sake of example, say that the terms my factical context has provided for under-standing my existence are those of a Cartesian subject, fully determined in the time dimension of presence and identical throughout the duration of my life. Through my investigation I discover that things are in fact a bit different: my existence is temporally distended in the form of thrown projection and, consequently, the understanding of myself as identical through time is a distortion generated when the ground of my existence in ecstatic temporality is concealed (that is, it is a mode of inauthenticity). I reinterpret my existence in terms of this more appropriate ground and *eo ipso* my existence is modulated (I understand myself to have a different kind of relation with other beings in the world, I project a different future, and so on). The modulations coming about are not simply changes in my point of view, but transformations of my very existence. The existential operation by which I interpret changes the very thing it is directed towards – *the constitution of my being* (my *Seinsverfassung*). By doing so, the inter-pretive act drives aspects of my existence beyond the scope of understand-ing that it generates.

It would be a mistake to think this type of scenario occurs only with major reinterpretations, like that prompted by discovering one's identity is a farce. Rather, the subject matter investigated, by its very nature, con-tinuously slips out from under its own feet, and this exhibits something about the structure of that subject matter itself. Since the interpretive, discursive process is always at work as a part of the structure of thrown projection, the withdrawal of an aspect of Dasein's being from itself is a constitutive feature of that very being (*Sein*). In fact, this is the feature constituting the *ecstasis* of ecstatic temporality. Without it, the temporal and existential distention that is drawn from facticity through the dis-cursive elements of interpretation and understanding and out into the domain of projection would be impossible. Dasein would collapse into a mere thing like a table or a dirt clod. In other words, this would be death. Though Heidegger might be in that state, we luckily are not . . . at the moment. For the living, the process of interpretation is always operative in Dasein's existence, regardless of whether one is investigating their own being or not. When the investigative gaze *is* directed in this way and one does fundamental ontology, the interpretive process takes a trajectory *into* the ontological ground of whichever structural elements of their existence have thus far been articulated by their discursive understanding. This is one important mode of what Heidegger calls 'transcendence'.

More generally speaking, in Heideggerian ontology the productive paradox at the heart of the reflexive problem drives or draws the subject matter enquired into beyond the account given of it at any moment in the process of questioning. This amounts to a reflexive, transformative relation between the account given and what the account is about, which characterises Heidegger's work. In terms of fundamental ontology, this operation of questioning drives forward the problematic of Dasein's existence, and, with it, that of the ground of ontology and the task of working out the nature of being. In other words, the reflexive relation drives an immanent evolution of the account given at any moment beyond itself, superseding earlier stages. In this case, the possibility of a total and exhaustive account of Dasein's existence is always deferred beyond the one articulated in any particular instance.

For Heidegger, this logic of deferral characterises not only the epistemological and existential situation of Dasein, but an abyssal logic or logic of excess belonging to being. In 'Vom Wesen des Grundes', he discusses this in terms of 'freedom' as 'the abyssal ground [Ab-grund] in Dasein'.[46] In *Beiträge*, he develops this in terms of abyssal ground as one of the essential dimensions of the grounding character of being as event.[47] Fascinatingly, this text begins to think of the abyssal ground in terms of a logic of ontologically originary, inexhaustible differentiation, which places Heidegger's work into conversation with thinkers like Deleuze and Derrida in new and interesting ways.

The fact that this logic belongs to being, moreover, has an important effect on the structure of Heidegger's methodology. If the problematic of being includes an abyssal logic in which an aspect of being is always deferred beyond each account given of it, and each account is, moreover, necessarily disrupted by its reflexive relation with this subject matter, how is the project of ontology to contend with this situation? One answer is simply 'deconstruction' or the 'hermeneutics of suspicion': we can focus on using the problematising element of being to undermine the pretensions of any concept or account and philosophy can become the worship of our own powerlessness and the confrontation with our own guilt of thinking in a way that always bears the inscription of such concepts (Derrida). Another answer is to become outright theologians: to take the problematising element of being to be the mark of God, pretending that the abyss loves us, and thereby turning philosophy into the exploration of a spiritual comfort blanket (Marion). A different answer is to pursue the abyss with a sense of adventure, enquiring into its structure and provenance, and trying to articulate being in a way harnessing its genetic character in an ongoing conceptual experimentalism. Heidegger, I believe, oscillates between the first and third of these, with a remarkable degree of success.

The way Heidegger's philosophy navigates the abyssal logic can be clarified by looking at what, in *Sein und Zeit*, he calls the 'productive logic' belonging to his methodology. It describes the way his ontology renders progressively more grounded or appropriate (*eigentliche*) accounts of being that advance along a diagenic axis. Importantly, a set of modulations of the concept of ground play a central role in defining his productive logic. This logic shows that though deconstruction is an important part of Heidegger's methodology, it does not simply remain within those bounds, but from early on employs a rigorous, creative conceptual experimentalism or genetic methodology.

Heidegger's discussion of productive logic is situated in his argument for the priority of the question and science of being with respect to other sciences (the main examples he comments on are mathematics, physics, biology, and theology). The ideas he uses here, though, are not confined to making this distinction. They apply to any problematic insofar as it includes an account articulating its subject matter and this account experiences a *Grundlagenkrisis* (crisis in its grounds or foundations), forcing it to revise them by developing a more appropriate understanding of its subject matter and, in turn, to fundamentally reconfigure the broader account by which the problematic field is articulated. These ideas apply to Heidegger's own ontology, which consistently tracks the abyssal logic entailed in and perpetually disrupting the fundamental terms of the problematic of being and reconfigures its account of being on the basis of more originary articulations that this enables.

In Heidegger's analysis, all sciences have a *Sachgebiet* (subject matter).[48] This can either be a *Bezirk* (domain) of beings, as in the cases of 'history, Nature, space, life, Dasein, language', or the being of beings in general, as in the case of fundamental ontology.[49] To a domain, which I have also called a problematic field or simply a *problematic*, belongs a set of *Grundstrukturen* (basic/ground structures) understood to characterise its subject matter and determine proper terms for scientific (*wissenschaftliche*) research about it.[50] Here, 'the basic structures [Grundstrukturen] of any such area' are not the product of pure theoretical investigation; they bear a factical character, having 'already been worked out after a fashion in our pre-scientific ways of experiencing and interpreting that domain of being [Seinsbezirkes] in which the area of subject-matter is itself confined'.[51] To illustrate this, our pre-scientific experience of regularity in nature might lead to theoretical research producing an account of laws of nature. Here, we develop *Grundbegriffe* (basic/ground concepts) to articulate the *Grundverfassung* (basic/ground constitution) of the subject matter at hand: for example, Newton's three laws of motion as used to articulate the basic constitution of the problematic field of nature.[52] The *Grundstrukturen* we understand to characterise a problematic field are revisable on the basis of scientific research. The objects thematised by such research provide one means for clarifying them. For example, research on natural objects helps to clarify the laws of nature: we can test to see if $F = MA$ or $F = M/A$. *Grundbegriffe* serve as a ground *for* more derivative concepts and operations within a science, like calculating the trajectory of a cannon ball or explaining planetary motion. As Heidegger puts it, 'basic concepts [Grundbegriffe] determine the way in which we get an understanding beforehand of the area of subject-matter underlying all the objects a science takes as its theme, and all positive investigation is guided by this understanding'.[53]

What does Heidegger mean by 'positive' investigation here? Ordinarily, a science's *Grundbegriffe* take on an axiomatic role, go unchallenged, and become more or less transparent to their practitioners. In Heidegger's terminology, positive investigation or positive science is scientific research done in such conditions. Positive science includes the type of research characteristic of logical positivism in which systems of propositions are analysed for internal semantic and syntactic consistency, consistency with the rules of an established logical language, and, regularly, consistency with the theoretical and methodological propositions of the natural sciences.

However, according to Heidegger, 'real progress' in research comes not in its positive operations, but by 'inquiring into the ways in which each particular area is basically constituted [Grundverfassungen]'.[54] Thus, we see two modalities of science: positive research that operates within the logic of a set of *Grundbegriffe*, which are not themselves in play, and what I will call 'radical' science, which problematises its *Grundbegriffe* in order to develop a more appropriate (*eigentlich*) account of the *Grundverfassung* of its subject matter. In fact, for Heidegger:

> The real 'movement' [eigentliche 'Bewegung'] of the sciences takes place when their basic concepts [Grundbegriffe] undergo a more or less radical revision which is transparent to itself. The level which a science has reached is determined by how far it is *capable* of a crisis in its basic concepts. In such immanent crises the very relationship between positively investigative inquiry and those things themselves that are under interrogation comes to a point where it begins to totter.[55]

Heidegger uses this framework to argue for the priority of fundamental ontology with respect to all other sciences. His central point is that, whether they recognise it or not, the *Grundbegriffe* of other sciences contain presuppositions about the being of the domain of beings constituting their subject matter. Certainly, the factical concepts framing fundamental ontology also contain presuppositions, indeed faulty ones, but it is an explicit task of fundamental ontology to root them out (its deconstructive dimension). In other sciences, the very delineation of a problematic field entails an interpretation of the being of the set of beings making up that field: 'Since every such area is itself obtained from the domain of beings themselves, [the] preliminary research, from which the basic concepts are drawn, signifies nothing else than an interpretation of those beings with regard to their basic state [Grundverfassung] of being.'[56] However, since such sciences are unable to clarify sufficiently the being of beings in general, they require one that does. That science is fundamental ontology. Without it, faulty presuppositions about the being of beings built into a science's *Grundbegriffe* get transmitted throughout that science as a whole. Without first being grounded by fundamental ontology, a science's *Grundbegriffe* cannot provide an appropriate account of the *Grundverfassung* of its subject matter. Fundamental ontology must *lay the grounds* for other sciences. Since the historical condition of the sciences is such that their *Grundbegriffe* bear faulty interpretations of the being of beings, fundamental ontology enacts the second, radical type of science. It challenges the *Grundbegriffe* of other sciences and provides the ground in terms of which they can be appropriately revised.

Here, we can see the fault in Carnap's critique of Heidegger. The Carnapian charge results from attempting to make sense of Heidegger's bizarre linguistic constructions from a position external to the ontological problematic within which they were produced. In other words, it fails because it does not recognise the distinction between (1) technical conceptual or linguistic formulations that operate within an established syntax – at the level of positive science – to which grammatical analysis within that syntax properly applies, and (2) formulations that aim to articulate the ground enabling an established syntax to be, that is, formulations operating in the service of radical science.

In Heidegger's account, 'ground-laying [Grundlegung] for the sciences is different in principle from the kind of "logic" which limps along after, investigating the status of some science as it chances to find it, in order to discover its "method"'.[57] *Grundlegung* does not operate like positive science within the logic of an established set of *Grundbegriffe*, but as radical science, problematising them and cutting into deeper ground on the basis of which they may be reconfigured. It is this process that Heidegger calls 'productive logic'. *Grundlegung*, he writes, 'is a productive logic – in the sense that it leaps ahead, as it were, into some area of being, discloses it for the first time in the constitution of its being [Seinsverfassung], and, after thus arriving at the structures within it, makes these available to the positive sciences as transparent assignments for their inquiry'.[58] This process is *productive* because it discloses new aspects of the being of a science's subject matter and produces new, more ontologically appropriate *Grundbegriffe* to articulate it. The productive logic characterising

Grundlegung does not simply deconstruct the *Grundbegriffe* of a problematic field; it does that *and* ventures new *Grundbegriffe* or accounts to articulate the *Grundverfassung* of its subject matter in an ontologically appropriate way.[59]

Of course, the function of fundamental ontology for Heidegger is not simply to lay the grounds for other sciences, but to work out the nature of being. In doing so, fundamental ontology enacts the same radical movement with respect to the problematic of being. This is seen in a number of contexts, including its disruption of the historical framework of metaphysics forming its factical situation. This disruption begins by grounding ontology in the existential analysis of Dasein, which leads to the complex, reflexive evolution of ontology and the abyssal logic entailed in its problematic. This complexity and logic characterise the problematic of being in Heidegger's analysis from early to late, not merely the methodology of *Sein und Zeit*.

The terminology of Heidegger's productive logic helps clarify this. The radical movement of his thought is precisely along a diagenic axis, drawn out by the abyssal logic. The evolution of his ontology enacts an incessant line of *Grundlegung*. Each of Heidegger's renditions of the ontological problematic is generated by problematising the *Grundbegriffe* of a previous rendition (say, that of the historical framework of metaphysics). He tracks the implicit but previously unrecognised logic entailed in the ontological features articulated by those *Grundbegriffe*, but exceeding the account they offer, to a standpoint more originary and appropriate (for example, the nexus of thinking and being constituted by a being that has its own being as an issue). He then recasts the *Grundbegriffe* to articulate his subject matter in a more originary and appropriate way, that is, he lays new grounds for the ontological problematic (for example, the concept of Dasein and consequent programme of existential analysis). The account constituted by laying these grounds enables a reconfiguration of the entire problematic field at hand. In each rendition, then, Heidegger advances the ontological problematic by employing this productive logic. In the language of abyssal logic, each rendition is opened up to the abyssal logic entailed in its ground, destabilised by tracking that logic deeper into the abyss, and casting a set of *Grundbegriffe* articulating the dimensions of the problematic thus disclosed. This renders a conceptual distance or oblique angle with respect to the terms of the previous account, enabling them to be fundamentally rethought.

This productive logic describes not only the macrological movement of Heidegger's ontology, but micrological movements involved in the transformation and generation of concepts within his texts, sections, paragraphs, and sentences. Making sense of his concept of event or other difficult, post-*Kehre* terms requires situating them in their proper location in the evolution of his account and reconstructing them with respect to their function in advancing the productive logic entailed in the problematic of being. In Chapters 3 and 4, I shall give a detailed example of this productive logic via an analysis of Heidegger's transformation of the ontological problematic of truth and how this renders a first properly grounded account of being as *Ereignis*.

It is worth pointing out three features of Heidegger's concept of event on the basis of this movement. First, the historical sense of the event, as a rupture in the foundations of metaphysics, has its ontological origin in the abyssal logic characterising the problematic of being. He pursues this problematic and its logic perpetually drives his thought beyond each rendition of being he generates. The concept of event is meant to articulate being in a way free of metaphysical import. Second, Heidegger's concept of event *develops* in different works.[60] Since an abyssal logic is built into it, a totalised concept of the event is impossible in principle. Instead, it offers an open-ended ontology and renders the evental nature of being essentially 'problematic'. Third, Heidegger does not introduce the concept of event into his ontology in an external, adjunct way such that it could be defined independently of it. He arrives at the concept by pressing through the project of *Sein und Zeit*. That project generates methodological and conceptual horizons that are eventually driven beyond themselves by the logic of the problematic of being. The concept of event articulates this problematic in the advanced stages of the evolution of Heidegger's account. It is within these horizons, or rather through their evolution, that the event is defined. Heidegger's use of this concept marks a supersession of earlier forms of his method and its concepts.

4 Solutions

The complex structure of the movement of Heidegger's ontology – necessitated by the abyssal logic belonging to the problematic of being and the reflexive relation between being and his methodology – calls for an interpretive realignment of his texts and concepts. The conventional approach to Heidegger's corpus is, ironically, chronological or 'historiological' (*historisch*). In it, the relations of his texts and their conceptual renditions of various problematics are analysed according to their positions along the timeline of his career, while observing the general pre-/post-*Kehre* rubric. In contrast, in the approach I suggest, their relations should be based on the simultaneously methodological and ontological relation animating the movement of his thought that I have discussed: that of grounding and grounded terms. My view is that Heidegger's corpus should be arranged according to the degree of grounding each text or conceptual scheme is able to attain. That is, they should be analysed according to their position along a diagenic axis rather than a chronological one. This provides a rigorous way to deal with the type of complex evolution found in Heidegger's work, to solve the four problems stated above, and to reconstruct his concept of event properly.

4.1 Solution to the problem of consistency

My methodological claim is that the philosophical evolution of Heidegger's ontology occurs along a diagenic axis. With each rendition of new *Grundbegriffe* comes a clarification of syngenically related features within the problematic field at hand. The apparent inconsistency of some of Heidegger's accounts of the same subject matters arises by viewing them as if they treated their matter at the same diagenic level in his ontology or were produced at the same diagenic stage of the evolution of that ontology – that is, as if they were syngenically related. This, however, utterly misconstrues Heidegger's thought. The systematic consistency of such accounts can be explained by way of their position in the methodological evolution of his work. Said differently, their consistency is found in the relation they have via the reflexive, iterative logic of the diagenic axis of his problematic of being.[61] The distinction between diagenic and syngenic axes allows us to clarify the supersession involved in the evolution of Heidegger's ontology and the relations between many of his difficult concepts. This solves the problem of consistency because it explains the internal relation of concepts as they develop within his texts and how one and the same subject matter can be explained in different terms at different stages of the ontology. In contrast to simply grouping elements of Heidegger's thought according the macrological distinction between the pre- and post-*Kehre* periods, diagenic analysis allows us to account for the *particular* characteristics of *particular* micrological conceptual transformations.

A few of the important moves made in *Sein und Zeit* Division I can serve as a good example. (1) Heidegger begins with a diagenic move, enquiring into the condition of possibility for the science of being. He pays special attention to the way that science has been construed in key *Grundbegriffe* offered by major systems from the history of metaphysics (time, subject, substance, etc.) and the failure of those concepts to sufficiently articulate their own ground. He establishes Dasein as the needed condition, thereby recasting the ground of ontology. (2) On that basis, he establishes the basic/ground constitution (*Grundverfassung*) of Dasein as being-in-the-world, and then develops a number of syngenic aspects of being-in-the-world: all the elements involved in the worldhood of the world, being-with, being-in, and so on. (3) At the end of Division I, his focus again turns to the diagenic axis in the search for a more originary unity grounding all the different syngenically related aspects of being-in-the-world. He writes:

> The totality of the structural whole [Die Ganzheit des Strukturganzen] is not to be reached by building it up out of elements . . . The being of Dasein, upon which the structural whole as such is ontologically supported, becomes accessible to us when we look all the way *through* this whole *to a single* primordially unitary [ursprünglich einheitliches] phenomenon which is already in this whole in such a way that it provides the ontological foundation for each structural item in its structural possibility [so daß es jedes Strukturmoment in seiner strukturalen Möglichkeit ontologisch fundiert].[62]

It is no accident that Heidegger refers to this ontological foundation as the *being* of Dasein. The force driving forward the problematic of being is the question of the ground whence the elements of a current rendition of that problematic are enabled or originated. In the passage just cited, the analysis of anxiety serves that methodology, allowing him to arrive at a conception of *Sorge* (care) as such a ground and as the being of Dasein.

4.2 Solution to the problem of arrangement

The solution to the problem of arrangement is simply an extension of that of the problem of consistency. The arrangement of different stages and elements of Heidegger's ontology is determined by diagenic and syngenic axes. We can systematically make sense of the transformations his ontology undergoes, and thereby avoid the confusion arising from mixing up elements of different stages, by being attentive to the position of those elements on these axes. Indeed, because the character of being includes the operations of ground it performs, Heidegger's axis of ground forms both an essential methodological and an ontological order. Thus, his accounts of being, of its various proxies (ἀλήθεια, φύσις, Anwesenheit, Ereignis, etc.), and of related matters like the origin of the work of art and the fourfold should be sequenced diagenically rather than chronologically. Sequential renditions are produced through the self-modulating, reflexive, productive logic of *Grundlegung*. This draws out the diagenic axis. Each new account is generated by working out how its problematic drives or draws the conceptual horizon of the extant account beyond itself, then developing new concepts to articulate that newly uncovered dimension, and finally rethinking the terms of the extant account on that basis.

This means that that problematic is driven or drawn to a more originary grounding.

4.3 Solution to the problem of terminology and grammar

Do Heidegger's bizarre linguistic formulations amount to nothing more than mysticism? Is his philosophy linguistically rigorous? I have already indicated the error in the Carnapian critique in terms of the distinction between positive and radical science. Now that error can be reformulated. The Carnapian position fails to recognise the structure of the evolution of Heidegger's ontology whereby new and often bizarre technical formulations are generated out of methodological need. It fails not only to recognise the distinction between positive and radical science, but between (1) formulations that operate on a syngenic axis, to which grammatical analysis within the syntax of that axis properly applies, and (2) formulations that operate along a diagenic axis, which aim to articulate the ground enabling the syntax of a syngenic axis to be. It thus fails to register the *relations* of Heidegger's technical terms, mistaking them for the relations that can be accounted for within a positivistic, established syntactical system.

The concern about Heidegger's language is especially apparent when dealing with the concept of event. The rupture with metaphysics that he intends this concept to establish introduces philosophical material with which the language of the tradition is unequipped to deal. Without a doubt, Heidegger failed to recognise sophisticated theories of events in the work of predecessors like Leibniz, Lucretius, and the Stoics. He rather flatly condemned such philosophers as restricted to thinking within the metaphysical framework oriented by the question of *Seiendheit* or the beingness of beings: τί τὸ ὄν. Putting my misgivings with this diagnosis aside, Heidegger's view entails that such conditions resulted in understanding the nature of events to be secondary to that of beings. The view that events are merely modifications of the attributes of a subject is a prime example. As I emphasised earlier, this metaphysical framework is infused into our very grammar, as can be seen in our use of a subject and predicates as the basic building blocks of a sentence. Moreover, our technical philosophical vocabulary has been adapted to the traditional problems that lay within that framework. Heidegger's concept of event aims to give a more fundamental account of being than is possible within the framework of *Seiendheit*, which involves problematising the very ground of metaphysics and, consequently, its language. His project engages the rupture in the tradition's conceptual structure that the event figures. Consequently, uncovering new aspects of the event and of ontological structures related to it requires developing new technical language, language that gains its philosophical purchase in the context of the evental problematic. Defining and evaluating it thus requires first taking into account the conceptual and methodological transformations that generate it.

To be clear, my claim is not that *all* of Heidegger's bizarre formulations are philosophically rigorous, but that those that *are* can be clarified on the basis of their roles on syngenic and diagenic axes. These axes offer a powerful tool for explaining the relations of terms and thereby determining what aspect of the ontological problematic they are used to articulate. Moreover, they provide a way for understanding the systematic function of terms that violate an established syntax by operating in a radical mode. Sheehan and others have expressed frustration with the hyper-jargonised, inconsistent state of the terminology on which much Heidegger scholarship has relied (especially English language scholarship) and I strongly agree with this sentiment.[63] Such lingo clouds the compelling accounts Heidegger gives as he grapples with the issues of his concern. However, at the same time some of these issues *do* require disrupting our language and grammar and developing new constructions for radically reconfigured philosophical landscapes. I do not believe this justifies perpetuating needlessly bizarre, often unintelligible jargon in scholarship. Instead, we should give precise accounts of Heidegger's concepts even, and *especially*, when what they aim to grasp has aspects that are conceptually indeterminate (as in the case of *Ab-grund*, for instance) or that are on the cutting edge of his thought and yet to be fully worked out. The challenge is simply to be precise about the syngenic and diagenic horizons within which certain concepts work, how and where they problematise those horizons, and the aspects of the problematic organising those horizons that they aim to articulate.

4.4 Solution to the problem of textual priority

On this basis, I return to the fourth problem: how to interpret the place and priority of Heidegger's various texts within his corpus. In the context of research on his concept of event, this issue is prompted by a debate over the importance and validity (or lack thereof) of *Beiträge* and the related private manuscripts. I will offer my solution within this frame. In my view, we ought to reject a popular interpretive approach that sidelines these texts. It claims that *Beiträge* should be disregarded (1) in light of later, published texts that address many of its core themes, especially *Ereignis*, and (2) because of its fractured, rough character.[64] Thus, this approach advocates the priority of the accounts of themes like *Ereignis* in certain later texts over those found in the private manuscripts.

Broadly speaking, that interpretive approach presupposes the chronological or 'historiological' axis for organising Heidegger's work. His texts and their accounts are sequenced loosely along a timeline, again usually observing a general distinction between pre-*Kehre* and post-*Kehre* periods. Within these groupings, certain texts are said to provide more genuine statements of Heidegger's thought than others. A text's chronologically advanced position in the corpus is taken to indicate a *philosophically* advanced status. The reasoning is that such a text had the benefit of more refinement and thus is the more mature statement of the author's thought. I do not deny that this is often the case. But the reason a later text is more philosophically advanced than another is not *because of* its chronological position. Rather, one is more advanced than another because it advances the enquiry into the nature of being or any of this enquiry's sub-problematics farther. Thus, if a chronologically earlier text advances the problematic of being farther than a later one, the former should be arranged interpretively as more philosophically advanced. Since the various renditions of these problematics are organised along diagenic axes, what it means to be more philosophically advanced is to hold a more originary position on a diagenic axis: one account is more philosophically advanced than another if it articulates the ground whence the elements of the other are enabled to be.

When it comes to *Beiträge* and the related private manuscripts, the chronological approach places these on a linear axis according to the dates of their writing, situated among Heidegger's other texts. With respect to the concept of event, therefore, chronologically later texts like *Der Satz der Identität* (1957) and *Zur Sache des Denkens* (1962) are taken to hold more philosophically advanced and genuine statements of Heidegger's thought on the topic. This position justifies dismissing aspects of the event in *Beiträge* that are not prominent in later texts. When those later texts, for example, explain the event to be a co-dependent, co-appropriation between being and human existence, chronological interpreters often take this to be grounds for dismissing the position in *Beiträge* that the event is independent of beings.

The chronological approach often correlates with the second suggestion noted, that texts Heidegger made publicly available during his lifetime should be given preference over rougher, private manuscripts. For instance, Richard Capobianco has posited the philosophical superiority of *Einführung in die Metaphysik* (1935) over *Beiträge* on these grounds.[65] Troublingly, this pre-empts certain objections to his overall interpretation of Heidegger, according to which being is thought 'as *physis* as *alētheia*' and 'Ereignis' is simply a different word for the same thing (objections to such a position can clearly be raised on the basis of texts like *Beiträge*).[66]

Despite the merit of Capobianco's analyses of ἀλήθεια, φύσις, and many other of Heidegger's concepts, the reasoning for such an interpretive decision is unconvincing. First, even though Heidegger suggested that *Beiträge* did not have the 'form' of a publishable 'work', he very much affirmed the text's project and as far as I have determined, beyond occasional minor points of critique, did not find its philosophical content to be of sub-par quality.[67] Second, and more importantly, even if Heidegger did believe the content of his private manuscripts was sub-par, it would not mean it in fact *is*. Authors are often poor interpreters of their own work. Their reflective statements can certainly be helpful in unlocking obscure aspects of their text. But the richness of the text often far exceeds what is recognised by the author him- or herself. Monet famously judged many of his *Water Lilies* to be unacceptable and Virgil died issuing the order that his *Aeneid* be burned. Even if Heidegger had disavowed *Beiträge* as philosophically faulty which to my knowledge he did not – he obviously could have been wrong. Third, the richness of a text and the account it offers is not necessarily a function of its compositional elegance, unified structure (take Nietzsche's aphorisms, for example), or aesthetic qualities one happens to prefer. As an example of the problem identified by this last point, Capobianco expresses a preference for a tempered, 'gentile' account of *Ereignis* in Heidegger's later texts over an 'eruptive event-ful-ness and momentousness' he finds to characterise *Ereignis* in *Beiträge* and the related writings.[68] He does not, however, offer reasons as to why these are preferable characteristics.

With respect to *Beiträge* in particular, I am sceptical about the sentiment that diminishes the status of the text because of its fractured, unpolished character: if the content is there, then the content is there, even if it is a rough read. I am especially sceptical about diminishing its status on the basis of the fact that Heidegger did not publish it. If one hopes to study the skills of a master samurai, a choreographed display sanitised for public consumption falls short. One wants to observe the warrior in the throes of real battle: how do they navigate the onslaught of their adversary? How do they improvise in changing conditions with setbacks and injuries? How do they handle their sword, use a particular environment to their advantage, and exploit their adversary's unique weaknesses? How do they conserve energy and avoid fatigue? The same goes when studying the work of a thinker. Texts polished for publication are obviously indispensable, but one should hope to study how a thinker actually thinks as they are in the throes of their problematic. This is precisely what we find in Heidegger's *Beiträge* and the related private manuscripts. Here, Heidegger is writing openly, for himself. In contrast to the later texts and lectures dealing with *Ereignis* made public during his lifetime, *Beiträge* offers an unsanitised account. It is the battlefield version of the concept, not the Discovery Channel version. Moreover, to study the *limits* of a warrior's skills, one would want to see them in action as they employ all within their power to handle a superior adversary, as the adversary begins to overwhelm them, and, finally, as the warrior's body is splintered and disintegrated in an ultimate charge into the abyss of the adversary's sword. *Beiträge* and the related private manuscripts are the texts in which Heidegger pushes his thought to its farthest limits and, as a result, where it begins to fragment. But this also means that some of their accomplishments are Heidegger's greatest. *Beiträge* (together with the related manuscripts) does not provide just another rendition of Heidegger's problematic, it provides the one farthest advanced along the diagenic axis: the account of the event in *Beiträge* articulates the ground whence the structures used to articulate his problematic in other, public texts are originated.

Since I hold that the key to Heidegger's philosophy is a grounding movement along the diagenic axis coupled with clarification of syngenically grounded structures at each stage, this is what organises my interpretive approach and reconstruction of his work. Heidegger's texts and concepts should be sequenced not along a chronological axis, but a diagenic one. They should be arranged according to the degree of grounding each is able to attain. Sometimes this overlaps the chronological progression. In the problematic of the essence of truth – which serves as the conceptual entryway to his account of the event – the account in 'Vom Wesen der Wahrheit' is more originary than that in *Sein und Zeit*: it provides the ground whence the more derivative structures of truth in *Sein und Zeit* are enabled to be. Similarly, the account of truth in *Beiträge* articulates the ground whence the structures in 'Vom Wesen der Wahrheit' are enabled to be, and thus it is more advanced on the diagenic axis. But the chronological axis is not the governing structure of Heidegger's work, and this fact becomes critical if we look at a text like the 1949 Bremen lecture, 'Einblick in Das Was Ist'.[69] In it, Heidegger rethinks the nature of beings in terms of the fourfold on a non-metaphysical ground – the evental account of beyng. But since his texts explicitly dealing with the nature of the event work out the ground for an account of the fourfold, they must be read as more advanced on the diagenic axis, even though 'Einblick in Das Was Ist' is chronologically later than some of them. Likewise, since Heidegger's account of the event in later published texts like *Der Satz der Identität* and *Zur Sache des Denkens* articulates the event at the level of the mutual appropriation of human existence to being and of being to human existence – whereas in *Beiträge* the event is the very ground enabling such an appropriation – the former must be read as less originary on the diagenic axis than the latter (even if they happen to provide better accounts of parts of their themes!). Indeed, in my view *Beiträge* and the related texts articulate the most profound degree of grounding in Heidegger's corpus. They should be taken as its philosophical apex, that is, as having advanced Heidegger's problematic the farthest.

5 Conclusion

Diagenic analysis provides a consistent method able to navigate the reflexive difficulty, solve the problems that arise from it, and reconstruct particularly tricky parts of Heidegger's ontology in a rigorous manner. Without a way to explain the consistency and relations of his various renditions of the ontological problematic, our efforts to make good sense of them become haphazard and arbitrary, and scholars face the danger of appropriating his language without being able to provide rigorous definitions for his unusual terms. The diagenic approach satisfies these conditions by explaining the engine driving the evolution of Heidegger's thought, the consistent structure of that evolution, and its necessary violation of the terminology and grammar of metaphysics.

'Event' – the central concept of Heidegger's later work – has presented scholars with particular difficulty. In the remaining chapters, I use diagenic and syngenic axes to critically reconstruct his account of beyng as event.

Notes

1. GA65 73/58–9.
2. *SZ* 10/30.
3. In Heidegger's work related to the event, he often spells 'Sein' ('being') with the archaic 'Seyn' ('beyng'), and this carries a technical significance that I discuss in later chapters.
4. 'The Being of beings "is" not itself a being' (*SZ* 6/26). Macquarrie and Robinson translate 'Seiendes' as 'entity' or 'entities' (see *Being and Time* 19, fn. 1). I substitute 'being' or 'beings' when I cite their translation or similar translations of other texts.
5. *SZ* 6/26. This formulation relies on the ontological difference, without which the question of being would collapse into the question of beings as beings (Aristotle's ὄν ἦ ὄν).
6. GA65 348/275, italics removed.
7. GA65 386/305.
8. For dozens of examples of this, just read the posts exchanged on the Heidegger Circle forum.
9. Braver, 'Analyzing Heidegger' 240.
10. GA11 45/36.
11. Richardson, *Heidegger: Through Phenomenology to Thought* passim.
12. For instance: Dahlstrom, *Heidegger's Concept of Truth*; Alejandro Vallega, *Heidegger and the Issue of Space*; Young, *Heidegger's Philosophy of Art*.

13. *WW* 177nA/136nA; GA65 379/299.
14. Saussure, *Course*.
15. Temporal lines will not work because in texts like *Beiträge* one of Heidegger's concerns is with the very origination of temporality.
16. GA65 371–88/293–306.
17. *SZ* 53/78.
18. GA24 322/227, translation modified, '. . . worin die Grundstrukturen . . . gründen'.
19. GA24 323/228, translation modified.
20. Heidegger, 'Der Ursprung des Kunstwerkes', in GA5 1/1.
21. As Heidegger puts it, 'Reflection on what *art* may be is completely and decisively directed solely toward the question of *being*. Art . . . belongs . . . to the Event out of which the "meaning of being" (compare *Being and Time*) is first determined' (GA5 73/55).
22. GA5 45/33.
23. GA5 51/38.
24. Much more could be added to this summary, of course. It is worth pointing out that an alternative outline of the diagenic axes in this text could focus on how 'art is history in the essential sense: it is the ground of history [sie Geschichte gründet]' (GA5 65/49).
25. GA14 7/*On Time and Being* 3.
26. GA14 8/*On Time and Being* 4, translation modified.
27. GA14 9/*On Time and Being* 5.
28. GA14 10/*On Time and Being* 6.
29. GA14 24/*On Time and Being* 19, translation modified.
30. Ibid., translation modified.
31. Heidegger, 'Vom Wesen des Grundes', in GA9 171/132, italics removed.
32. GA9 172/132, italics removed. 'Transcendental' is used here in relation to Dasein's transcendence or *Überstieg* (surpassing) (GA9 137/107). The term 'transcendental' 'names all that belongs essentially to transcendence and bears its intrinsic possibility thanks to transcendence' (GA9 139/109).
33. GA77 164–5/106.
34. GA77 164/106.
35. GA77 165/107.
36. GA77 171/111.
37. GA77 176–7/115, italics removed.
38. GA77 187/122.
39. GA77 179/116.
40. GA77 181/118, my italics.
41. GA77 192/125.
42. It is worth noting that Heidegger references the historical sense of the event here in terms of the sojourn: 'For the essence of history [Geschichte] is determined from that which is, to us, called "the sojourn." If we are successful in turning to enter this sojourn, then a liberation from history could come about' (GA77 184/120).
43. GA77 200/130.
44. GA77 199–200/130.
45. Deleuze assigns a distinctive ontological importance to this paradox, which he discusses in relation to Lewis Carroll and calls the 'paradox of regress, or of infinite proliferation' (*Logique du sens* 41/28).
46. GA9 174/134, translation modified, italics removed.
47. GA65 379/299.
48. *SZ* 9/29.
49. Ibid.
50. Ibid.
51. Ibid.

52. Ibid., translation modified.
53. *SZ* 10/30.
54. *SZ* 9/29.
55. Ibid.
56. *SZ* 10/30. There is an additional, implicit logic supporting Heidegger's claim for the priority of fundamental ontology with respect to ontic sciences. The problematic field of an ontic science is defined by the set of beings or aspects of beings it takes as its subject matter (the problematic fields of biology and ethics both include human beings, but each with respect to different aspects). In other words, there are sets of beings or aspects of beings that are *excluded* by each ontic science except one. That, in Heidegger's view, is metaphysics, which is guided by the question of what beings are insofar as they are beings, that is, *Seiendheit* or Aristotle's ὄν ᾗ ὄν. Since no ontic science can contain all beings under all aspects (insofar as they are beings) in its problematic field without becoming identical with metaphysics, none can give a sufficient account of the being of beings *in general*. Likewise, metaphysics is incapable of this because it fails to mark the ontological difference between being and beings. It investigates beings insofar as they are beings, but not the being of beings. Otherwise, it would become fundamental ontology, which is precisely what Heidegger is aiming to accomplish. Consequently, neither metaphysics nor any other ontic science is capable of supplying an appropriate account of the being of beings. Yet their basic concepts contain presuppositions about this. Thus, fundamental ontology is needed to clarify the being of beings and properly ground the ontic sciences.
57. *SZ* 10/30, translation modified. I translate 'Grundlegung' as 'ground-laying', rather than Macquarrie and Robinson's and Stambaugh's 'laying the foundations' throughout.
58. *SZ* 10/30–1, translation modified.
59. Heidegger cites Kant as an example of this sort of productive logic: 'the positive outcome of Kant's *Critique of Pure Reason* lies in what it has contributed towards the working out of what belongs to any Nature whatsoever, not in a "theory" of knowledge. His transcendental logic is an *a priori* logic for the subject-matter of that area of being called "Nature"' (*SZ* 10–11/31; Heidegger is not using 'positive' here in the sense of 'positive science').
60. This is not always a smooth or seamless development, but one of fits and starts. Heidegger's reflections on this process in *Beiträge* §42, entitled '*From "Being and Time" to "Event"*', are helpful: 'On this "way," if to keep falling down and getting up can be called a way, it is always and only the same question of the "meaning of beyng" that is asked. Therefore the positions of the questioning are constantly different. Every essential questioning must radically change whenever it questions more originally. There is no gradual "development" here. Even less is there that relation of the later to the earlier according to which the later would already lie enclosed in the earlier. Since everything in the thinking of beyng is directed toward the unique, to fall down is, as it were, the norm here! This also rules out the historiological procedure: to renounce the earlier as "false" or to prove that the later was "already meant" in the earlier. The "changes" are so essential that their scale [Ausmaß] can be determined only if in each case the *one* question is pervasively asked out of its own site of questioning' (GA65 84–5/67–8). Polt restates a key point as follows: 'Neither should we say that *Being and Time* already includes what comes later; the movement toward the *Contributions* is not a deduction of what is implied by some previous propositions, but trailblazing' (*EB* 44).
61. This is not to say that *all* of Heidegger's work is consistent. It is difficult to imagine that in a corpus so extensive every single idea proposed would be consistent. Yet if we look at the overall arc of his work, diagenic analysis shows that the vast majority is.
62. *SZ* 181/226.
63. See Sheehan, 'A Paradigm Shift'.

64. As an instance of a position favouring the importance of *Beiträge*, Daniela Vallega-Neu writes that it 'may be considered Heidegger's second major work after *Being and Time*' (*HCP* 1). For a position downplaying its importance, see Capobianco, *EH* 35–6 and *HWB* 20 and 51–2.
65. *HWB* 50–1.
66. *HWB* 50. Also see *EH* 35–6.
67. GA66 427/377. I thank Richard Polt for drawing my attention to this passage.
68. *EH* 150n6.
69. Heidegger, 'Einblick in Das Was Ist' in GA79.

Chapter 2

The Historical and Ontological Senses of 'Event' and their Relation

Despite the prominent role of the concept of 'Ereignis' or 'event' in Heidegger's philosophy, there has been little scholarly agreement about its nature. To mention just a few of the most developed positions, the event has been suggested to be (1) a mutual appropriation between human existence and being that is responsible for the constitution of meaning in an historical world,[1] (2) just another name for being as *physis* or *alētheia*,[2] (3) an occasional, emergent transformation of history,[3] (4) the name for a thoroughly *historical* essence of being,[4] (5) the term via which Heidegger aims to perform a poietic saying of 'being as and in its historical happening',[5] and so on. I shall suggest that such positions are incomplete and that in Heidegger's most developed text on the topic – *Beiträge* – there are *two* core senses of 'event'. They are distinguished diagenically and I designate them the 'historical' and 'ontological' senses.

In this chapter I focus on two things. First, I outline the distinction and relations between the two senses of 'event'. I argue that the historical sense has a methodological priority over the ontological sense, while the latter has an ontological priority over the former. These relations determine the structure of the rest of this book. Second, given this methodological priority, I turn to an outline of Heidegger's ontology of history and a more detailed account of his concept of an historical event. This involves some preliminary contextual work. Reconstructing Heidegger's 'event' – in both versions – requires explaining it in light of a methodological and conceptual continuity with the groundwork for ontology established in *Sein und Zeit* §§1–7. That groundwork is the point of departure for the diagenic evolution of his ontology. Its analysis of the 'ontico-ontological condition for the possibility of any ontologies' establishes the proper setting for the science of being's productive logic of *Grundlegung*.[6] As noted earlier, that condition is Dasein: the being whose existence includes thinking about that existence.[7] The result is that in Heidegger's early work the methodological arena for pursuing the question of being is the existential analysis of Dasein. His early ontology of history works on this basis: Dasein is the existential-ontological ground of history and the history of metaphysics is that of the transmission of a distortion in Dasein's existence and factical world. Outlining this allows me then to shift to his later philosophy of history in *Beiträge* and its conception of an 'other beginning' (*anderer Anfang*) for history and for thought that results from an historical event.[8] In contrast to what I call 'fatalist' interpretations of Heidegger's event, I argue that Dasein has an important role in bringing about an historical event. The core term describing this role is '*Er-gründung*', translated by Rojcewicz and Vallega-Neu as 'fathoming the ground'. In its core meaning, fathoming the ground is a collection of operations whereby historically alienated Dasein endeavours to reground itself.

Before going farther, it will be helpful to locate the Heideggerian concepts of event in relation to some broader concerns in his philosophy. The historical and ontological senses of event correspond with the first two of three major problems that consistently structure his thought.

Problem 1:   The first problem is that of resolving distortion and alienation. The historical sense of event corresponds with it and I explore their connection in detail in this chapter. To use one of Heidegger's images, the solution to this problem is analogous to a movement up a river toward its source. Fathoming the ground addresses this problem.

To help clarify, let me define my use of 'distortion' and 'alienation' in this context. By 'distortion' I mean the process by which something constitutes a self-obfuscation or, in cases where two things are in a diagenic relation, the process by which one obfuscates the other. Heidegger sometimes discusses this in terms of *Verborgenheit* (concealment) and *Unverborgenheit* (unconcealment) or *Entdecktheit* (uncoveredness), although these terms extend to cases of syngenic occlusion that are not instances of distortion (for example, when my table conceals the chair behind it). (To be clear, at the level of structural features of the phenomenological disclosure of a world, concealment and unconcealment or uncoveredness are irreducible. At certain other levels that I shall discuss, they are not.) By 'alienation', I mean the state of obfuscation insofar as that state *obfuscates* the process by which it is constituted, that is, insofar as something in that state appears as if it were not the result of distortion (namely, that distortion that it is in fact a result of). In *Sein und Zeit*, the most essential register in which Heidegger understands distortion and alienation is Dasein's *Uneigentlichkeit* or inauthenticity in conjunction with the history of metaphysics that reinforces that inauthenticity. In *Beiträge*, he reframes it in terms of a more originary historical 'epoch' or framework of metaphysics that involves ontological features diagenically prior to Dasein and that is expressed in 'machination', 'representation', and 'lived experience'.

Problem 2:   The second problem is to develop an account of the nature of being (the river's source) that is freed of the distortion and alienation involved in the framework of metaphysics. The ontological sense of event corresponds with this.

Problem 3:   The third problem is to explain the genesis of metaphysical distortion and alienation (the return from the source back down a transformed river).

Problem 3 is meant to be addressed on the basis of 2. Problems 1 and 2 do not mean the elimination of distortion, but the elimination of *metaphysical* distortion: that which arises on the basis of the history of metaphysics in conjunction with the existential dynamics of Dasein. We should contrast this with what we might call ontological distortion: that inherent to and irreducible from the structure of being itself. This plays an important role throughout Heidegger's philosophy and is discussed in *Beiträge* in terms of the 'Un-wesen' or 'distorted essence' of truth and the 'Unwesen des Seyns' or 'distorted essence of beyng'.[9] According to these terms, beyng generates self-distortion. Sorting out what this means will be important in Chapter 5.

Without a doubt, Heidegger's philosophy maintains not only that there is such ontological distortion, but also that certain forms of *alienation* are irreducible from human life (for example, there is no such thing as becoming perfectly authentic). Nonetheless, his work is geared towards minimising alienation and metaphysical distortion and understanding ontological distortion in a way that keeps the processes generating it in view, that is, that does not devolve into alienation. Together, I shall refer to these tasks as the tasks of 'resolving'. At the epistemological level, 'resolving' means the incremental elimination of illusion or delusion.

Heidegger's concept of an historical event forms the core of his later work's attempt to resolve the distortion and alienation belonging to the historical framework of metaphysics (problem 1). His ontological event is the concept he uses to rethink being in a non-metaphysical way (problem 2). Heidegger's response to problem 3 usually comes in the form of promissory notes that do not offer much of an actual solution, though I will say a bit more about this in what follows.

The historical and ontological senses of 'event' are closely related, and Heidegger does little to differentiate them terminologically. In fact, I would wager that he was not entirely clear about the distinction at work in his text. Commentators have generally conflated the two, most often by reducing the ontological sense to the historical. This is commonly expressed by defining Heidegger's project in *Beiträge* and the related private manuscripts in terms of 'seynsgeschichtliche Denken' (beyng-historical thinking). Is this the essential descriptor for these texts? Only if 'event' signifies nothing other than a transformative rupture in the ontological foundations of the epoch of metaphysics, in other words, the production of a new configuration of being, where being is understood as the manifestation of history in its many facets. On the other hand, if in some manner there is an excess of being over the domain of history and if Heidegger uses 'event' to articulate the structure and character of that excess and its relation to history, that is, to articulate the ontological structures or processes themselves grounding the domain of history, then the term has a second sense irreducible to its historical one – it has a distinctively ontological sense. I shall argue that this is a central idea advanced in *Beiträge* and that failing to take it into account leads to a confusion of the rest of the philosophy he built around the concept of event.

Distinguishing the two senses of 'event' is indispensable. Yet their connection is equally important. As mentioned, I will argue that the historical sense has a methodological priority over the ontological one, while the latter has an ontological priority over the former. In brief, the idea is that we cannot give an account of beyng as event without passing through a transformative rupture in the ground of metaphysics, that is, without moving to another beginning for thought. But only if beyng is in fact such that it cannot be sufficiently articulated by metaphysics is such an historical event possible at all. 'Event', in its ontological sense, describes just such aspects of beyng that are ontologically and diagenically prior to metaphysics, that enable metaphysics to be at all, and that likewise make possible a transformative rupture in the foundations of metaphysics. To be clear, I do not mean to say that Heidegger's historical sense of event is not ontological. It is. But the precise way it is must be defined: it is ontological to the extent that it has to do with the ontological constitution and transformation of history.

1 The historical sense of 'event'

Heidegger argued that there is a problem in the current historical situation of human existence: the human being and all its various endeavours are existentially determined by the historical framework of metaphysics. In its historical sense, 'event' designates a transformative rupture in that framework that generates new forms of human existence freed of the errancy and alienation metaphysics entails. Incidentally, many Heidegger scholars work under the assumption that the historical epoch of metaphysics extends to our time in the early twenty-first century.[10] I will bracket this assumption and simply say that I find it questionable after thinkers like Deleuze and Badiou.

For Heidegger, our historical situation is largely bad because the framework of metaphysics governing it is constituted by a distortion and consequent alienation. In *Sein und Zeit*, the distortion in question is found in the existential structure of Dasein; in *Beiträge*, it is a more fundamental distortion shaping the historical field in which Dasein exists. In both cases, it takes hold in the ground of the practical, intellectual, conceptual, linguistic, creative, interpersonal, political, technological, and other dimensions of historically situated human life (in shorthand, the 'historical' dimensions of human life). Consequently, it saturates all those grounded dimensions.

Clearly, in this picture 'metaphysics' refers to more than just (1) the philosophical science of that name. It also encompasses (2) the distortion that grounds that science, (3) this distortion's manifestation in the historical dimensions of human existence, and (4) the historical epoch governed by this distortion and extending from the ancient Greeks to the twentieth century (or whenever). These different aspects of metaphysics have somewhat complicated relations. The distortion (and consequent alienation) grounding the history of metaphysics took hold in ancient Greece and became fast in the discursive, philosophical frameworks advanced by Plato and Aristotle.[11] This came to provide the *Grundbegriffe* defining the scope and character of the other sciences as well as the broader historical dimensions of human life, all of which in turn reinforce that general framework by forming the factical context absorbed and repeated by each generation of thrown Dasein. There are a variety of negative consequences for human existence. When it comes to philosophy, some of the most pressing are errors in our understanding of the nature of beings, the human being, thought, truth, time, and, of course, being.

The philosophical science of metaphysics plays an interesting role in Heidegger's larger treatment of our historical errancy. Its terms capture that errancy in precise discursive forms. They compose structurally determinative points organising the evolving framework of metaphysics (in the broader sense). This is interesting in its own right, but it also tells us something about how philosophers might effectively respond to this situation: if we undermine the determinative points of metaphysics and generate a new form of thinking based on better grounds, we will have taken some first steps towards resolving the alienation in question and accomplishing the type of historical event with which Heidegger is concerned. What, then, are the principle commitments defining metaphysics in its form as a philosophical science? Heidegger's answer varies in different texts. Nonetheless, there are core ideas he often repeats. This list is not meant to be exhaustive and not all metaphysical systems do all the things on it. Metaphysics:

1. is oriented by the question of ὂν ᾗ ὄν (beings as beings), which Heidegger argues Aristotle articulated in its most general form as τί τὸ ὄν (what are beings?). (Note: Heidegger translates Aristotle's question in the plural.)
2. understands being in terms of the temporal frame of presence (*Anwesenheit*), exemplified by Aristotle's παρουσία and οὐσία.
3. conceives of beings as fully determinate or objectively present and self-identical through time.
4. understands being on the basis of characteristics attributed to beings.
5. posits an ultimate foundation – usually in the form of God or an unconditioned absolute – for everything that is.
6. conceives of 'the world' as a universe or totality of things there are.
7. conceives of 'reality' or 'actuality' as something thoroughly calculable or measurable by the mathematical sciences.
8. conceives of the human being as subject.
9. conceives of thought as representation.
10. understands truth to be *adaequatio*, correspondence, or certainty.

Heidegger often places 1 and/or 2 at the ground of the others; 6 and 7 are especially prevalent in the modern era but are rooted in Greek philosophy. Different items on this list will be important in different parts of the following chapters. In Chapter 3, 10 will be especially important; in Chapter 4, 1, 4, and 10; in Chapter 5, 1, 4, and 5; and in Chapter 6, 2, 4, and 5.

In *Beiträge*, Heidegger puts special emphasis on defining metaphysics in terms of point 1, that is, in terms of an orientation to the question of beings as beings (ὂν ᾗ ὄν), sometimes expressed in the form τί τὸ ὄν (what are beings?).[12] 'All metaphysics', he writes, is 'founded [gegründet] on the leading question: what are beings?'[13] In fact, he recognises that metaphysics has had certain successes in answering this question. The problem, however, is that this orientation entails a distinctive myopia and consequently sets into place a philosophical horizon governed by that myopia: because metaphysics explains things in terms of the ontic character of beings as beings (*Seiendheit*), it is unable to provide a suitable account of being (*Sein*). Since metaphysics is oriented by the question of beings as such, when it comes to ask about being, it treats being as if it were *a* being and renders it as a transcendent idea or form, a substratum, God, an abstract universal, or some such thing. As long as our efforts to understand being operate within the framework of metaphysics, he argues, we are doomed to failure. The specific character of the foundations of metaphysics and their self-myopia prevents success in the science of being. Thus, a genuine rupture with metaphysics must be made. Since we live within the historical framework of metaphysics, though, this rupture has to be generated from *within* that framework. Heidegger works to do this by enquiring into the ground enabling the historical configuration of metaphysics, a ground that in his early work is understood in terms of the existential constitution of Dasein – the ontico-ontological condition for the possibility of any ontology.

Importantly, this does not mean that metaphysics is simply to be done away with. The enquiry into its ground has a dual role: along with effecting the kind of rupture he is after, reconceptualising this ground has the promise to give metaphysics a refreshed basis for its own projects, especially that of providing an account of beings. Ultimately, Heidegger's efforts to fulfil this promise have limited success, appearing largely as a reconceptualisation of beings in terms of *das Geviert* (the fourfold) in 1949 and the 1950s.[14] This effort is meant to be non-metaphysical for reasons I cannot go into here and it does not make major appearances in *Beiträge*.

In *Sein und Zeit*, Dasein's existential constitution is the ground enabling any ontology, including the diminished form as metaphysics. Thus, fundamental ontology or the project to rethink being on proper grounds operates via the existential analytic of Dasein. Since this addresses the very ground of metaphysics, it enacts the beginnings of the rupture Heidegger is after. It performs the movement of radical science with respect to the *Grundbegriffe* set in place by metaphysics. Yet, as his own later critique of *Sein und Zeit* points out, the project of fundamental ontology did not go far enough: its understanding of being – and of human existence – remained essentially determined by metaphysics because it continued to think being on the basis of beings (namely of Dasein). Because of this, it repeated the error of the Aristotelian orientation of philosophy and inadvertently determined being in terms of *Seiendheit* or 'beingness'. Thus, for Heidegger, a more profound rupture with metaphysics is required. This rupture is figured as the transition from the project of a fundamental ontology of Dasein to the project of thinking being as event. Heidegger thinks that if we were to accomplish this, a genuinely distinct other beginning (*anderer Anfang*) for thought would become possible. This rupture, which he continually strives to bring about but never thinks he has sufficiently accomplished, is the first, 'historical' sense of 'event': the event as a rupture in the framework of metaphysics that drives or draws thought beyond metaphysics, but which can only be pursued from within its factical, historical horizons. I think Heidegger was more successful in this than he realised.

2 The ontological sense of 'event'

In its second sense, 'event' is the core concept in terms of which Heidegger's *Beiträge* attempts to rethink being and, in turn, the plight of human existence in a way freed of metaphysical errancy.[15] I give an outline of the concept here and introduce many of the technical terms it involves. The main explanation of these terms, the arguments for the account outlined here, and most of the textual support for it will be provided in the rest of the book.

In short, beyng *is* the event. Heidegger usually avoids the verb 'to be' (and its conjugated form 'is') when making this point to keep from importing the metaphysical understanding of being as substance, quiddity, or *Seiendheit*. Instead, he usually substitutes it with a verbal form of the German noun 'Wesen' ('essence'), namely 'wesen', or uses a nominal modification of that verb ('Wesung') that is meant to emphasise the verbal, non-substantive character of the term.[16] For instance: 'Beyng essentially occurs as the event' ('Das Seyn west als das Ereignis') or 'The essential occurrence of beyng constitutes the event' ('das Ereignis die Wesung des Seyns ausmacht').[17] The use of this terminology has two immediate implications. First, the event must not be mistaken as the substance, quiddity, 'whatness', or *Seiendheit* of beyng. Second, as highlighted by the verbal form of 'Wesen' ('wesen'), beyng as event is not static, but rather occurs. This is not to say that the event occurs now and then in time. Neither is it outside of time. Rather, I will suggest that it is characterised by a structural instability that generates or constitutes time. The event *occurs* because it is a dynamic process motivated by the structural instability at its heart.

This second sense of 'event' has an ontological and diagenic priority over the historical sense and I take it to be the richest in Heidegger's thought. As Heidegger points out, 'history [Geschichte] is not the event'; the 'other' beginning initiated by a rupture with the history of metaphysics is possible only because beyng is evental.[18] It is true that when the project of developing an ontology of the event is no more than a glimmer on the philosophical horizon, the historical, ruptural sense might appear primary. Yet, the historical event is unthinkable without whatever ontological element drives or draws thought beyond metaphysics. In other words, if metaphysics provided a sufficient ontological framework, it would be impossible for thought to discover aspects of being that are irreducible to that framework, and so there would be no possibility of a rupture with it (historical or otherwise). However, I hold that in Heidegger's ontology, thought is constitutively connected to a logic of being (as event) that undermines the foundations of metaphysics, and, further, that this is a necessary condition for the occurrence of the event in its historical sense. The logic of beyng as event provides the ontological form of the 'other' historical beginning: 'the beginning – grasped primordially – is beyng itself', indeed 'beyng as the event is the beginning'.[19] Obversely, since our factical conditions dictate that we exist and think within the framework of metaphysics, if we want to develop an account of that ontological element (the evental character of being), we can do so only beginning within and sculpted by these conditions.

The structural instability of the event that makes it a dynamic process or occurrence provides its genetic power or its function as a ground for worlds of beings. Its instability undermines any tendency to collapse into a static, substantive identity. Identity – even if only quasi-stable – can exist only on the ground of the event. This means that beyng as event is diagenically prior to all constituted identity. Thus, Heidegger understands the event's structural instability in terms of *difference*. In the ontological sense of 'event', beyng as event is a dynamic or logic of what I have called 'pure' difference (*Unterschied, Unterscheidung*, and in a particular sense *Entscheidung*).[20] This logic is driven by the differentiation of that difference from itself such that it self-determines in processes of appropriation (*Er-eignis*) and expropriation (*Ent-eignis*), which, elaborated in the registers of truth, ground, and time-space, constitute the genetic ground of worlds of beings, that is, of the 'Da' expressed in the term 'Da-sein'. 'Da-sein' does not designate human existence here, but the determinate field or finite world in which human beings exist. This is signified by Heidegger's use of the hyphen. Outside of the context of his 1957 lecture '*Der Satz der Identität*', little scholarship has focused on the importance of 'difference' in his concept of event (an excellent exception is Krzysztof Ziarek's 2013 *Language after Heidegger*) or the function of difference as a genetic ground of the 'Da', so I anticipate my view on this might run into some resistance. To quell objections from the get-go, I support these points with the following quotations. I provide argumentation for this position in the following chapters. Using Heidegger's words, the event is 'the difference [Unterscheidung] as the essential occurrence of beyng itself, which differentiates *itself* [*sich* unterscheidet] and in that way lets beings arise in emergence'.[21] Beings *are* in the field of the 'Da' or 'there', and 'beyng essentially occurs as the event of the grounding of the "there" [Ereignis der Dagründung]'.[22]

In this picture, the event entails an abyss or excess of difference, which takes the position of the abyssal logic I discussed in Chapter 1. Although abyss and excess may seem to be opposites, Heidegger's language of the 'abyss' is part of the discourse of 'ground' I have already begun to explore: abyss is *Ab-grund* – the prefix 'ab-' evoking both a 'lack' and an 'origin' of ground. Heidegger holds that while the abyssal dimension of the event involves a sense of total lack, this is a genetic or originary lack – a lack that grounds all that is. Simultaneously, the abyss is excessive in three senses: (1) it is the ground whence all that is *is* as the abyss's overflow or abundance, (2) it withdraws from or exceeds that which it grounds, and (3) it thus exceeds the measurability characteristic of that which it grounds.[23] Heidegger sometimes refers to this abyssal or excessive character as an *ab-gründige Unerschöpfung* (abyssal undepletion) or *Unerschöpflichkeit* (inexhaustibility).[24]

The event's self-differentiation is a perpetual displacement that simultaneously generates and undermines determinacy (in the form of ontological structures, worlds, and beings). The event's self-determination unfolds in a 'turning' of processes of *Er-eignis* (appropriation) and *Enteignis* (expropriation).[25] It has often been suggested that Heidegger's event simply *is* appropriation or appropriation in conjunction with expropriation. I shall argue that this is incorrect: these form part of the dynamics of the event, but its abyss of difference exceeds the logic of appropriation and expropriation. The logic of appropriation and expropriation form the event's basic logic of determinacy, which enables the manifestation or coming to presence of beings. That is, it enables beings to *be*. Heidegger understands the process of this manifestation in terms of his concepts of ground, timespace, and especially truth.

Truth, at one level, is a dynamic relation between what Heidegger terms originary concealment or withdrawal (λήθη) and unconcealment (ἀλήθεια). Most scholarship on the subject maintains that this *a-lēthic* framework gives the most originary conception of truth in *Beiträge*. I will argue that this is not so. Ἀλήθεια and λήθη are grounded in difference, and so the concept of truth expressed in that text is most originarily differential, not *a-lēthic*. In the context of the event, Heidegger's concept of truth forms part of an account of the advent of the world: at the *a-lēthic* level, the event is a process by which the structures of originary concealment and unconcealment are appropriated in a co-determinate relation of simultaneous 'strife' and 'intimacy', and this unfolds in a way that gives determination or finitude to a world. Explaining what exactly these unusual concepts mean will have to wait until later.

This process is integrally related to time (as the temporal character of being) and history. In part, the event figures an originary process that is ontologically prior to the historical and out of which historical epochs unfold. History is an *epochal* history, where an epoch is not simply a 'span of time' but a determination or formation of being that is enabled or given its determination (that is, is sent or 'destined' [*geschickt*]) by an originary holding back or withdrawal ontologically prior to that formation of being: 'A giving which gives only its gift, but in the giving holds itself back and withdraws.'[26] Here, the 'sequence of epochs' or transformations of being is determined by withdrawals that enable them.[27] Richard Polt argues that for Heidegger *Ereignis* is an occasional event that occurs as the inception of an historical epoch ('it happens only at a few, inconspicuous moments').[28] I think this is only part of a larger story: the inception of such historical epochs is one aspect of a more primordial event. This primordial event can be characterised neither as occasional nor continual – either approach would locate the event within the domain of temporality, whereas this event is originary *of* temporality. In other words, *Ereignis* grounds the time in which any occasional event might occur.

Metaphysics, characterised by the 'forgottenness', eclipse, or obfuscation of the withdrawal of being in favour of the presence it enables, understands being in terms of presence.[29] Thus, Heidegger argues, the event and the withdrawal essential to it are ontologically prior to the metaphysical determination of being as beingness (*Seiendheit*). Since metaphysics, furthermore, understands human existence on the basis of being as presence, the event is also ontologically prior to human existence, metaphysically determined. In contrast, Heidegger recasts the human being on a more originary ground, resulting in an account in which a mutual appropriation of being to human existence and human existence to being is one dimension of the event. Sheehan and Meillassoux take this mutual appropriation to form the heart of Heidegger's event, resulting in the view that his ontology is categorically anti-realist. This, however, is incorrect, at least within *Beiträge* and the related private manuscripts. It is certainly true that the mutual appropriation of being and Dasein is a dimension of the event, but there are other dimensions not captured by the logic of appropriation. Perhaps more straightforwardly damning of the anti-realist view is Heidegger's insistence that in its most originary sense beyng as event is not dependent on relations with beings, most notably human beings (nonetheless, it must be emphasised that this does *not* imply that the event is metaphysically transcendent).

3 The criterion of radical critique

At this point, I would like to introduce a criterion that I think should be satisfied by any ontology, even if that ontology is open-ended like

Heidegger's. I adopt it from a different context: Deleuze's reading of Salomon Maimon and Nietzsche in relation to Kant's critical philosophy. This was formative for Deleuze's approach to ontology in *Différence et répétition*. Simply put, Maimon and Nietzsche offer Deleuze a way to argue that the *critique* in Kant's critical philosophy does not go far enough. Supposing Kant were successful in deriving the conditions of possibility for experience and marking the boundaries of knowledge in terms of the legitimate functioning of the cognitive faculties, his philosophy is nonetheless insufficient because it does not give an account of the *genesis* of those faculties or the real experience they enable. It does not show 'the genesis of what has been criticized', as Hughes puts it.[30] Only in doing so can the critical philosophy be sufficient or rise to the level of what can be called 'radical critique', which is the criterion that I would like to introduce.

Différence et répétition attempts to recast Kant's *Kritik der reinen Vernunft* and satisfy this criterion, albeit in its own terms. For Deleuze, the prime critical target is the regime of representation and its categorial systems, together with the ontological priority of identity presupposed by such systems. He argues that prioritising identity over difference renders an ontology insufficient. In a move similar to the one I am attributing to Heidegger, Deleuze tries to fix this by proposing an ontology in which difference is primary, and the regime of representation and identity are generated secondarily.[31] Following Maimon and Nietzsche, he recognises that this project's success requires more than a condition-focused critique of systems grounded in identity and representation. Merely replacing such systems with an ontology of difference is insufficient as well, for representation and identity (at least a quasi-stable form of identity) are real – they cannot be simply subtracted from the scope of ontology. Rather, the differential ontology proposed must explain the genesis of identity and representation, giving an account of how they come to eclipse their differential ground, that is, an account of the ontological and epistemological distortion that is constituted.

I would like to suggest a similar requirement be made of Heidegger. This requirement is not by any means alien to his philosophy and is directly related to problem 3 pointed out at the beginning of this chapter. The prime target of Heidegger's critique is metaphysics, which is to be supplanted with an ontology grounded in the concept of event. According to the criterion of radical critique, if this ontology is to be sufficient – within the bounds of Heideggerian methodology – it must not merely show the errors and limits of metaphysics and develop an account of being as event, but also explain the genesis of metaphysics on that basis. More precisely, it must satisfy the following criteria. (1) It must account for the way in which that which exceeds the framework of metaphysics does so.

One way Heidegger does this is by showing the insufficiency of metaphysics to account for its own ground. (2) It must account for the genesis of metaphysics. In Heidegger's work, this involves two aspects: (a) the 'Destruktion' or deconstruction of the historical and conceptual foundations sustaining metaphysics and the alienation it constitutes, which gives us a better picture of the ground of metaphysics, and (b) the promised, though perhaps never actualised, recuperation of a metaphysics grounded in the event and reconstructed on its basis. The latter would constitute a fundamental transformation or re-appropriation of metaphysics on proper ontological grounds and require a robust theory of distortion. In Chapter 5 I discuss the mechanism of distortion in Heidegger's account of beyng as event in terms of the noted 'Un-wesen' or 'distorted essence' of truth and the 'Unwesen des Seyns' or 'distorted essence of beyng'. I find Heidegger's work to fall short when it comes to satisfying criterion 2(b).

4 The methodological and ontological relation between the two senses of 'event'

Heidegger's 'event' has the two senses indicated: at the historical level, it is a transformative rupture in the historical and conceptual framework of metaphysics that produces another beginning for thought; at the ontological level, it articulates the nature of beyng. Though the second has an ontological and diagenic priority, the first has a temporary methodological priority because it is the concept available within the horizon of metaphysics. A properly grounded articulation of beyng as event is not available within this horizon, thus that horizon must be breached – enacting the historical event – by an ontological method able to generate access to aspects of beyng that are more originary than those of the historical framework of metaphysics. In Heidegger's philosophy, this method is the productive logic of *Grundlegung*, which moves ontology along a diagenic axis.

In the advanced stages of this evolution something remarkable occurs. The methodological priority of the historical event holds only insofar as the horizon of thought is defined by the framework of metaphysics. But once this horizon is breached, that priority begins to dissolve. Said differently, the priority of the historical event holds only until a sufficiently originary state of grounding is attained: the state in which a well-grounded, non-metaphysical account of being is generated that is, at least in principle, sufficient for providing a genetic explanation of metaphysics, i.e., of fulfilling criteria 2(b) of a radical critique (even if that explanation is not in fact given). At that point, the difference between methodological and ontological priority collapses: the two merge and the ontological sense of event gains methodological primacy. What this means is that rather than operating with the distance belonging to metaphysical or representational thought, philosophical methodology takes on the logic of being as event, develops an account of the event from a standpoint immanent to that logic, and establishes the ground for a non-alienated reconceptualisation of the domain of history and its metaphysical epoch.

A philosophical effort focused on the historical event alone is insufficient for developing a non-metaphysical account of being and, consequently, for bringing about the historical event itself. The concept of the historical event is a concept of a transformative rupture with metaphysics, but this means that it is co-determined by metaphysics. The historical event can occur only as the by-product of developing a properly grounded non-metaphysical account of being. Though Heidegger devotes a great deal of attention to working through the problematic of the history of metaphysics, developing a robust theory describing it and analysing a variety of canonical texts, this should not be mistaken as the core of his project. In turn, the destructive or deconstructive mode of his method can have only a temporary role, at least in principle. Prior to reaching a state in which ontology is grounded in the logic of being as event, the productive logic of *Grundlegung* necessarily includes the negative or deflationary operation of deconstruction. The productive, conceptually experimental, or affirmative operation of *Grundlegung* by which ontology generates new accounts of its subject matter remains structurally mitigated by the task of deconstruction, and this is because the terms of the ontological problematic are defined by the alienation from being manifested in the history of metaphysics. In this state, the affirmative operation is bound to the task of remedying this alienation, that is, grounding human existence, Da-sein, history, and so on, in being.

However, once this task is accomplished by attaining a methodological grounding in the logic of the event, the negative, deconstructive dimension can be sidelined. Heidegger describes this as the moment of 'join[ing] the free conjuncture [Fuge] of the truth of beyng out of beyng itself'.[32] Doing so grounds an affirmative method that elaborates the logic of the event and enacts a logically immanent, inflationary conceptual experimentalism. Heidegger seems to think that *Beiträge* does not get to this point, but it seems to me that it at least begins the affirmative process. In Chapter 6, I try to show how this works in terms of his concepts of ground and time-space. The concepts that an affirmative method generate would both articulate the event and serve as the *Grundbegriffe* for accounts of diagenically derivative things like beings, worlds, historical configurations, and a variety of ontological structures. Since in Heidegger's terms the defining task of metaphysics is to explain beings as beings, these *Grundbegriffe* would offer a basis for what we might call an appropriately grounded *experimental metaphysics*.[33] To suggest this does go beyond Heidegger's text to a degree (the use of such a term certainly does), nonetheless it is a logical entailment of his ontology of events: 'the age [Zeit] that would elaborate the essential form of beings from out of the truth of beyng'.[34]

These relations determine the structure of the rest of this book. In contrast to approaches to Heidegger's concept of event that focus on its historical sense, my reconstruction in Chapters 3 to 6 focuses on its onto-logical sense. The remainder of the current chapter sets this up by looking at the groundwork for ontology in *Sein und Zeit* and then going into more detail about his ontology of historical alienation and the historical concept of event. This elaborates on the methodological and conceptual continuity between the two senses of event and allows me to expand on the reasons that working out the ontological sense of the event simultaneously enacts the historical event. In *Beiträge*, 'truth' is the primary ontological term through which proper conceptual grounding in the logic of the event is secured. Thus, in Chapter 3 I look at the diagenic evolution of Heidegger's account of truth from *Sein und Zeit* to 'Vom Wesen der Wahrheit' and in Chapter 4 I turn to an analysis of truth in relation to the event in *Beiträge*.

5 The groundwork for fundamental ontology in *Sein und Zeit*

τὸ γὰρ αὐτὸ νοεῖν ἐστίν τε καὶ εἶναι

Parmenides, Fragment 3

The relations of priority between the two senses of event reflect a broader issue structuring Heideggerian thought from the beginning. If the hori-zons of our practical and intellectual lives are factically defined by our position within the historical epoch of metaphysics *and* we hold that those horizons are insufficient for giving an account of being, then we are com-mitted to the idea that in one manner or another there is an excess of being over the domain of metaphysics. Ontology must move beyond metaphys-ics if it is to give an appropriate account of being and, on that basis, of beings. But how can this be possible? Either we are locked into the domain of metaphysics entirely, in which case Heidegger's project and the histori-cal event he describes are impossible, or we are not, in which case there is some Ariadne's thread that leads out. Heidegger thinks the latter is true.

This thread is discovered by critical enquiry into the ground of meta-physics, that is into being. The opening sections of *Sein und Zeit* provide a methodological grip on it by placing the productive logic of *Grundlegung* in its proper setting: they ground that logic in the distinctive ontico-ontological structure that operates as the condition for the possibility of ontology – Dasein – and thereby establish the philosophical and methodological ground from which Heidegger's programme proceeds. The foundations of metaphysics do not somehow not exist (otherwise there would be no problem), so the thread *itself* is the continuity between the logic of those foundations and the logic of being, that is, the order of onto-genesis that produces or constitutes the framework of metaphysics, despite (or *because of*) the fact that doing so is a self-obfuscation by being.[35] We can understand the thread's trail that we follow, then, to be the diagenic axis that draws forward the evolution of Heidegger's ontology.

Heidegger began developing his specialised concept of event in the 1930s as the result of a diagenic evolution of the ontology he had worked out in his earlier period. This means that in order to reconstruct his concept of event it is necessary to track the thread of that evolution from its point of origin: the groundwork of *Sein und Zeit*. If traditional approaches to the question of being work within the framework of representational thought and its implicit distance from its objects, *Sein und Zeit* transforms the question into a concrete structure of Dasein's existence. There, the historical errancy of metaphysics is grounded on a distortion and alienation in Dasein's existence. Since we pursue the *Seinsfrage* via the existential analysis of Dasein, this pursuit *simultaneously* enacts incremental progress in the project of ontology *and* in resolving Dasein's historical alienation. This movement prefigures that in *Beiträge* of Dasein's efforts to bring about the historical event – the movement of *Er-gründung* or 'fathoming the ground'.

The history of metaphysics is the history of the forgetting (*Vergessenheit*) of being; the transmission and transformation of error with respect to the ground of ontology. Plato's ἰδέα and Aristotle's οὐσία emblemise the initiation of this history in discursive or 'scientific' form. The question τί ἐστι or τί τὸ ὄν is answered in terms of a thing's participation in a Platonic idea that transcends this world and its time or in terms of the thing's position in the Aristotelian categorial system grounded in the absolute foundation of οὐσία and its identity. In both cases, the being (*Sein*) of a thing is reduced to what defines it as the kind of being (*Seiendes*) it is, its *Seiendheit* or beingness. By orienting philosophy in this way, later philosophical systems replicate the view that being is *Seiendheit*, or that *Seiendheit* in the form of *quidditas, essentia, realitas, actualitas*, etc., simply is the fundamental subject matter of ontology. Because of this, philosophy since the ancient Greeks has failed to properly work out the ground of ontology. The fundamental task Heidegger confronts in *Sein und Zeit* is to break the hold of the foundations of metaphysics and rehabilitate the question of being, which he does by marking the difference between being and beings and enquiring into the condition for the possibility of any ontology. Needless to say, he is not modest in his ambitions to rectify over 2,000 years of philosophy.

Ordinarily, Heidegger's approach to determining the ground for ontology is understood in terms of his phenomenology. No doubt, phenomenology plays an important role. But his conception of phenomenology in *Sein und Zeit* is governed by the logic of *Grundlegung*. Only because phenomenology can effectively advance that logic is it a proper method for ontology. Instead of focusing on the phenomenology involved, I would like to highlight the implicit critique of representationalism contained in that text's 'Introduction'. This allows me to focus on the structural character of the ground for ontology, which I take to be the essential point – the point that grounds the logic of *Grundlegung* in the problematic of being.

The Heideggerian critique of representationalism is motivated by a problem that has come to shape current realist ontologies, such as that of Markus Gabriel. Heidegger's response to this problem, I believe, places him closer to new realisms than to the forms of phenomenological thought criticised by Quentin Meillassoux for remaining 'correlationist' anti-realisms.[36] The problem, as Gabriel puts it, is that of 'an alienation of thought from being', and in Heideggerian terms this has resulted from an historical failure to properly work out the ground of ontology.[37] Defining being as reality, for instance, makes what *is* into the objects of the real world, while thought is relegated to the status of a merely ephemeral or ideal means for knowing (or failing to know) about those objects. Intellectual processes are taken to be internal to the subject, while what the subject aims to know is external and objective.[38] This divorce has tethered Western philosophy to a series of representationalist epistemologies, a basic problem for which becomes establishing how thought or the 'mind' can have proper access (or *any* access) to its object. How can the relation of externality between mind and object be overcome?

Heidegger takes Thomistic epistemology to be a paradigm for this problem, which persists in a range of modern variations.[39] For Thomas, thought is to achieve an *adaequatio intellectus ad rem* (adequation of the intellect to the thing), thereby forming a true account of the object of thought in the intellect. This is proposed to operate by an analogical relation between the intellect's representation and the thing it represents. However, barring reliance on God as a guarantor, this type of approach results in well-known problems, not the least of which is how to explain the ontological status of the connection between intellect and thing that supposedly enables an analogical relationship to be established at all.[40]

Now, obviously Heidegger holds that the subject-object split and its representationalist approach to thought are deeply flawed. His work in

Sein und Zeit intends to leave these metaphysical artefacts behind. But we cannot simply jump to his conclusion without being clear about how he gets there (at least, for our purposes here, with regard to the science of being). The phenomenology of being-in-the-world provides part of this story, but to focus on it alone misses the essential point – the point that allows the phenomenology of being-in-the-world to be performed in a non-representational mode of thinking in the first place. If the subject matter enquired into is being, then to escape the trap of representationalism Heidegger must undermine the thought-being divide. To get the project of fundamental ontology off the ground, it must address the access problem from the very get-go.

Heidegger begins explicitly dealing with this problem in §2. He is of course committed to the idea that being (*Sein*) is the being of beings. What is important is that according to the picture of thought alienated from being, being assumes a position external to the subject who wants to know about it – the mind positing the *Seinsfrage*. Structurally speaking, in that picture the problem becomes: how can the mind gain an adequate representational knowledge of being?[41] In other words, the question of how ontology is possible is presented as a problem of correct means of access. For Heidegger, being is the being of beings, and not their *Seiendheit*. Nonetheless, ontology must proceed by analysing the being of appropriate beings. The problem of access, then, takes the form of a problem of access to the being of such beings. 'When we come to what is to be interrogated, the question of being requires that the right way of access [der rechten Zugangsart] to entities shall have been obtained and secured in advance.'[42] Heidegger of course rejects the term 'mind' as another artefact of metaphysics, opting for hermeneutically and phenomenologically dynamic terms like 'understanding', 'interpretation', and 'thought'.[43] Yet, if philosophical thought poses the *Seinsfrage*, it must have the right kind of access to being (via the appropriate beings) – and must proceed on that basis – if ontology is to have success.[44] Borrowing a Cartesian term, why doesn't a *real* distinction hold between the two? Or, why aren't the question and its subject matter condemned to a purely external relation? Structurally, for ontology to be possible an appropriate point of intersection must be secured through which thought can access being. Some internal relation must be established.

Heidegger's solution to this problem does not work by proposing some new way for thought to bridge the subject-object divide. In fact, he does not attempt to solve the problem directly in these terms. Rather, his position entails that the terms in which the problem of representation is posed are mistaken. Representationalism is not in fact a problem at all, because thought and its 'objects' are not in a relation of exteriority, *partes extra partes*. The idea of such a relation is an artefact of metaphysics that gets the situation wrong. Heidegger's work on being-in-the-world addresses this in relation to the way we think about beings. When it comes to thinking about being, though, he undermines the problem by reformulating our approach in terms of a fresh analysis of the ground of ontology. From the perspective of representationalism, this will mean that Heidegger reconfigures the relation of thought and being and shows there never was a gap needing to be bridged. Thought and being are not condemned to a relation of exteriority; instead, they have one of coincidence or interiority.

This point is established in a fundamental insight that Heidegger shared with a number of philosophers – Parmenides, Schelling, and Hegel, to name a few. Namely, thought is not an ontologically negligible or ephemeral faculty of representing objects that are, over and against it, ontologically real. Thought *is*.[45] To be clear, Heidegger in no way simply equates thinking and being – this is no vulgar form of idealism. Rather, thinking is one domain of being: not all being is the being of thought, but all thought *is*. The insight that thought *is*, or that thinking (interpreting, understanding, disclosing meaningfully, etc.) is part of the very existence of the one who thinks, provides the solution to the problem of access when it comes to thinking about being.[46]

Ontology is possible because thought constitutively entails at least a minimally meaningful articulation of at least a minimal domain of being: its own being, the being of a meaningful articulation (even if unclear, errant, and incomplete).[47] The being who thinks (Dasein) constitutes this moment of coincidence: 'in its very being' it has 'that being as an issue for it'.[48] As such, its existence is the ground for the possibility of ontology. The fact that thought *is* means that ontology can proceed via a direct connectivity between the procedures of questioning and the subject matter questioned into. The logic of thought is not divorced from the logic of being, but continuous with it. In Heidegger's words, the 'understanding of being is itself a definite characteristic of Dasein's being'.[49] Because thought is already situated in the milieu of being, to begin doing ontology it must only turn towards its own being, and this requires no extrinsic methodological principles. In this sense, Heidegger establishes a path of methodological immanence via which the project of ontology can bypass the pitfalls of representational thought. This also means that the evolution of fundamental ontology proceeds as an evolution of the existence of the being who thinks, insofar as they pursue the question of being. Solving the access problem in this way marks a transformation of the question of being from a state of alienated abstractness into a structure of the very flesh of existence.

Heidegger uses a slightly different terminology to make some of these points. The enquiry into being 'is itself the behaviour of a questioner', he writes.[50] Rather than investigating the being of something other than oneself, which might raise problems of representation, one's own being has a priority. The questioner is distinct from other beings insofar as it is both a being *and* posits the question about being. Thus, the question and the being (*Seiendes*) to be interrogated with respect to its being coincide in the questioner. Indeed, the questioner *is* in a distinctive manner: it is a being for whom 'the very asking of this question' is its 'mode of *being*'; and as such it gets its essential character from what is inquired about – namely, being'.[51] The being who enquires into being does so by existing as the enquiry into its own existence. This is of course the core feature defining Dasein in Heidegger's use of the term – Dasein is the being that 'is ontically distinctive in that it *is* ontological'.[52] In Dasein there is an intrinsic relation of thinking and being that makes possible any understanding of being. Thus, Dasein exists as the condition for the possibility of any ontology.

In my view, establishing the intrinsic link between thought and being in Dasein is the single most important ontological move that Heidegger makes in the introduction to *Sein und Zeit*. It grounds the project of ontology in the condition for its possibility and generates the methodological horizon in which that project is carried out in the rest of the text – the existential analysis of Dasein. Without it, Heidegger's project would be impossible. The remainder of his life's philosophical work, including his efforts to supplant the history of metaphysics, depart from this point. Dasein's distinctive character provides a conceptual and indeed *constitutive* grasp on the subject matter of fundamental ontology – on the Ariadne's thread eventually leading out of the historical framework of metaphysics.

Sheehan has argued that throughout Heidegger's career, the core subject matter of his thought was not being, but the human being and its meaning-making procedures. In Sheehan's view, by 'being' (*Sein*) Heidegger really meant 'meaning' (*Sinn* or *Bedeutung*) and the entire effort of his philosophy was directed towards the way in which meaning is constituted in the human sphere.[53] Sheehan's position is clearly incorrect considering Heidegger's analysis of the condition for the possibility of ontology in *Sein und Zeit*, which shows that it is indeed the question of being that governs his investigation of human existence, not the reverse. In the introduction to that text, Heidegger raises the question of being and investigates how a scientific treatment of that question could be possible. It is only as a *consequence of* the nature of the condition for this possibility (namely, that it is Dasein) that the question of being is then methodologically situated in the existential analysis of Dasein. The existential analysis of Dasein – as insightful and extensive as it is – is not Heidegger's primary

concern, but rather the necessary methodological arena for doing fundamental ontology. As Heidegger decisively puts it, 'fundamental ontology
. . . must be sought in the existential analytic of Dasein', but 'the analytic
of Dasein remains wholly oriented towards the guiding task of working
out the question of being'.[54]

Heidegger's *Seinsfrage* is nothing abstract, but a structure of Dasein's
existence. Working out an account of being is a distinctive procedure carried out by Dasein: namely, that of thinking in an immanent trajectory
into its own being.[55] The evolution of Heidegger's ontology proceeds by
applying the productive logic of *Grundlegung* in this trajectory. Its course
of methodological immanence is the famous 'pathway' he continued along
for the remainder of his life. Even within the scope of *Sein und Zeit* alone,
there is a complex sequence of diagenically related accounts of Dasein's
being (the metaphysical subject, being-in-the-world, care, thrown projection, ecstatic temporality). The transition from one to the next is generated
by analysing the terms of the first, enquiring into the ground enabling
them, and then reflexively recasting those terms on a more originary basis.
By doing this, Dasein incrementally takes ownership of itself or evolves
towards a more 'authentic' state of existing and understanding being.[56]
Said differently, insofar as Dasein's existential and historical alienation is
constituted by the 'forgetting' of being, by pursuing the ontological problematic Dasein enacts a self-grounding. This drives forward the horizon in
which it understands itself – and, in turn, being – along a diagenic axis.
In the early 1930s this evolves to a point where Heidegger rethinks being
in terms of ontological structures more originary than human existence,
structures grounding the very possibility of human existence. It is in this
context that he develops his account of beyng as event. But it is only by
passing through the grounding of the ontological problematic in Dasein's
existence and the subsequent existential analysis that Heidegger's account
of the event can be accessed.

6 The ontology of history in *Sein und Zeit*

The problematic of being has been distorted by the history of metaphysics.
In the view of *Sein und Zeit*, this distortion is grounded in the historical
character of Dasein's existence. The historical alienation we call 'metaphysics' is rooted in an existential alienation, though one simultaneously
inscribed into and reinforced by the artefacts, languages, institutions, and
rituals of the *Mitwelt* (with-world) into which Dasein is thrown. This
fact means that *doing* fundamental ontology via the existential analytic of
Dasein incrementally remedies the errancy of the historical configuration

of metaphysics (though to me this effort must extend to transforming the relevant elements of the *Mitwelt*). The self-grounding that Dasein accomplishes via the existential analytic *is* an incremental disruption and reconfiguration of the ground of metaphysics. This process prefigures the concept of an historical event that Heidegger developed in the 1930s. The concept of event is a result of increasingly radical reconfigurations of the ground of metaphysics and its history, which were produced as Heidegger developed accounts of ontological structures more originary than Dasein. Before looking at this in *Beiträge*, I will outline some of the central features of his ontology of history in *Sein und Zeit*. Since my intention though is to get to that later work, I forego reconstructing the full arguments in *Sein und Zeit* and simply summarise the position presented. This is intended to give a basic picture of the way historical alienation is grounded in the problematic of being (in the form of Dasein's existence), such that addressing the latter simultaneously addresses the former (or at the least establishes the basis for doing so).

First, *Sein und Zeit* distinguishes between two registers of history: *Weltgeschichte* or world-history and Dasein's *Geschichtlichkeit* or historicality.[57] World-history is comprised of the sequence of entities and occurrences in the world that would make up its history if, for instance, arrayed on a timeline. Heidegger calls the science of world-history 'Historie' ('historiology', in Macquarrie and Robinson's translation).[58] In contrast, historicality describes first and foremost the fact that Dasein's existence *is* historical. The idea isn't simply that Dasein is a part of world-history, but that 'what is *primarily* historical is Dasein'.[59] History in the form of historicality is a function of Dasein's existence and must be understood on its basis.

How so? Dasein's historicality is a function of its temporality. As *Sein und Zeit* famously argues, Dasein's existence is 'grounded in temporality', that is, it exists as thrown projection or 'ecstatico-horizonal temporality' (*ekstatisch-horizontalen Zeitlichkeit*).[60] It is because Dasein exists as temporal that it can be historical: Dasein 'is not "temporal" because it "stands in history"', instead, 'it exists historically and can so exist only because it is temporal in the very basis of its being'.[61] What does it mean to say Dasein exists as temporal? In brief: as thrown into a concrete factical situation, Dasein is always 'in the process of having-been [gewesend]' and, as projection, is always 'essentially futural [zukünftig]'.[62] 'Having-been' designates the factical, 'past' dimension of Dasein's existence:

> In its factical being, any Dasein is as it already was, and is 'what' it already was. It *is* its past, whether explicitly or not. And this is so not only in that its past is, as it were, pushing itself along 'behind' it, and that Dasein possesses what is past as a property which is still present-at-hand and which

> sometimes has after-effects upon it: Dasein 'is' its past in the way of *its* own being, which, to put it roughly, 'historizes' [geschieht] out of its future on each occasion.[63]

As the last clause in this passage indicates, the relation between Dasein's having-been and futural dimensions is complex. The former is factical – it determines the distinct finitude belonging to each human being. This means that it governs the specific terms in which Dasein projects its futural dimension, including the possibility of thinking about its own having-been. Now, because the way we orient ourselves towards our having-been dimension is by projecting the possibility of interpreting and understanding that dimension, our having-been includes a distinctively futural aspect. Likewise, since our projections are based on our factical conditions, which include our having-been, our futural dimension includes a distinctively past or having-been aspect. When, in Chapter 6, I return to Heidegger's account of time-space in *Beiträge*, this structural co-implication of the futural and having-been dimensions of temporality will once again be important.

Within the register of history, the unified structure of Dasein's historical, ecstatico-temporal existence – that is, of its having-been and futural dimensions – is named its 'historising' or 'occurrence' (*Geschehens*).[64] World-history and historiology are grounded in Dasein's historising or occurrence, without which they could not be at all.[65]

> Historicality [Geschichtlichkeit], as a determinate character [Bestimmung], is prior to what is called 'history' [Geschichte] (world-historical historizing).
> 'Historicality' stands for the state of being that is constitutive for [Seinsverfassung] Dasein's 'historizing' [Geschehens] as such; only on the basis [Grunde] of such historizing is anything like 'world-history' possible or can anything belong historically [geschichtlich] to world-history.[66]

World-history and historiology are both modes of Dasein's historising: that is, they are 'world-historical historising' (*welt-geschichtlichen Geschehens*).[67] Dasein's historising is its ecstatic structure insofar as Dasein is 'stretching along [Erstreckung] between birth and death'.[68] By 'birth' and 'death', Heidegger of course does not mean datable events on a world-historical timeline, but essential limits of Dasein's existence; limits that structure Dasein and grant its finitude. Death, as the inescapable, most essential possibility belonging to Dasein and determining its futural limit, and birth, as Dasein's factical limit, do in a sense form the ultimate limits of its existence: beyond these, Dasein does not exist. But death and birth, as the very horizons of finitude characterising its futurally oriented projection into possibilities and factical conditions, are *dynamic* horizons, limits that are always with Dasein. They are the articulated limits of its dynamic, concrete finitude. Since birth and death are inescapable and structurally determinative for the entirety of Dasein's existence, that existence always bears a structural reference towards these limits: Dasein is at once 'being-towards-death' and 'being-towards-the-beginning'.[69] It is stretched or distended between these futural and factical limits; it *is* this 'between'.[70] Dasein's historising is the dynamic of its existence as stretched between these limits.

Late in *Sein und Zeit* Heidegger differentiates between inauthentic (*uneigentliche*) and authentic (*eigentliche*) modes of world-history. In the former, 'the being of the world-historical is experienced and interpreted in the sense of something present-at-hand which comes along, has presence, and then disappears' (this is the sense in which I have just been using it).[71] Here, Dasein makes a diagenic error: it mistakes world-history and historiology to be primary, failing to understand them properly on the ground of historising. In turn, it understands its own historical condition inauthentically because it does so in terms of a world-history of present-at-hand entities and events. Thus, since world-history is possible only on the basis of Dasein's historicality, when Dasein understands its historical condition in terms of the former, this constitutes an inauthentic mode of the latter.[72]

Authentic world-history, on the other hand, 'has a double significa-tion'.[73] First, it is 'the historizing of the world in its essential existent unity with Dasein'.[74] That is, it is the historical character of the world freed of its alienated state and grounded in Dasein. In this case, historiology inves-tigates not past entities and events – taken as present-at-hand – but 'the *disclosure* of historical entities'.[75] It investigates the ontological structure that enables such things to be historical at all and allows Dasein to thema-tise the past.[76] Second, authentic world-history signifies 'the "historizing" within-the-world of what is ready-to-hand and present-at-hand, insofar as entities within-the-world are, in every case, discovered with the facti-cally existent world'.[77] In this case, authentic historiology does investigate entities and events of the past, but precisely on the basis of the ontological structure addressed in the first signification – the disclosure of historical entities.

Thus, authentic world-history can be taken to designate both the historical character of a world, insofar as that character is grounded in Dasein's historicality, and the historical character of entities and events insofar as they are, in turn, part of such a world of significance. Historical artifacts, for instance, are characterised by being things of the 'past'. But this past is 'nothing else than that *world* within which they belonged to a context of equipment and were encountered as ready-to-hand and used by a concernful Dasein who was-in-the-world'.[78] 'That *world* is no longer.

But what was formerly *within-the-world* with respect to that world is still present-at-hand.'[79]

Additionally, it should at least be noted again that because Dasein as being-in-the-world is *Mitsein*, the world-historical fabric is woven through the *Mitwelt* or with-world. More fundamentally: 'if fateful [schicksalhafte] Dasein, as being-in-the-world, exists essentially in being-with Others, its historizing is a co-historizing [Mitgeschehen] and is determinative for it as destiny [Geschick]. This is how we designate the historizing of the community, of a people.'[80]

These considerations about Dasein's historicality and world-history frame two important conditions for the project of fundamental ontology. First, the conceptual, linguistic, equipmental, affective, interpretive, and so on, matrices in terms of which Dasein understands its own existence and, in turn, being are defined by the factical, historical context into which it is thrown. We seem to be thrown into the context of the metaphysical tradition which determines the terms in which we understand our own existence and understand being. The problem is that metaphysics is insufficient for ontology. This is a rather standard Heideggerian point. But it leads to the second and more fundamental condition.

Namely, the way that Dasein's existence is shaped by the historical framework of metaphysics produces a fundamental alienation of Dasein from itself. As seen above, Dasein *is* its factical having-been and *is* its futural projection, that is, Dasein *is* historical. Although this historicality is the ontological ground for any distinct world-historical configuration, it always and only exists as situated within a concrete world-historical configuration. That is, Dasein exists always as thrown into a concrete factical situation and projects its future on its basis. Moreover, understanding and interpretation are part of Dasein's very historical existence. By interpreting, understanding, and projecting itself in terms of its metaphysical-historical situation, Dasein *exists* as metaphysical. It *exists* as alienated from itself. Obviously, this does not mean that Dasein is in fact a metaphysical thing (for instance, a substance or a subject), but that in its existential make-up, the horizon of its understanding of its own existence and the horizon of possibilities it projects for itself are determined by the horizon of metaphysics. The problem is that this is a false horizon. It obscures the possibility that Dasein might enquire into the nature of being by enquiring into its own existence.

The analysis of history in *Sein und Zeit* develops a basis for addressing these conditions and setting ontology on the right track. It operates on different, but intertwined, levels: (1) it problematises the historical-conceptual foundations of metaphysics and thus the grip they have on our understanding. This generates a space in which metaphysics as a whole can be problematised. It also indicates specific ways we might break with the foundations of the metaphysical tradition, develop better ontological concepts and methods, and employ them to reformulate the question of being. (2) The analysis of history advances a transformation of human existence itself: by problematising the foundations of metaphysics, the human being's understanding of itself in metaphysical terms is problematised.[81] It is forced to confront the question of its own existence without the benefit of metaphysical concepts in terms of which it might define itself. The transformation is initiated when the human being reinterprets itself phenomenologically on the basis of its distinctive ontico-ontological characteristic (that it is a being for whom its own being is an issue), and thus as Dasein. By reformulating the question about being on this basis, Dasein can work to remedy its state of alienation, understand its own existence more authentically, and develop a better understanding of being. This transformation is obviously complex. It does not amount to simply disavowing the history of metaphysics or its impact on one's existence, for Dasein *is* historical, and so 'the inquiry into being . . . is itself characterized by historicality'.[82] Nevertheless, Heidegger holds that we have been thrown factically into the framework of metaphysics and its history. Thus,

> the ownmost meaning of being which belongs to the inquiry into being as an historical inquiry, gives us the assignment of inquiring into the history of that inquiry itself, that is, of becoming historiological. In working out the question of being, we must heed this assignment, so that by positively making the past our own, we may bring ourselves into full possession of the ownmost possibilities of such inquiry. The question of the meaning of being must be carried through by explicating Dasein beforehand in its temporality and historicality; the question thus brings itself to the point where it understands itself as historiological.[83]

The focus on historical alienation gets carried over to *Beiträge* in a new form that moves beyond the frame of the existential analysis of Dasein. There, the issue of breaking with the history of metaphysics becomes magnified in the concept of an historical event generating another beginning for thought.

7 The historical alienation of Dasein from its ground in *Beiträge*

Heidegger's concept of event – in both its historical and ontological forms – is defined in the context of his post-*Kehre* philosophy. That philosophy is generated via an evolution along an axis of ground proceeding from the formulation of Dasein as the condition for the possibility of ontology.

Yet, one of the defining features of Heidegger's *Kehre* is its shift from explaining being on the basis of Dasein's existence to explaining Dasein's existence on the basis of being. We can make sense of this by applying a diagenic distinction: the turn happens when Heidegger's methodology drives him beyond the existential analysis of Dasein to a more profound level of ground at which he begins to articulate being in terms of features, structures, or processes diagenically and ontologically prior to Dasein. In a certain sense (though not with respect to the movement along a diagenic axis), this parallels the Schellingian shift from a transcendental idealism describing the subject to a *Naturphilosophie* that tells the story of the constitution or emergence of the subject on the basis of non-subjective ontological processes. As an extension of Heidegger's shift, the distortion and alienation belonging to metaphysics are no longer understood as simply grounded in Dasein's existence and preserved in artefacts of the *Mitwelt*, but rather as part of the ontological and ontic make-up of the field or world itself in which Dasein exists.

With Heidegger's *Kehre* comes a terminological distinction between 'Dasein' and 'Da-sein'. While the former continues to refer to the human being, the latter is a technical term for both (1) the field or world in which Dasein lives, which in the epoch of metaphysics is a field of distortion and alienation, but in another epoch might be quite different, and (2) the ontological features of that field or world that are diagenically prior to Dasein and make its structure of existence possible. 'A history [Geschichte]', that is, an historical epoch, is 'a style of Da-sein'.[84] It is important to emphasise the position of this field in the ontology *Beiträge* presents: 'Da-sein has its origin [Ursprung] in the event and in the turning of the event'.[85] This means that ultimately we will have to understand the constitution of Da-sein in terms of the structure of beyng as event (see Chapter 5). More specifically, as Heidegger's post-*Kehre* work comes to designate the event's onto-genesis of worlds of beings in terms of the 'essence of truth' or 'truth of beyng', 'Da-sein is to be grounded only as, and in, the truth of beyng'.[86]

We must be careful, though, for this 'grounding' has two senses, both of which will be important. In one, it is indeed the story of the onto-genesis of Da-sein. But there is another sense: in the epoch of metaphysics Da-sein is a field alienated from its ground and, in this context, grounding additionally refers to the process whereby that alienation is resolved and Da-sein is realigned with or set back into its ground. Moreover, since Da-sein comprises the structures of beyng that make Dasein possible, while Dasein's alienation is an alienation from its own being (narrowly) and from beyng (broadly), the remedy to Dasein's alienation is directly related to the grounding of Da-sein in the second sense. 'The grounding – not creating [Erschaffung] – is, *from the side of humans* . . . a matter of letting the ground be [Grund-sein-lassen]. Thereby humans once again come to *themselves* and win back selfhood [Selbst-sein].'[87]

To be sure, 'self' and 'selfhood' here refer in no way to a metaphysical subject identical with 'itself' through the duration of time. In Heidegger's use, I take 'selfhood' to mean Dasein's existence in a state of minimal self-alienation, previously expressed in *Sein und Zeit* in terms of authenticity. I take 'self' to refer to Dasein's ground in the form of what Heidegger calls 'das Eigentum'; as he puts it, 'the origin of the self is the domain of what is proper [Eigen-tum]'.[88] Rojcewicz and Vallega-Neu translate 'das Eigentum' as 'domain of what is proper', but I often use 'domain of propriety' or simply 'propriety' instead. *Das Eigentum* is the structure of propriety that makes selfhood possible – a structure generated in the logic of beyng as event, namely, its 'Er-eignis' or 'appropriation'. But more on this in Chapter 5.

Heidegger's 'event' at the historical level is a function of the alienation emblemised by metaphysics – namely, it is a transformative rupture in which that alienation is remedied. What, then, are the forms of aliena-tion with which he is concerned in *Beiträge*? The prime terms describing the field of distortion in which alienated Dasein lives, that is, Da-sein as constituted in the historical epoch of metaphysics, are *Seinsverlassenheit* ('the abandonment by being') and its counterpart, *Seinsvergessenheit* ('the forgottenness of being'). While 'the abandonment by being' applies espe-cially to forms of the self-alienation involved in the structure of being, 'the forgottenness of being' names the abandonment of being insofar as it is manifested in human thought and experience; it is the abandonment by being that is operative in human existence. The two can be distinguished diagenically: 'the abandonment by being is the ground of the forgotten-ness of being'.[89] Both are expressed in a variety of modes, the most central of which Heidegger calls 'Machenschaft' (machination), 'Vor-stellung' (representation), and 'Erlebnis' (lived experience).

These modes are consequences of a more originary distortion essen-tial to the structure of beyng as event itself. Namely, in Heidegger's words, the abandonment by being has 'arisen from the distorted essence of beyng [Unwesen des Seyns] through machination'.[90] Explaining the precise nature of this distorted essence will be important when we come to Heidegger's ontological concept of event, again in Chapter 5. In fact, explaining its ontological constitution in terms of historical alienation is impossible, since the former is the ground making the latter possible. For now, the important idea is that the different modes of the abandonment by being 'are merely emanations [Ausstrahlungen] from an intricate and obdurate dissimulation [Verstellung] of the essence of beyng, especially of its fissure [Zerklüftung]', a dissimulation that results from a tendency structurally inherent to beyng.[91] As we will see later, this tendency is a counterpart of the event's logic of *Er-eignis* or appropriation, namely, that of 'Enteignis' or 'expropriation'.[92] If 'Er-eignis' names the genesis of structural propriety (*das Eigentum*), 'Enteignis' names the genesis of a corelative structural alienation. Together these are the basic lattice of Da-sein. The tendency belonging to the logic of the event to generate self-distortion and alienation is what Heidegger calls the 'distorted essence' of beyng. And just as appropriation serves as the ground for whatever selfhood Dasein might attain, expropriation serves as the ground for the different modes of historical alienation. At the historical level, referring in part to Nietzsche, Heidegger writes that 'in this era [of metaphysics], "beings" (that which we call the "actual," "life," "values") are expropriated [enteignet] of beyng'.[93] Beings – especially Dasein – are in a state of expropriation from their ground (beyng or the event).

Something further and truly elegant must be added to this picture, even if it cannot be unpacked until later. In Heidegger's ontology, 'Er-eignis' and 'Enteignis' name the *very same* logic of the event (*Ereignis*) – as we shall see, the differential logic noted earlier – insofar as it simultaneously generates propriety or 'self' and alienation from propriety. Propriety and alienation from propriety are co-determinate: each is what it is insofar as it is differentiated from the other. But this means that each has a constitutive structural reference to the other, without which it would not be at all. The consequence for Dasein is that its 'self' is co-constituted by alienation from that self; its 'self' is rooted in both propriety and alienation, and thus it is fractured from the ground up. Better said, Dasein's 'self' is a tension or distension between propriety and alienation, each constituting and simultaneously undermining the other. This is the logic at the root of Dasein's 'disclosedness': to exist, for Dasein, is to be continuously torn apart.[94] This *also* means that ultimately we must understand Dasein's alienation not simply in terms of expropriation from propriety, but in terms of expropriation from the structural distension or self-problematising logic upon which Dasein is grounded, that is, the obscuration or concealment of that distension. Such an obscuration is found, for example, in the metaphysical conception of Dasein as a self-identical subject persisting through time (a stable domain of propriety of which various attributes can be predicated). This all sounds very mysterious at this point, though, and it will remain so until we reconstruct the logic of the event by way of Heidegger's ontology of truth.

In the epoch of metaphysics, machination, representation, and lived experience are the core modes of alienation determining Da-sein and, consequently, Dasein. To reconstruct the basic form of Heidegger's concept of an historical event, two tasks remain: explaining the nature of these modes and explaining the way they might be resolved and broken with.

In Heidegger's account, beyng as event is essentially self-problematising and structurally incomplete – it is not objectively present, fully determinate, or exhaustively representable. Because of this, it is interminably question-worthy. The idea here is not simply that questioning beyng leads to rich results, but rather that any ontology produced as an answer to the question of beyng is necessarily incomplete and, if its method is properly grounded, is perpetually driven to question again and again. Machination is the obscuration of this problematic or question-worthy character of beyng that is enabled by the distorted essence of beyng and manifested historically in a prevalence of the *Seiendheit* of beings and their ontic presence, determinacy, representability, measurability, and makeability: in short, 'within machination, there is nothing question-worthy'.[95]

The eclipse of beyng and its question-worthy character is expressed and reinforced in a variety of ways that contribute to the overall dominance of machination. These revolve around the determination of everything there is on the basis of ontic ποίησις ('making' or 'bringing-forth') in correlation with τέχνη ('know-how'). I shall distinguish 'ontic poiesis' from 'ontological poiesis': the former has a negative connotation and refers to the makeability of beings as such within the framework of *techne*; the latter has an affirmative connotation and refers to the genetic character of beyng and to the ways in which human beings can articulate and preserve that character in creative works like art, poetry, and philosophy. When beyng is obscured by the presence of beings, the ontic poietic character of beings as such – that is, in their *Seiendheit* – is freed to dominate. In the age of machination 'everything "is made" and "can be made," if only the "will" to it is summoned up'.[96] As Vallega-Neu emphasises, Heidegger's conception of machination is rooted historically in Greek thought: 'in the overpowering of *phusis* through *techne*'.[97] Nonetheless, Heidegger suggests that the historical dominance of machination becomes *total* for the first time in Christianity.

In Christianity, God is the ultimate craftsman. He takes on the role of an absolute foundation for beings, a foundation that – in place of the self-problematising character of beyng – is not intrinsically problematic or self-destabilising at all. Despite theological claims to the contrary, the traditional characteristics assigned to God are characteristics of *Seiendheit* carried to the maximal degree: if every being must be *one*, God is perfectly simple; if every being must be self-identical through the duration of its existence, God is self-identical to such a degree that He is beyond duration; if beings have causal power, God is perfectly powerful and the cause of all that exists; if beings might have only imperfect knowledge, God has perfect knowledge; and so on. As a being, God is the prime ontic cause of the universe and its beings, which are His product: 'every being is *explained* in its origin as an *ens creatum*, the creator is what is most certain, and beings are the effect of this cause which *is* most eminently'.[98] To be a being, in other words, is to be something essentially makeable and made by another being, and reality is understood on the basis of an ultimate principle of ontic production.

If the early Christian tradition universalised the framework of machination by grounding reality in God the maker, the early modern scientific revolution places the makeability of beings in human hands. The domain of beings becomes mathematically quantifiable, calculable, and manipulable down to the finest detail via human technology – at least in principle. Simultaneously, representability gets pushed to a total saturation of reality. Machination is

> that interpretation of beings as representable and represented. Representable means, on the one hand, accessible in opinion and calculation and, on the other hand, providable in production and implementation. All that is thought on the grounds that beings as such are the represented, and only the represented is a being.[99]

Leibniz's reciprocal principles of sufficient reason and the identity of indiscernibles provide a good image of the kind of infinite representability Heidegger has in mind.[100] If Leibniz's system understands determination in terms of the predication of a subject, while a concept is sufficient to the degree that it represents the subject's infinite chain of predicates, then no things in reality are in principle unrepresentable. Indeed, according to these principles there is one sufficient concept for each distinct thing and one distinct thing for each concept; that is, for each thing there is a concept that has an infinite comprehension and an extension of one.[101] For a concept to adequately represent its object it must have infinite comprehension: it must contain *all* the object's predicates (in the right order). Since two things between which no difference can be discerned are in fact one and the same thing, such a concept applies to one and only one thing. In contrast, if a concept has a finite comprehension, that is, if it does not contain all its object's predicates, its extension increases (in principle indefinitely, even if not in fact). The concept is no longer adequate to its object, since there are determinations in the object not represented in the concept. Any concept with an extension greater than one is therefore a generality: it ranges over any object bearing the concept's predicates, but it is inadequate to any of them. The objects ranged over can be distinguished numerically as particular instances of the concept, but not adequately, since the concept fails precisely with respect to the differences individuating one from another. The goal of representation is thus to become total: to infinitely saturate the predicates of the beings represented.[102]

As a more current illustration, the ideal of machination is carried to the 'gigantic' (*das Riesenhafte*) in the Kardashev scale dreamt of by astrophysicists and science-fiction writers.[103] This scale proposes to measure the development of a society according to three grand levels of energy control. The first marks a hypothetical society that has grown able to capture, store, and use all the energy radiated to its planet by the star at the centre of its solar system. A 'level two' society could capture the energy produced by its star *in total* and control that energy – as well as the star itself – for its own purposes. A 'level three' society would have attained total control of the energy output of an entire galaxy. When carried to the logical conclusion – total poietic and technological control of the universe – the Kardashevian dream merges the modern image of the human being as poietic wielder of technology with the Christian image of God as maker. To compliment this image of machination at the level of the gigantic, Rick Sanchez's car battery powered by a fabricated internal 'microverse' containing a 'miniverse' containing a 'teenyverse' carries it to the infinitely small.[104] Both the Sanchez battery and the Kardashev scale express the idea of total poietic technological dominance over a reality made measurable and manipulable by the mathematical sciences. Vallega-Neu captures the idea well:

> machination and lived experience are completed insofar as they encounter no more boundaries. In the gigantic, beings are discovered through their boundless calculability and makeability. Any being is always already discovered as quantitatively calculable. Indeed, what beings are, their *quale*, is understood as quantity.[105]

Within the framework of machinational metaphysics, the eclipse of the self-problematising, question-worthy character of beyng goes hand in hand with a general view that there is nothing at all that is irreducibly problematic. As Heidegger puts it, for machination 'there is no problem that is not solvable, and the solution is merely a matter of number applied to time, space, and force'.[106] This view is opposed to what I call the 'ontological realism about problems' argued for by Albert Lautman and Gilles Deleuze (who very much drew upon Heidegger to make their cases).[107] Nonetheless, in Heidegger's view the problematic, question-worthy character of beyng is structural and thus cannot be entirely eliminated from the world. Under the determination of machination, this question-worthy character is encountered in sublimated forms defined within the bounds of the machinery of representation. Heidegger calls the kind of experience available within such bounds 'Erlebnis' or 'lived experience'. He critiqued lived experience in several contexts during his career and a full picture would require piecing together his engagement with post-Kantian philosophy. But this would take us far afield. The important connection to make here is that in *Beiträge* Heidegger emphasises the way lived experience expresses a transformed, tamed form of the self-problematising, question-worthy character of beyng. Lived experience reduces the question-worthy and the inherently problematic to simple curiosities and the type of problems that disappear once their solutions are discovered.

> Since ... machination dispels and eradicates question-worthiness and brands it as downright deviltry, and since this destruction ... is perhaps at bottom not fully possible, therefore this age is still in need of that which allows – in the manner proper to the age, i.e., machinationally – some validity to what is worthy of question and yet at the same time makes it innocuous. That is the accomplishment of *lived experience*.[108]

Lived experience reinforces the alienation of Dasein by sublimating Dasein's encounter with the pre-representational, problematic, question-worthy character of its self and of being and rendering it innocuous. The key is that it does this in forms of experience that are enticing enough to hold one's attention (or the attention of a community), but that are captured within the machinational focus on *Seiendheit* and its apparatus of representation. Rather than being struck by the problematic character of oneself, one's attention is captured by skydiving or watching crime dramas on TV. Rather than looking into the question-worthy character of being, one becomes obsessed with conspiracy theories or solving logistics problems to make a business more profitable. '"Lived experience," understood here as the basic form of representation belonging to the machinational and the basic form of abiding therein, is the publicness (accessibility to everyone) of the mysterious, i.e., the exciting, provocative, stunning, and enchanting.'[109]

Crucially, for Heidegger the domination by machination, representation, and lived experience extends to the form of truth predominant in our historical framework. As is well known, he describes part of the problematic, question-worthy character of being in terms of concealment, which – together with unconcealment – is one of the syngenic elements in his conception of the essence of truth. However, in machination the very fact of concealment is eclipsed: being conceals itself and its inclination to do so is carried into the modes of concealment shaping worlds of beings. In machination there is no room to recognise that this sort of thing has occurred. 'Not only is it denied in principle that anything could be concealed; more decisively, self-concealment as such is in no way admitted as a determining power.'[110] Consequently, machination entails an obscuration of the essence of truth and the predominance of a sublimated, derivative form of truth: '"machination" is the name for a specific truth of beings (of the beingness of beings). We grasp this beingness first and foremost as objectivity (beings as objects of representation).'[111] In Heidegger's view ontological structures of concealment and unconcealment form the diagenic ground of propositional truth. But with machination truth as propositional representation in the form of adequation, correctness, correspondence, and measurability reigns supreme and reinforces the modern ontic poietic view of reality. As we will see in the following chapter, precisely this is part of the reason Heidegger argues that to generate an historical event or rupture with the framework of machinational metaphysics our philosophical efforts must be directed to an enquiry into the essence of truth.

Before moving on it must be emphasised that machination and its manifestation in derivative forms of truth are not simply products of human negligence. Their ultimate ground is not in Dasein's existence, as that of historical alienation was in *Sein und Zeit*. Rather, they are grounded more originarily in the structure of beyng and expressed in the historical formation of Da-sein in which Dasein exists. '"Machination' is at first a type of human comportment, and then suddenly and properly it means the reverse: the essence (distorted essence) of beyng in which the ground of the possibility of "undertakings" is first rooted.'[112] In Heidegger's post-*Kehre* conception of truth, the essence of truth is a dynamic of being that enables the determination of Da-sein and, in turn, worlds of beings. In this picture, machination is moreover a way in which the distorted essence or abandonment by beyng is determined in truth. 'The abandonment by being is basically [im Grunde] an essential decay [Ver-wesung] of beyng. Its essence is distorted [verstört] and only in that way does it bring itself into truth, namely, [in the epoch of metaphysics] as the correctness of representation.'[113]

8 *Er-gründung* (fathoming the ground) and the historical sense of 'event' in *Beiträge*

In its first form, Heidegger's event is a rupture within the historical framework of metaphysics and its expression in machination, representation, and lived experience. If it were to happen, it would entail a remedy of Dasein's existential alienation (to the degree possible), establish the ground for a transformation of the historical character or style of Da-sein, and initiate the other beginning for thought suggested to be necessary for philosophy. But how is this all supposed to happen?

Heidegger's way of talking about this type of historical transformation is often suggestive of a mysterious quasi-agency of beyng that does not appear to me to have serious justification. Obviously, he would deny the way I have just stated this since he holds that 'agency' is a concept belonging to metaphysics. Nonetheless, his emphasis on the 'sent' or 'destined' (*geschickt*) character of history, for example, can make it appear that the occurrence of an historical event is really up to beyng, while human beings are just along for the ride, ready in the wings to 'preserve' beyng whenever it happens to reveal itself. Many Heidegger scholars seem inclined to accept this picture in one form or another. I call it the 'fatalist' interpretation of Heidegger's event. In this view, perhaps the best one could hope for is having some extraordinary luck and seemingly mystical insight that would allow them to capture something of beyng in a great work of art or poetry. This sort of mystical inclination is certainly present in Heidegger's work – to its detriment – but not exclusively so: it is doubled by a proper argumentative methodology, and this is what we should focus on if his ontology of events is to have value for philosophy today. The mystical fatalist interpretation is not only philosophically unsatisfying, it brings to a halt a critical approach to this topic. Generally speaking, scholarship which relies on such mysticism to deal with the later Heidegger sidesteps the formidable philosophical work his texts contain, which should be worked out and evaluated in explicit terms. Not doing so opens the door to ideological appropriations of his ontology – something of which we must remember Heidegger himself was guilty. Without a doubt, in his philosophy historical events – including the one in question now – might occur because of historical forces out of the hands of any particular human being(s). But contrary to the fatalist interpretation, the event pertaining to the historical framework of metaphysics is also something that can be accomplished by human effort. In Heidegger's texts we can find a distinctive method for this and we should deal with the topic in philosophical, not mystical terms.

In my view, the fatalist interpretation fetishises the powerlessness of Dasein in the face of the history of being. No doubt, the historical event would occur in the historical framework in which human beings live. It would be a transformation of Da-sein, and thereby of ontological structures that exert a determining force on Dasein. In this way, the event would be something that happens *to* human beings. But, if we look at what Heidegger's philosophy actually does (not simply what it says) and the connection of his productive logic of *Grundlegung* with the concept of *Er-gründung* used in *Beiträge*, it undeniably supports an 'active' role for human beings in bringing about the historical event. For those who dislike the term 'active', we can say that Dasein can put in an effort, endeavour, or comport itself towards bringing about the event. A first piece of evidence for this is the work that Heidegger produced: despite his meditations on the 'destiny' of history and his serious personal shortcomings, much of

Heidegger's career was an effort to accomplish such an event *by doing philosophy*.

The human effort involves a self-transformation of the human being, a transformation from the state in which one is existentially determined by metaphysical alienation to one realigned with beyng as event. In part, this would involve a revision of one's understanding of the world such that it would no longer be governed by the erroneous commitments of metaphysics but rather be worked out on an appropriate ontological basis. We have already begun to see how this works generally in terms of the diagenic evolution of Heidegger's ontology. In *Sein und Zeit*, if I do ontology and this endeavour progresses along a diagenic axis, with transformations of the account produced marking different stages along that axis, *and* ontology proceeds via the existential analytic of Dasein, then this endeavour entails a transformation of my very existence. This is the process of becoming more authentic. Heidegger's *Kehre* prompts a recalibration and broadening of this idea. *Beiträge* presents it as a collection of processes under the heading 'Er-gründung' or 'fathoming the ground', which I take to be the central term describing Dasein's role in resolving its own alienation and bringing about the historical event. We can clarify this term by putting it into context with the broader conception of 'ground' in *Beiträge* and marking an important diagenic distinction.

The core notion of ground in *Beiträge* is 'Grund der Möglichkeit' ('ground of possibility'), which appears in a more developed form as 'das Sichverbergen im tragenden Durchragen' ('self-concealing in a protruding that bears').[114] Explaining what on earth that odd formulation means will have to wait until Chapter 6. For now, we can mark two main sub-divisions of this concept. The first is 'das ursprüngliche Gründen des Grundes' ('the original grounding of the ground') which is also expressed in shorter form as the 'gründende Grund' ('grounding ground'); the second is 'ergründen' ('to fathom the ground') or 'Er-gründung' ('fathoming the ground').[115]

The first designates the grounding character belonging to beyng as event, that is, the nature of the event insofar as it generates, maintains, undermines, and distorts itself as a ground that can bear things grounded on or in it. Grounding ground is tightly related to the event's structures of truth and time-space and it has the three modalities listed earlier: *Ab-grund* (abyssal ground), *Ur-grund* (primordial ground), and *Un-grund* (distorted ground).

In contrast, *Er-gründung* or fathoming the ground designates not a character of beyng, but a set of grounding operations at the level of human existence. It can be called 'fathoming' in English in the sense of plumbing the depths of an ocean's abyss (the *profond* in French) to discover and grasp what might be there. Its verbal form – 'er-gründen' – highlights the fact that grounding is something human beings can *do*. We can, for instance, do ontology to plumb the depths of the ground structure of beyng (grounding ground). The different operations comprised by fathoming the ground are diagenically derivative in relation to grounding ground, which makes them possible in the first place. If fathoming takes place in the game of grounding and grounded terms, grounding ground is the origination of the game itself. Insofar as human existence is alienated from itself and from beyng, fathoming the ground comprises modes in which we might remedy that alienation and keep from forgetting beyng. It pertains to the relation of human existence to beyng as event and, in a distinctive way, to the event's character as grounding ground. In Heidegger's words, fathoming the ground describes ways in which 'grounding ground, as such, is attained and taken up' by human existence.[116]

The kind of thought that belongs to fathoming the ground is *anfängliche Denken* (inceptual thinking) or *Besinnung* (meditation). In contrast to representational thought and its form in propositional judgements, inceptual thinking moves to the ontological ground enabling the former to be possible at all. In doing so, it replicates the three movements of ontology in *Beiträge*: (1) It moves from a state of alienation towards that state's ground in beyng as event. It does this via different stages elaborated in the text ('Anklang' or 'resonating', 'Zuspiel' or 'interplay', 'Sprung' or 'leap', and 'Gründung' or 'grounding').[117] In this sequence, meditative inceptual thinking has a distinctive focus: it questions into different aspects of the problematic of beyng, but especially 'into the truth of beyng' where 'the questioning of truth is the leap into its essence and thereby into beyng itself'.[118] The question of truth, in other words, plays a special role in inceptual thinking and the fathoming it performs. In this context, the 'leap' must not be confused with anything like a 'leap of faith' or blind commitment. Rather, it names the diagenic methodological movement whereby *Grundlegung* goes beyond an existing set of *Grundbegriffe* to articulate the ground supporting them.[119] Inceptual thinking does this in its treatment of truth. The second movement (2) performed by inceptual thinking or meditation is to think the structure of beyng as event, that is, the ground of the other beginning. This is where thought lands in its 'leap'. On that basis, the third movement (3) is the one promised but somewhat neglected by Heidegger: inceptual thinking is to return from the event to what the event grounds. It is to rethink the domain of Da-sein in a properly grounded way: if, when 'grasped primordially', 'the beginning is beyng itself as event', then 'inceptual thinking' is 'thinking out of the beginning'.[120]

Heidegger distinguishes two main types of *Er-gründung*, each of which in turn has various modes. The first is a 'creative' form of grounding connected to his concept of 'building' ('bauen'). It is creative in the sense of building on a ground or 'bring[ing] something to the ground' and Heidegger sees it exemplified in the ontological poietic character of great art and poetry.[121] In contrast to 'forgetting' beyng, creative grounding is an operation through which human existence builds such a work that preserves an exposure of the essence of truth and the nature of the event in the world. Art and poetry certainly have important places in Heidegger's philosophy of events. However, for the reasons given in my Introduction I think it is a mistake to take them – and this creative mode of *Er-gründung* – as the prime context in which to understand this concept. Heidegger's description of creative grounding also relies a bit heavily on the idea of historically fated watershed figures (van Gogh, Hölderlin, etc.) who seem to be granted some mystical facility with beyng.[122] I have received no such gift, so my hope is that philosophy might through an explicit sequence of thinking access and articulate a proper conception of beyng in an intelligible manner. In my mind, if we were to de-mystify the artistic facility, this would be an improvement on Heidegger's philosophy of art and poetry.

The philosophical approach is captured better in the second main type of *Er-gründung*, which is described as 'den Grund als gründenden *wesen* lassen' ('to let the ground *essentially occur* as grounding').[123] The 'letting' involved here entails a complex relation between ways Dasein might comport itself towards its ontological ground and ways that ground determines Dasein. Though I briefly address the second half of this in a moment, I will return to it in more detail in Chapter 3. For now, my focus is on the former, since it encompasses the human effort, which can be applied to the task of doing the philosophy of the event and generating another beginning for thought – that is, to bringing about the historical event. It again includes a subset of related modes found not only in Heidegger's description of the concept, but in the work his texts perform.

The first, which we see consistently active in Heidegger's texts, is the methodological movement of *Grundlegung* described in Chapter 1. This makes the subsequent modes of this kind of fathoming the ground possible. In this mode, fathoming is the way in which human existence engages in a radical science that enquires into the nature of being, progressing along a series of renditions of the ontological problematic arrayed on a diagenic axis. Each rendition is generated by problematising the *Grundbegriffe* of a previous rendition. One tracks the logic implicit in the features of being that are articulated by those *Grundbegriffe* (but exceeding the account they offer) to a more originary standpoint. On that basis, one then recasts *Grundbegriffe* to articulate being in a more appropriate way, that is, one lays new grounds for the ontological problematic. The account constituted thereby enables a reconfiguration of that problematic field. This sense of fathoming the ground describes precisely the diagenic evolution of Heidegger's ontology that I have begun to trace.

When this methodological movement is applied within the sphere of human existence, we find a second, closely related sense of fathoming the ground. Namely, this is the way human existence uncovers its own ground, regaining ownership of itself from the alienation involved in inauthenticity, machination, representation, lived experience, and the historical framework of metaphysics more broadly. In this human perspective, Heidegger describes the grounding involved as a matter of 'letting the ground be' (*Grund-sein-lassen*) whereby 'humans once again come to themselves and win back selfhood'.[124] In this context, *wesen lassen* or *sein lassen* is an extension of a mode of comportment involved in what Heidegger calls 'freedom' in his essay 'Vom Wesen der Wahrheit' (see Chapter 3, section 2). Freedom is not the volition of a subject, but a way Dasein contributes to letting beings be (*das Seinlassen von Seiendem*) by being attentive to their ontological ground and preserving the experience of those beings as so grounded. *Beiträge's* discussion of this emphasises the attention of human existence to its own ground or its 'self'. As we saw earlier, this self is not the personal self of a subject: 'selfhood is more originary than any I or thou or we'.[125] It is rather the event's structure of propriety (*Eigentum*) (and, I suggest, alienation from propriety), which forms a basic structure of Da-sein. Winning back 'selfhood' refers to the way alienated human existence might incrementally resolve its alienation or become properly grounded. This entails rearticulating oneself and one's understanding of the world on the basis of the event rather than the terms of metaphysics. Heidegger puts this as follows: 'the relation back [Rückbezug] which is named in terms of "self," to "itself," with "itself," and for "itself" has its essence in appropriation [Eignung]'; 'the domain of what is proper [Eigentum]' is 'the ground of selfhood'.[126]

There is another important operation of fathoming the ground that is a bit counterintuitive: according to Heidegger, Da-sein needs to get grounded by Dasein. Since the configuration of Da-sein in the epoch of metaphysics is one of alienation, it makes sense that Da-sein should get grounded. But the way this is suggested to happen here is strange, since Dasein is grounded by Da-sein. How should what is grounded ground its ground? The idea clearly cannot be that Dasein is to serve as the ground making Da-sein possible. Rather, in Heidegger's words, what occurs is that humans 'place themselves back into Da-sein, thereby grounding Da-sein, in order thus to place themselves out into the truth of beyng'.[127] I take this to mean that Dasein's act of regrounding itself simultaneously contributes to grounding Da-sein. How? The idea relies on the fact that for Heidegger the ground of something is not somehow metaphysically transcendent in relation to it, but immanent in its constitution.[128] Since Da-sein is the ground enabling human existence, when the human being 'forgets' its ground it becomes alienated or expropriated from that ground and seems unconnected to it. But what this means in terms of Da-sein is that Da-sein has expropriated or alienated part of itself from itself via human errancy. Thus, when the human being 'places itself back into' its ground (Da-sein) and rethinks itself on that basis, Da-sein re-appropriates itself: it is regrounded. Human existence grounds Da-sein.

Together, these senses of fathoming the ground describe the forms that the human effort would take in working to develop a properly non-metaphysical account of beyng (as event), to reground itself therein, and to contribute to a transformation of Da-sein that would remedy its alienation. In other words, they describe a human effort to bring about the historical event described by Heidegger. What I hope to have indicated with this brief look at *Er-gründung* is that in his account, this is something we can work to do. This does not negate the occurrence of other historical events that might simply be out of our hands. Yet is shows that we are not stuck within a fatalistic world when it comes to a transformative rupture with the historical framework of metaphysics and the generation of another beginning for thought.

9 Conclusion

My intention in this chapter has been to distinguish between the historical and ontological senses of Heidegger's concept of event, outline their relations, and develop a broader account of the historical event. In the following chapters I will shift to a reconstruction of the ontological sense of event.

Dealing with both, I have argued, requires beginning with the groundwork for ontology set in *Sein und Zeit* and showing the nature of the methodological continuity between that groundwork and the conception of the event in Heidegger's post-*Kehre* work. By looking at the early account of how the historical alienation we call 'metaphysics' is rooted in Dasein's existence, I have argued that fundamental ontology in the form of the existential analytic incrementally remedies this alienation. This prefigures the transformation to be found in the historical event described in his later work. That transformation must be understood within the context of the immanent, complex evolution of Heidegger's problematic of being in the *Kehre*, which goes beyond the form it took in the earlier existential analytic. We have now seen how this changes the way historical alienation is understood. And we have seen the forms Dasein's effort might take to bring about the historical event. But we have not seen the specific way those efforts are actually carried out in Heidegger's philosophy.

In Chapter 3, I begin to deal with just that. There I track the diagenic evolution of Heidegger's ontology of truth via the productive logic of *Grundlegung* as it moves from *Sein und Zeit* to perhaps the earliest text in which the *Kehre* is evident: 'Vom Wesen der Wahrheit'. Doing so allows me to show that Heidegger's post-*Kehre* efforts to articulate ontological structures diagenically prior to Dasein generate increasingly radical reconfigurations of the historical framework of metaphysics. I focus on this within the problematic of truth because it has a distinctive importance for Heidegger's problematic of being. In this context, my earlier treatment of the groundwork for ontology in *Sein und Zeit* serves a second purpose: it provides a basis for the methodological and ontological continuity between the problem of resolving historical alienation and that of enquiring into the essence of truth. In *Sein und Zeit*, both are grounded in Dasein's existence and addressed via the existential analytic. When Heidegger's post-*Kehre* work surpasses the existential analytic by moving farther along a diagenic axis, this generates a new account according to which the historical alienation discussed above is grounded in structures of being that are articulated by the problematic of truth. In other words, we begin to get a fuller account of the structure of Da-sein. I argue that the operations of *Er-gründung* can be carried out (rather than just described) by pursuing the problematic of truth; this is how historical alienation can eventually get resolved, that is, how the historical event can be accomplished. But this happens precisely because via the problematic of truth we are able to generate an account of beyng as event, that is, of the ontological sense of event.

As indicated, my approach to the event in the following chapters is governed by a crucial point. It is true that the historical sense of event has a temporary methodological priority insofar as giving an account of beyng as event is beyond the metaphysical horizon of the 'first beginning'. Thus, giving such an account entails a transformative rupture of that horizon. However, this is not contingent on the historical event, the situation is the reverse. An account of beyng as event is not generated by analysing intrahistorical terms or even the domain of history, but by way of the question of the ground enabling the domain of history, that is, of the structures of beyng that make possible the determination of any historical configuration. These are articulated via the question of the ontological essence of truth. As Heidegger puts it, 'the other beginning must be brought into effect entirely out of beyng as event and out of the essential occurrence of its truth and of the history of that truth'.[129] Despite Heidegger's concern with history and the occurrence of another historical beginning, this beginning is to be accessed via the ontological problematic, that is, by working out an account of beyng as event and thereby properly grounding the domain of history. Said differently, the historical event occurs as a by-product of the generation of a non-metaphysical account of beyng, that is, of the event in its ontological sense. Chapters 3 to 5 deal with this, which then allows me to elaborate Heidegger's ontological concept of event in terms of 'ground' and 'time-space' in Chapter 6.

Notes

1. Sheehan, *Making Sense of Heidegger*.
2. *EH*.
3. *EB*.
4. Herrmann, *Wege ins Ereignis*.
5. Vallega-Neu, *Heidegger's Poietic Writings* 1.
6. *SZ* 13/34. It should be noted that in *Beiträge* Heidegger argues that there is an important difference between a condition of possibility and a ground. I discuss this in Chapter 4.
7. Heidegger reserves the term 'existence' ('Existenz') for the being of Dasein.
8. GA65 5/7.
9. GA65 347/274, 107/85.
10. In Heidegger's 1936 summer lectures on Schelling he states the age he understands himself to be working within: '"Today," that does not mean this very day, nor this year nor even this decade, but rather the whole transitional age from the nineteenth to the twentieth century and at the same time this transition in its whole European expansion' (GA42 39/22).
11. Although, because Plato and Aristotle occupy transitional positions, their work is liminal with respect to metaphysics, maintaining an exposure to a non-metaphysical philosophical ground, which is why Heidegger returns to them so frequently.
12. GA65 75/60.
13. GA65 12/12.
14. On Heidegger's concept of the fourfold, see Mitchell, *The Fourfold: Reading the Late Heidegger*. Elsewhere, Mitchell notes that this concept first appears in Heidegger's 1949 Bremen lectures (GA79) (Mitchell, 'Translator's Foreword' to Heidegger, *Bremen and Freiburg Lectures*, vii).
15. To be clear, Heidegger does not think he fully accomplishes this task, but has at least made an attempt: 'here [in *Beiträge*] already the thoughtful speaking of a philosophy within the other beginning must be attempted' (GA65 4/6).
16. For more on this, see GA65 §166. Also, see for example *WW*, where he states that 'essence is understood verbally' (*WW* 201/153).
17. GA65 30/25, 8/9.
18. GA65 27/23.
19. GA65 58/47.
20. See Introduction pp. 5–6 above.
21. GA71 127/108, Heidegger's italics on 'sich'.
22. GA65 183/144.
23. Heidegger captures these senses in relation to his vocabulary of truth as follows, for instance: (1) 'the abyssal ground [Ab-grund] is also, and primarily, the originary essence of the ground, of its grounding, *of the essence of truth*', (2) 'What is *its* [the

abyssal ground's] mode of grounding? The abyssal ground is the staying away [Weg-bleiben] of the ground', and (3) 'the excess [Übermaß] in the essence of beyng (self-concealment)' is 'the self-withdrawing of measuring out [Ausmessung], because it first lets arise and holds open the strife' (GA65 379/299, 249/196).

24. GA65 29/25, 382/302.

25. On the 'turning' in question here, see GA65 185/145: 'das *in sich kehrige Ereignis*' ('the *intrinsically turning event*'), 29/25, 34/29, 57/46, 95/76, and §255. For more on 'appropriation' and 'expropriation', see, for example, GA14 24–8/*On Time and Being* 19–23.

26. GA14 13/*On Time and Being* 9, 12/*On Time and Being* 8.

27. GA14 13/*On Time and Being* 9.

28. *EB* 81. For Polt's discussion regarding whether *Ereignis* is a singular, occasional, or continual event, see *EB* 74–87.

29. *WW* 195/149.

30. Hughes, *Deleuze's* Difference and Repetition 3. For more, see ibid. 2–5. For an instance where Deleuze addresses this, see *Différence et répétition* 224–6/173–4.

31. Deleuze did engage Heidegger's philosophy of difference, particularly in the form of the ontological difference between being and beings and the form presented in the 1957 *Identität und Differenz*. However, Deleuze did not have access to *Beiträge* or the related manuscripts, and thus he could not have seen Heidegger's work on the concept of difference in them.

32. GA65 4/6.

33. Cf. Lautman's account of mathematical theorisation, which I discuss in Bahoh, 'Deleuze's Theory of Dialectical Ideas'.

34. GA65 5/6.

35. Metaphysics is unable to sufficiently account for its own ontological grounds and this is a result of an inherent blockage: the constitution of metaphysics *is* a certain eclipse of the ground enabling that constitution to occur. Metaphysics is constituted by ontological distortion.

36. Meillassoux, *After Finitude* 8.

37. Gabriel, *Transcendental Ontology* vii.

38. Sokolowski has a nice discussion of this 'egocentric predicament' (*Introduction to Phenomenology* 9).

39. Heidegger discusses this in terms of the problem of truth in *WW* 178–82/137–40.

40. For a discussion of how Heidegger's work can address issues in contemporary episte-mology, see Gabriel, 'Is Heidegger's "Turn" a Realist Project?'.

41. Of course, for Heidegger, part of the solution is that being is not an object at all.

42. *SZ* 6/26.

43. By 'thought' here I do not mean the technical conception of thought developed in Heidegger's later work. I mean 'thought' in the sense that might be given in terms of *Sein und Zeit*: the existential structures and processes that make up human existence's disclosure, interpretation, and understanding of meaning, while all of this takes place via one's concernful absorption in networks of significance and equipment (being-in-the-world) and is co-determined by the structures of factical, thrown projection.

44. Perhaps, it might be objected, the project of ontology is in fact impossible. In that case, Heidegger has no business working from the presupposition that it is possible. However, the point to his argument is that the claim that ontology is possible is not a presupposition at all. The very fact that we have any understanding of being whatsoever – which is demonstrated, for instance, by the fact that we have a concept of being, or even by the fact that we use the verb 'to be' in a sensible way – proves that a thematic enquiry into the nature of being (ontology) is possible. This does not guarantee success in ontology, just that it is not categorically impossible. The first task, then, is to clarify the ground that enables the possibility of such a project. Note that this broader point is a Heideggerian version of Schelling's principle that

'like is known by like' (alternative translation: 'like is recognised by like') which Schelling borrows from Sextus Empiricus's *tois homoiois ta homoia gignoskesthai*. See GA42 93/54; Schelling, *Philosophische Untersuchungen über das Wesen der menschlichen Freiheit* 10; Sextus Empiricus, *adv. Grammaticos* L. I, c. 13, p. 283, quoted in Schelling, ibid. Schelling reformulates the point again as follows: 'he alone grasps the god outside through the god in himself' (ibid. 10). On the same page, Schelling additionally associates this principle with Pythagoras, Plato, and Empedocles. The point is found again in Parmenides, Fragment 3, which Heidegger cites at the beginning of his discussion of truth in *SZ* §44: τὸ γὰρ αὐτὸ νοεῖν ἐστίν τε καὶ εἶναι (*SZ* 212/256). In Plato, we find it in *Republic* at 508a–b, where 'the eye' 'is the most sunlike of the organs', being that in which 'sight' exists, and sight is 'naturally related' to 'the sun' (Plato, *Republic*, trans. Bloom 188). Heidegger refers to this as follows: 'Here one remembers at the same time the Platonic-Plotinian: *Ou gar an popote eiden ophthalmos hellion, helioeides me gegenemenos.* "For the eye could not see the sun if it were not itself 'sun-like'"' (GA42 96/55). He points out again that the same idea is expressed in a passage from Goethe's introduction to *Zur Farbenlehre*: 'If the eye were not sun-like / How could we look at light? / If God's own power didn't live in us / How could we be delighted by the god-like?'.

45. 'Being' might be rephrased awkwardly as 'isness'. Cf. Gabriel and Žižek, who make this point in relation to post-Kantian Idealism: 'the whole domain of the representation of the world (call it mind, spirit, language, consciousness, or whatever medium you prefer) needs to be understood as an event within and of the world itself. Thought is not at all opposed to being, it is rather being's replication within itself' (Gabriel and Žižek, *Mythology, Madness and Laughter* 3).

46. Heidegger thinks Descartes's insight on this point was significant but insufficient because he substantialised thought's being.

47. 'The meaning of being' is 'already . . . available to us in some way', even if for the most part 'infiltrated with traditional theories and opinions about being' (*SZ* 5–6/25).

48. *SZ* 12/32, italics removed.

49. Ibid., italics removed.

50. *SZ* 5/24.

51. *SZ* 7/27.

52. *SZ* 12/32. Dasein 'is ontically distinguished by the fact that, in its very being, that being is an *issue* for it . . . [T]his is a constitutive state of Dasein's being, and this implies that Dasein, in its being, has a relationship towards that being – a relationship which itself is one of being. And this means further that there is some way in which Dasein understands itself in its being . . . It is peculiar to this being that with and through its being, this being is disclosed to it' (*SZ* 12/32).

53. See Sheehan, *FE*, *Making Sense of Heidegger*, and 'Astonishing!'.

54. *SZ* 13/34, italics removed, 17/38.

55. This shouldn't be confused with a solipsism about being, of course, since Dasein is being-in-the-world.

56. Understanding and interpretation constitute only part of Dasein's existence. Though these are laced through Dasein's factical dimension, as thrown, Dasein's factical dimension includes historical, corporeal, linguistic, etc., aspects that go beyond its understanding and interpretation.

57. *SZ* 20/41.

58. Ibid.

59. *SZ* 381/433. Historicality is 'the essence of history [Geschichte]' (*SZ* 378/429).

60. *SZ* 382/434, 393/445. 'Temporality [is] the primordial condition for the possibility of *care*' (*SZ* 372/424).

61. *SZ* 376/428, italics removed.

62. *SZ* 385/437, italics removed.

63. *SZ* 20/41.
64. *SZ* 375/427, alternative translation sourced from Stambaugh's translation of *SZ* 358.
65. *SZ* 20/41.
66. *SZ* 19–20/41.
67. *SZ* 389/441.
68. *SZ* 372–3/424–5, italics removed, translation modified.
69. *SZ* 373/425.
70. *SZ* 374/427.
71. *SZ* 389/441.
72. See *SZ* 389–90/441–2.
73. *SZ* 389/440.
74. Ibid.
75. *SZ* 393/445.
76. See ibid.
77. *SZ* 389/440–1.
78. *SZ* 380/432.
79. Ibid.
80. SZ 384/436, italics removed.
81. For a related discussion, see Polt's account of 'reinterpretive events' (*EB* 78–80).
82. *SZ* 20/42.
83. *SZ* 20–1/42.
84. GA65 34/29.
85. GA65 31/27.
86. Ibid.
87. Ibid., italics modified.
88. GA65 319–20/253. This marks a slight difference between my interpretation and that of Vallega-Neu, who takes 'the "self" Heidegger is thinking here' to be 'the authentic self which he also thinks in *Being and Time*, the self to which human beings come back only in resolute being-towards-death' (*HCP* 85).
89. GA65 114/91, italics removed.
90. GA65 107/85.
91. GA65 118/94.
92. I am aware of only two uses of cognates of 'Enteignis' in *Beiträge* (pp. 120/95 and 231/182), but the idea is present throughout the text nonetheless and the term itself is used frequently in the subsequent private manuscripts through which the project of *Beiträge* extends.
93. GA65 120/95. I use 'expropriated' to translate 'enteignet' rather than Rojcewicz and Vallega-Neu's 'dissappropriated'.
94. In Heidegger's view, the logic of *Er-eignis* and *Enteignis* is also that of 'Zeit-Raum' (time-space), which generates temporality and spatiality. This, it is worth pointing out, is the Heideggerian analogue to Deleuze's reading of Kant on the role of time in the constitution of the subject. According to Deleuze, for Kant '"form of interiority" means not that time is internal to us, but that our interiority constantly divides us from ourselves, splits us in two: a splitting in two which never runs its course, since time has no end. A giddiness, an oscillation which constitutes time' (Deleuze, *Kant's Critical Philosophy* ix). In *Différence et répétition* he puts the point as follows: 'it is as though the *I* [JE] were fractured [traversé d'une fêlure] from one end to the other: fractured by the pure and empty form of time' (Deleuze, *Différence et répétition* 117/86). Deleuze takes Hamlet to supply the slogan for this idea: 'The time is out of joint' (Deleuze, *Kant's Critical Philosophy* vii).
95. GA65 109/86.
96. GA65 108/86.
97. *HCP* 62. 'This process begins with the Greek experience of being as *phusis*, i.e., as an emerging of beings. But soon *techne*, the "know-how" to make things, determines the

Greek approach to being so that being comes to be presented analogously to make-able beings. Consequently, being is determined as beingness (*Seiendheit*) and appears to be makeable and quantitatively calculable, like beings' (ibid.).

98. GA65 110/88.

99. GA65 108–9/86.

100. In *Différence et répétition*, Deleuze analyses these ideas in terms of what he calls a 'vulgarized Leibnizianism' (*Différence et répétition* 21/11). It is 'vulgarized' because it is something of a caricature. Nonetheless, it expresses a set of major ontological problems that both Heidegger and Deleuze target: the universalisation of representa-tion, the dominance of conceptual generality, and the reduction of difference to the kind of differences thinkable within the bounds of a representational concept. For Heidegger, these form part of the lattice of machination that texts like *Beiträge* aim to supplant, while for Deleuze they form organising points for a history of insufficient ontologies that *Différence et répétition* works to overturn.

101. A concept's comprehension is the extent to which it accurately represents its object, that is, the exhaustiveness of its predicates in matching up with the predicates belonging to its object, while its extension is the range of objects for which it is a concept.

102. Incidentally, this helps show part of why Heidegger argues that being is not a general-ity: mistaking being for a generality captures it within the machinery of representation.

103. The Kardashev scale illustrates Heidegger's idea of the gigantic well, but I have seen no evidence that he was aware of it.

104. 'The Ricks Must be Crazy', *Rick and Morty*, television (Cartoon Network, 30 August 2015).

105. *HCP* 61. Vallega-Neu is referring to a passage found at GA65 135/106.

106. GA65 123/98.

107. See Bahoh, 'Deleuze's Theory of Dialectical Ideas'.

108. GA65 109/87.

109. Ibid.

110. GA65 123/98.

111. GA65 132/104.

112. GA65 84/67.

113. GA65 115/91.

114. GA65 297/234, 379/300.

115. GA65 307/243.

116. Ibid. Two of Heidegger's main published texts that address 'bauen' are 'Der Ursprung des Kunstwerkes' in GA5 and 'Bauen Wohnen Denken' in GA7.

117. See GA65 64/51.

118. GA65 43/36.

119. 'The leap first of all opens the untrodden expanses and concealments of that into which the *grounding* of *Da*-sein must penetrate as belonging to the call of the event' (GA65 82/66).

120. GA65 58/47, 57/46, italics modified.

121. GA65 307/243.

122. Describing 'the "sheltering" (Bergung) of the truth of be-ing [Seyn] into beings' that is involved in creative grounding, Vallega-Neu writes that 'humans do not "do this" as independent subjects, but rather find themselves enowned [that is, appropriated] in this very occurrence' (*HCP* 81).

123. GA65 307/243.

124. GA65 31/27, italics removed.

125. GA65 320/253, italics removed.

126. Ibid., italics removed.

127. GA65 317–18/251.

128. This is by no means to suggest that the ground is not also simultaneously transcendent

in the specifically Heideggerian sense (see, for instance, Lautman's analysis of Heidegger and the simultaneous immanence and transcendence of a thing's ontological ground in 'Nouvelles recherches' in *Les mathématiques, les idées et le reel physique*).
129. GA65 58/47.

Chapter 3

Dasein and the Precursory Question of Truth

Heidegger's concept of *Er-gründung* or fathoming the ground describes the form Dasein's endeavours take to remedy the alienation from being that it suffers in the framework of metaphysics. It thus describes in broad terms the kind of transformations that would be involved in bringing about the historical event. However, describing fathoming the ground is not the same as doing it. Nor is meditating on the historical condition of Dasein and Da-sein sufficient to generate a transformative historical rupture capable of sustaining another beginning for thought if this does not include a reference to a ground exceeding the historical framework to be transformed. Fathoming the ground is accomplished by doing ontology, for this is the diagenic operation by which Dasein undergoes existential transformation remedying its alienation and progressively developing better-grounded articulations of being. As I have argued, the historical event has a certain methodological priority over the ontological, since we pursue the problematic of being from within the historical framework of metaphysics. Yet, the historical event is to be accomplished precisely by generating a properly grounded account of the logic or structure of beyng that grounds history in the first place, that is, of the ontological sense of event.

More specifically, for Heidegger this is to be done via the ontological problematic of the essence of truth: 'inceptual thinking is the inventive thinking [Er-denken] of the truth of beyng and thus is the fathoming of the ground [Ergründung des Grundes]'.[1] Even more directly to the point, in *Beiträge* he claims that 'the question of the *essence of truth*' must be 'posed radically as the question that is preliminary [Vorfrage] to the basic question [Grundfrage] of philosophy (How does beyng essentially occur [west]?)'.[2] As we know, *Beiträge* answers this basic question by arguing that 'beyng essentially occurs as event'. Despite the status of the question of truth as a *Vorfrage* to this other *Grundfrage*, it is not simply a propaedeutic. Truth forms an essential register of the event itself – in the ontological sense – and its dynamic structure: 'beyng qua event essentially occurs as truth'.[3] In Chapters 3 and 4, I reconstruct how the problematic of truth serves both methodologically as a path to an account of beyng as event and as an essential aspect of the event itself. Though there is extensive literature on Heidegger's concept of truth, these two crucial relations have remained poorly explained. I will argue the standard picture of Heidegger's account of truth is in fact incomplete: there are important changes that account undergoes in *Beiträge* that directly impact how we should understand his concept of event, but that have not been registered by most scholarship.

As is well known, dating back to his early work, Heidegger argues that the primary form of truth cannot be logical (formal), propositional, calculative, epistemological, or, more broadly, representational. These models are unable to explain essential aspects of the inner workings of truth. His position follows from the view that a true statement or judgement, for instance, is not nothing, but *is* in its own right; it's truth cannot be reduced to some ontologically negligible, merely ephemeral quality that arises when humans get to know reality and do away with illusion. A true statement or judgement (and likewise a false one) is part of reality, or in Heideggerian terminology, something that *is*. Sufficiently accounting for truth, then, requires explaining the being of truth, not just its ontic components and criteria. Heidegger takes this a step further, maintaining that in its primary sense, truth is ontological in character.[4] That is to say, 'truth' or what he comes to call 'the essence of truth' designates aspects or structures of being. These structures serve as the ground making possible the epistemological qualities of truth and their representational forms (to whatever extent they might in fact hold), which are diagenically secondary or derivative.

As emphasised earlier, *Sein und Zeit* grounds the problematic of being in the existence of Dasein, the analysis of which forms the methodological arena for fundamental ontology. Consequently, Heidegger explains truth within that arena – at least until the *Kehre*, when this is diagenically surpassed. In this chapter I reconstruct the ontology of truth in *Sein und Zeit* and perhaps the earliest text in which the *Kehre* is visible, 'Vom Wesen der Wahrheit' (lecture 1930, print 1943). In Chapter 4 I turn to *Beiträge* and its account of the relation between truth and event. As this all suggests, Heidegger's conception of truth undergoes a series of important transformations. I focus on three, which correspond with these three texts and are sequenced along a diagenic axis.

In the 1920s and early-to-mid-1930s Heidegger develops what I will call an *a-lēthic* account of the essence of truth. That is, he casts truth and untruth in terms of the Greek ἀλήθεια and λήθη. Untruth or λήθη, is not falsity or the failure of truth, but a necessary, coessential dimension of it. Ἀλήθεια and λήθη structurally entail one another and together form an ongoing ontological dynamism. As the alpha-privative of 'λήθη', the word 'ἀλήθεια' ('ἀ-λήθεια') exhibits this correlation.

Two main stages of the *a-lēthic* account can be identified. The first is expressed in *Sein und Zeit*, where ἀλήθεια and λήθη are the 'Unverborgenheit' ('unhiddenness'/'unconcealment') or 'Entdecktheit' ('uncovered ness'/'discoveredness') and 'Verborgenheit' ('hiddenness'/'concealment') of beings in a world.[5] This is a phenomenological account of the nature of truth, since it describes the way beings become present as phenomena for Dasein and recede from that presence.[6] Ἀλήθεια and λήθη are grounded in (and thus dependent upon) Dasein's *Erschlossenheit* (disclosedness) and are co-extensive with the phenomenal world of beings disclosed by Dasein. Said differently, they are aspects of Dasein's own existence in its constitutive correlation with a world of such beings.

The nature of truth, particularly its relation to logic, was a central concern in Heidegger's early work before the 1927 publication of *Sein und Zeit*.[7] Yet in the decade after, the problematic of truth takes on a prominent role in his treatment of the *Seinsfrage* itself. It is during the same period that 'event' rises to the forefront of his characterisation of being. In this period a second stage of the *a-lēthic* account of truth emerges, which is expressed well in 'Vom Wesen der Wahrheit'. There, a shift occurs in Heidegger's ontology: he recasts the elements of the essence of truth, placing them in a position diagenically prior to human existence. He begins to use the hyphenated 'Da-sein' to refer to the determinate field or finite world grounding human existence and understands ἀλήθεια and λήθη to provide the ontological structure of this field. With this shift, Heidegger begins to shed the properly phenomenological stage of his methodology required for the existential analytic of Dasein. His account of the essence of truth retains much of the phenomenological terminology but deploys it in increasingly structural rather than descriptive senses. In this picture, the *a-lēthic* essence of truth comprises correlated ontological structures or processes that enable beings to come to presence as part of a world, that is, *to be*. Truth or ἀλήθεια becomes understood as *Freiheit* (freedom), *Offenheit* (openness), or *Lichtung* (clearing), which designate an ontological structure that enables the movement of unconcealment, disclosure of beings, or origination of a meaningful world.[8] Untruth or λήθη becomes originary *Verbergung/Verborgenheit* (concealing/concealment) or *verbergenden Entzugs* (concealing withdrawal), the ground enabling ἀλήθεια.[9] In this account, truth as ἀ-λήθεια articulates at least three correlated things: (1) the terrain of beings or meaning constituting a world, (2) the genetic process by which such beings come to presence or become manifest and recede from presence, and (3) the ontological structures enabling that genetic process.

Most scholarship on Heidegger's account of truth in *Beiträge* takes it to remain within the basic framework of the second stage of the *a-lēthic* account. I take this to overlook significant structural and conceptual changes expressed in that text. My analysis in Chapter 4 turns to this, arguing that Heidegger moves into a third stage, which can no longer be properly accounted for in terms of the *a-lēthic* framework. Namely, by enquiring into the ontological ground generating the very structures of ἀλήθεια and λήθη, he moves to a position more originary on the diagenic axis. In the account this produces, ἀλήθεια and λήθη are originated in the primal process of differentiation I've mentioned, which constitutes not only the essence of truth but part of the logic of the event. Thus, in this third stage Heidegger's ontology offers a differential account of truth that is more originary than the earlier *a-lēthic* accounts. To be clear, this is not to say that he gets rid of the *a-lēthic* terminology; it remains important in the differential account but is insufficient for explaining the essence of truth.

A great deal of the confusion that has surrounded Heidegger's concept of event, especially as presented in *Beiträge*, is the result of a failure to clarify the relations defining his idiosyncratic terms. I attribute much of this to a failure to register the diagenic shift to a differential concept of truth, since this provides access to the logic of the ground articulating those relations, that is, to the logic of the event. If the problematic of truth is the problematic preliminary to that of beyng as event, then how one understands Heidegger's account of the essence of truth directly impacts how one understands his account of the event. Understanding the essence of truth to be ultimately *a-lēthic*, leads to an account of the evental nature of beyng in terms of the *a-lēthic* framework.[10] However, this leads to confusion about a variety of related concepts, which appear out of joint, disconnected, or connected only extrinsically by Heidegger's fiat (how exactly are 'truth' and 'time-space' or 'concealment' and 'difference' related, for example?). Hence the reliance of so many reconstructions on the repetition of jargon, mysticism, or appeals to authority. The problem is that the *a-lēthic* framework falls short of the text's most originary level of grounding. Making sense of *Beiträge*'s concepts without this is like trying to understand the pieces of a game without the rules defining their characteristics. In contrast, by registering *Beiträge*'s differential concept of truth, we can develop a better-grounded account of the event on the basis of which those concepts snap into place to form a consistent ontology.

The programme of enquiring into the essence of truth grants us an appropriately grounded standpoint within the logic of Heidegger's concept of event. This programme enacts a process of *Er-gründung* whereby thought progresses through increasingly originary positions on a diagenic axis that correspond with a variety of conceptual transformations that I will explore. In Heidegger's ontology, the logic of thought, that is, the logic of the being of thought, is continuous with the logic of being. Thus, by tracking the former it is possible to gain access to the latter. Truth, particularly in the earlier Heidegger, is a good jumping-off point for this process because there 'truth' designates being, insofar as being is disclosed in a meaningful way in Dasein's thought.

I Truth and Dasein in *Sein und Zeit*

In *Sein und Zeit* §44 Heidegger makes two points about truth that are important for making sense of the evolution of his ontology in the 1930s. First, 'truth, understood in the most primordial sense, belongs to the basic constitution of Dasein', that is, it is an 'existentiale' (*Existenzial*) of Dasein, the human being.[11] Second, 'Dasein is equiprimordially both *in* the truth and *in un*truth'.[12] I examine these statements below.

Heidegger often begins his analysis of a topic by summarising canonical accounts that he will argue are insufficient or contain an essential insight that later in history becomes distorted. His treatment of truth in *Sein und Zeit* follows this pattern. Parmenides's Fragment 3 expresses the insight that there is a primordial association of being with truth (under the guise of νοεῖν): 'he "identified" being with the perceptive understanding of being: τὸ γὰρ αὐτὸ νοεῖν ἐστίν τε καὶ εἶναι'.[13] Heidegger sees Aristotle as simultaneously adopting and distorting this insight. For Aristotle, 'philosophy itself is defined as ἐπιστήμη τῆς ἀληθείας – "the science of truth."' But it is also characterized as ἐπιστήμη, ἣ θεωρεῖ τὸ ὂν ᾗ ὄν – as "a science which contemplates beings as beings" – that is, with regard to their being'.[14] Thus, Aristotle maintained the association of truth with being. However, he also 'assigned truth to the judgment [or assertion] as its primordial locus' and 'set going the definition of "truth" as "agreement"'.[15] Heidegger challenges these positions.

I should make one preliminary note about this engagement with Aristotle. As I have mentioned, in *Beiträge* Heidegger argues that the philosophical orientation to the question about ὂν ᾗ ὄν leads to insufficient accounts of being as *Seiendheit* and is a defining characteristic of metaphysics. Yet, in *Sein und Zeit*, Heidegger still speaks of this orientation in a positive light – one aligned with the project of fundamental ontology. This contrast shows an important evolution in Heidegger's thought during the *Kehre*.

In Heidegger's analysis, Aristotle proposed that 'the soul's "Experiences" [*Erlebnesse*], its νοήματα ("representations" ["Vorstellungen"]), are likenings [Angleichungen] of Things', and this set the precedent for 'the later formulation of the essence of truth as *adaequatio intellectus et rei*', which I touched on in Chapter 2.[16] Heidegger uses 'Angleichung' here to translate both 'adaequatio' and 'ὁμοίωμα'.[17] The history of defining truth in terms of *adaequatio* is extensive. In its pre-Kantian form, Heidegger highlights its transmission from Isaac Israeli to Avicenna and to Aquinas, who 'also uses for "*adaequatio*" (likening [Angleichung]) the terms "*correspondentia*" (correspondence) and "*convenientia*" (coming together)'.[18] Though neo-Kantian epistemology might suggest the model of *adaequatio* is untenable after the critical revolution, Heidegger insists that Kant's system retained it, citing Kant's initial response in *Kritik der reinen Vernunft* to the question 'What is truth?': 'The nominal definition of truth, that it is the agreement of knowledge with its object, is assumed as granted; the question asked is as to what is the general and sure criterion of the truth of any and every knowledge.'[19]

The jumping-off point for Heidegger's critique of the model of *adaequatio* is his claim that 'the agreement of something with something has the formal character of a relation of something to something. Every agreement, and therefore "truth" as well, is a relation.'[20] The problem is that in the canon the ontological status of this relation and its implications for what is related are unclear. We might be tempted to think this means that Heidegger's point is to jettison the model of *adaequatio*, but this is not so. Rather, he takes it as a cue to investigate the nature of this relation, asking 'what else is tacitly posited in this relational totality of the *adaequatio intellectus et rei*? And what ontological character does that which is thus posited have itself?'[21] More pointedly, his critique proceeds by 'inquiring into the foundations [Fundamenten] of this "relation"'.[22] Though he uses the terminology of 'Fundament' here, the result will not be an account of a metaphysical or absolute foundation, but of the ontological structures enabling *adaequatio*, that is, of its ground in the sense I have been using.

Thus, this critique begins with a diagenic step. In fact, Heidegger gives a broader statement of how this will proceed that includes the key moments of the productive logic of *Grundlegung*: First, 'our analysis takes its departure from the traditional conception of truth, and attempts to lay bare the ontological foundations [Fundamente] of that conception'.[23] Second, 'in terms of these foundations the primordial [ursprüngliche] phenomenon of truth becomes visible. We can then exhibit the way in which the traditional conception of truth has been derived from [die Abkünftigkeit] this phenomenon.'[24] In other words, the analysis will generate an account of structures of truth that are diagenically prior to those described in the traditional model, while the latter are derived from and explained by the former. In fact, articulating these originary structures means articulating that which enables the derivative elements of truth to be what they are, that is, the *essence* of truth. Clarifying that entails clarifying the being of truth, or, as Heidegger puts it, 'our investigation will make it plain that to the question of the "essence" of truth, there belongs necessarily the question of the kind of being which truth possesses'.[25]

We usually consider *intellectus* and *res* to be different kinds of things, so with regard to what do they agree when in a relation of *adaequatio*? What grounds their relation such that *adaequatio* is possible? In an historically standard epistemology, one has knowledge (as opposed to falsity, illusion, or opinion) when one has truth together with justification. Such knowledge is manifest in judgements (subject predication), which are formulated linguistically in assertions/propositions (*Aussage*) or claims (*Sätze*). But 'in judgment one must distinguish between the judging as a *Real* psychical process, and that which is judged, as an *ideal* content'.[26] In turn, both of these must be distinguished from 'the Real Thing as that which is judged *about*'.[27] We have truth when the ideal content of a judgement has a relation of agreement to the real thing.

According to Heidegger, this model is insufficient and the reason can be seen in 'the ontologically unclarified separation of the Real and the ideal' or, inversely, the model's inability to say whether the relationship of agreement between ideal content and real thing is itself 'Real or ideal in its kind of being, or neither of these'.[28] Thus the question becomes, 'how are we to take ontologically the relation between ideal entity and something that is Real and present-at-hand?'[29] To pose the question in the general terminology of *adaequatio*, what is the ontological character of the relation between *intellectus* and *res*? Heidegger's solution entails a rejection of the fundamentality of the epistemological model supporting this version of the real/ideal distinction. The absolute distinction between real judgement, ideal content, and real thing is sustainable only so long as a system fails to discern the fact that the relation between judgement and thing, or between *intellectus* and *res*, *is*, that is, has its own affirmative ontological status. Since the terms of that model are unable to define this status, the being of the relation is irreducible to them.

Heidegger argues that to clarify the being of this relation (that is, the essence of truth) we can examine the way 'knowing demonstrates itself as true'; in other words, 'in the phenomenal context of *demonstration*, the relationship of agreement must become visible'.[30] The point is not that what is interesting about demonstration is the mechanism of how the *adaequatio* of proposition and thing is confirmed or disconfirmed. Rather, it is that all such mechanisms – to whatever degree they might be successful – are underwritten by the phenomenal access one has to the thing. If the being of the one who asserts or makes the proposition were such that access is impossible, the adequacy or inadequacy of the proposition could never be demonstrated. Truth as *adaequatio* would be structurally impossible (barring, for instance, a Thomistic appeal to a benevolent metaphysical guarantor).

Likewise, what is interesting about asserting or making a proposition here is not its role in *adaequatio*, but the fact that, as Heidegger puts it, 'asserting is a way of being towards the Thing itself that is'.[31] More specifically, it is a way of being in which the one who makes the proposition gains phenomenal access to the thing, that is, encounters it meaningfully in a world, and does so in such a way that it might be encountered '*just as* it is in itself'. This is not to suggest that one accesses the thing as noumenon in the Kantian sense. Rather, what Heidegger means by 'the thing' here is the thing exactly as an encountered phenomenon. Needless to say, Heidegger thinks his recasting of philosophy as fundamental ontology undermines Kant's epistemological framework not because it somehow gives us access to noumena, but instead because it denies the validity of the transcendental subject and its cognitive apparatus, and thus the validity of the phenomenon/noumenon distinction itself. Heidegger, of course, replaces the Kantian concept of phenomenon with his own: 'that which shows itself in itself, the manifest'; for Heidegger, phenomena 'are the totality of what lies in the light of day or can be brought into the light – what the Greeks sometimes identified simply with τὰ ὄντα (beings)'.[32] Thus, the diagenic move of enquiring into the essence of truth in this manner implies the eventual elimination of the illusion of the subject/object split.

Heidegger uses the term 'entdecken' (to uncover or discover) to describe the way we gain access to phenomenal beings. Making a proposition is one way (among others) of being towards something such that it might get uncovered. Asserting or making a proposition might also fail, of course. For Heidegger, 'to say that a proposition "*is true*" signifies that it uncovers the being [Seiende] as it is in itself. Such a proposition asserts, points out, "lets" the being be seen [läßt sehen] (ἀπόφανσις) in its uncoveredness.'[33] On this basis, Heidegger claims that we can identify the kind of being a proposition has when it is true: 'the *being-true* [*Wahrsein*] (*truth*) of the proposition must be understood as *being-uncovering* [*entdeckend-sein*]'.[34] Since, in his view, being-uncovering is what constitutes the truth of a proposition in this originary sense, as well as the ontological ground on which *adaequatio* might be possible at all, he claims that '"being-true" ("truth") means being-uncovering'.[35] In an effort to lend this thesis historical support, Heidegger suggests it was 'understood in a pre-phenomenological manner' by the ancients and translates it into Greek terms:

If a λόγος as ἀπόφανσις is to be true, its being-true is ἀληθεύειν in the manner of αποφαίνεσθαι – of taking beings out of their hiddenness and letting them be seen in their unhiddenness (their uncoveredness). The ἀλήθεια which Aristotle equates with πρᾶγμα and φαινόμενα . . . signifies the 'things themselves'; it signifies what shows itself – beings in the 'how' of their uncoveredness.[36]

For the purposes of my analysis, whether or not this is a justifiable interpretation of Greek thought is not important. What matters is that Heidegger takes truth or being-true to be uncoveredness, which is designated alternatively as 'ἀλήθεια'. His use of 'ἀλήθεια' marks a point of intervention into the tradition at which he sees himself both recuperating an original sense of the term and correcting later distortions of it.

The above derivation of a definition of truth as uncoveredness or ἀλήθεια operated by looking at the traditional model of truth, observing its insufficiency, and working out the ontological ground it presupposes. But how does this connect with the methodological horizon belonging to fundamental ontology? For, if '*truth* rightfully has a primordial connection with *being*, then the phenomenon of truth comes within the range of the problematic of fundamental ontology'.[37] Moreover, it is pretty vague to say that the primordial kind of being constituting truth is 'uncoveredness'. Can a more detailed account of the structure of uncoveredness be provided?

We can address both questions on the basis of Heidegger's earlier arguments claiming that Dasein is being-in-the-world, arguments that subvert the categories of *intellectus*, *res*, and so on, along with the metaphysical separation between these terms that leads to the epistemological problems involved in representationalism. 'Being-true as being-uncovering', Heidegger claims, is 'ontologically possible only on the basis [Grunde] of being-in-the-world. This latter phenomenon, which we have known as the basic state [Grundverfassung] of Dasein, is the foundation [Fundament] for the primordial phenomenon of truth.'[38]

This allows us to make sense of Heidegger's claim that in its originary sense truth belongs to the basic constitution of Dasein, that is, that it is an existentiale of Dasein. The problematic of truth is situated within the problematic of being, which has the form of the existential analytic of Dasein; and Dasein grounds truth, forming its ontological structure. Consequently, truth is structurally dependent upon Dasein's existence: 'Because the kind of being that is essential to truth is of the character of Dasein, all truth is relative to Dasein's being.'[39] This of course does not mean that the truth or falsity of a proposition or judgement is relativistic, but that when it comes to the ontological ground making such things possible at all, 'being-true as being-uncovering, is a way of being for Dasein'.[40]

Heidegger thinks this grounding of truth in Dasein can be stated more fundamentally. The structure of Dasein's being that enables all the dimensions of its being-in-the-world and its pre-theoretical openness to being is its *Erschlossenheit* (disclosedness). Disclosedness is the ground enabling Dasein's constitutive correlation with, or absorption in, a world of beings or meaning. Its basic structure is exhibited in the ecstatic structure of care, or thrown projection, and can be elaborated in terms of a set of existentialia that it comprises: *Befindlichkeit* (state-of-mind), *Verstehen* (understanding), *Rede* (discourse), and so on.[41] This is important because it means that the essence of truth can be articulated even more originarily in terms of disclosedness than of being-in-the-world. More precisely, 'truth, in the most primordial sense, is Dasein's disclosedness, to which the uncoveredness of beings within-the-world belongs'.[42] The enquiry into the nature of truth in *Sein und Zeit* leads ultimately to an enquiry into the disclosedness of Dasein. In Heidegger's words: 'only with Dasein's *disclosedness* is the *most primordial* phenomenon of truth attained'.[43] It should be noted that Heidegger sometimes casts Dasein's disclosedness as a *Lichtung* or 'clearing', in the sense that as its *Da* ('there'/'here'), Dasein holds open a clearing in which beings are accessible as phenomena. In fact, he writes, Dasein '*is* itself the clearing'.[44] This concept evolves after *Sein und Zeit* and will play an important role in his subsequent account of the essence of truth and the event.[45]

With all this in mind, we can explain Heidegger's claim that 'in so far as Dasein *is* its disclosedness essentially . . . to this extent it is essentially "true". *Dasein is "in the truth."*'[46] Truth is grounded in Dasein's disclosedness, but what is disclosed (along with Dasein) are beings or networks of meaning in the world. In other words, the structure of disclosedness extends into what is disclosed. In this sense, Dasein exists as enmeshed within the network of meaning or world of beings it discloses, that is, uncovers. The domain of truth (in its primordial sense) includes all that is disclosed or uncovered. It articulates the dynamic fabric of the world as disclosed by Dasein and within which Dasein exists.

How, then, is sense to be made of Heidegger's connected claim that Dasein is equally *in untruth*? Clarifying this requires looking to the 'full existential meaning of the principle that "Dasein is in the truth,"' which includes not only Dasein's 'disclosedness in general' but the fact that Dasein's existence is characterised by *Geworfenheit* (thrownness), *Entwurf* (projection), and *Verfallen* (falling).[47] Thrownness and falling are most important here. 'Thrownness' names the fact that Dasein does not choose the factical context in which it finds itself existing. Dasein is simply always already woven into and conditioned by it. On the basis of its factical context, Dasein 'projects' itself into the network of relations of significance and possibilities (world) through which it advances projects, navigates obstacles, and presses or is drawn forward temporally. Among Dasein's possibilities are those of striving to gain ownership of itself (authenticity) by pursuing the question of its own being or, on the other hand, slipping into the pre-fabricated language, interpretive matrices, and possibilities of action supplied by the masses (inauthenticity). 'Falling' is the process of slipping into inauthenticity, the gravity of which can never be conquered once and for all. It includes what Richardson called the 'negatived' aspects of the world of beings that Dasein discloses: the fact that aspects of the world are concealed and that what is disclosed as present is sometimes distorted and recedes in one way or another from presence in time (occlusion, being forgotten, death, etc.).[48] As part of this process, beings 'show themselves . . . in the mode of *semblance*'.[49] Dasein is disclosive, thrown projection to which belongs the essential characteristic of falling, but by the gravity of falling, 'what has formerly been uncovered sinks back again, hidden and disguised'.[50] Consequently, 'to be closed off and covered up belongs to Dasein's facticity'.[51] Thus, 'because Dasein is essentially falling, its state of being is such that it is in "untruth"', where untruth as coveredness is manifested in semblance, occlusion, or withdrawal in the field Dasein discloses.[52]

In this way, to say Dasein is in the truth entails that it is equiprimordially in untruth.[53] Dasein's existence is articulated in the two movements of unconcealment and concealment. It discloses networks of meaning or worlds of beings, which are phenomenally present only on the basis of its existence. The truth/untruth dynamic is the context, fabric, or terrain of meaning or beings in which Dasein is absorbed.

2 Truth and Dasein in 'Vom Wesen der Wahrheit'

During the 1930s, the problematic of truth takes on a more pronounced role in Heidegger's treatment of the *Seinsfrage*, coming to form a central register in terms of which he articulates the nature of being. The essay 'Vom Wesen der Wahrheit' is his central statement on this matter during the early part of that decade. A paragraph added in its 1949 edition emphasises the point: 'truth signifies sheltering that clears [lichtendes Bergen] as the fundamental trait [Grundzug] of being'.[54] More generally, through the problematic of truth Heidegger aims to work out the ontological structures or ground enabling beings to come to be, that is, to come to and recede from 'presence', become manifest in a world, or constitute a network of meaning for Dasein. 'The essence of truth' will name this ground, while 'truth' will name being, insofar as being is manifest in beings. The structures of the essence of truth prefigure important parts of beyng or the event in the account that emerges a few years later. Heidegger's account of those structures advances his ontology along a dia-genic axis and contributes to the effort of *Er-gründung*.

In distinction from *Sein und Zeit*, 'Vom Wesen der Wahrheit' presents the noted shift in the relation between the essence of truth and Dasein: rather than maintaining that the essence of truth is Dasein's disclosedness, Dasein will now be grounded in the essence of truth. In this new view, the essence of truth still entails an ontological structure of disclosedness, but now in a form diagenically prior to that belonging to Dasein. As I've indi-cated, the terminological distinction between 'Dasein' and the hyphenated 'Da-sein' marks this shift. Whereas 'Dasein' retains the meaning given in *Sein und Zeit*, 'Da-sein' refers to this more originary disclosedness, which I take to be constituted by co-determinate structures of originary 'openness' or 'ἀληθέα' and 'concealment', 'withdrawal', or 'λήθη' that I will discuss. Da-sein is (1) the determinate field or world in which Dasein lives, and (2) the ontological features of that field or world that are diagenically prior to Dasein and make its structure of existence (and that of other beings) possible, that is, the determinate openness or ἀληθέα that enables them to be things related to one another at all and the concealment or λήθη that is required for its determinacy. The essence of truth is made up of these *a priori* ontological structures, which, it should be emphasised, are not metaphysically transcendent but rather constitutively immanent to the worlds of beings they enable to be.

This transformation is significant for several reasons. For one, it shows that Heidegger's philosophy supports a type of ontological realism further challenging both Kant's definition of the range of legitimate philosophi-cal thought and its subsequent forms in the twentieth-century phenom-enological tradition. To me, 'Vom Wesen der Wahrheit' is particularly fascinating because in it are found both the phenomenological apparatus of Heidegger's early work and his move to the logic of a pre-phenomenal ground enabling phenomenal presentation. Clearly, this ground is not a transcendental subject nor the elements of such a subject's cognitive apparatus (as it might have been for Kant); but furthermore it is not even indexed onto the meaning-making activities of Dasein (as it might have been for Heidegger himself in *Sein und Zeit*). Since it comprises ontologi-cal features structurally prior to the domain of phenomena, the account of it can no longer be called strictly phenomenological. Though he never states the claims overtly in this way, his ontology supports the realist views that (1) there are aspects of being that are ontologically prior to and thus independent of human existence, and (2) we can give an account of them, even if our methodology entails a necessary incompleteness and its account is subject to ongoing evolution.

Well aware that his treatment of the essence of truth continues to challenge Kant, Heidegger references the latter's famous metaphor of the light dove of metaphysics: 'With this question concerning essence do we not soar too high into the void of generality that deprives all thinking of breath?'[55] His answer is of course 'no'. This is remarkable because contrary to strong phenomenological readings of Heidegger, like that of Sheehan, his work begins directly undermining philosophy's tethers to the human being. Interestingly, this move parallels Deleuze's critique of Kant in *Différence et répétition* insofar as both he and Heidegger seek not only a pre-representational, but a 'pre-subjective' ontological ground on the basis of which human existence and its representational activities are possible. Though Heidegger argues against a certain form of 'transcendentalism', it makes good sense to think of this ground as a transcendental field somewhat akin to that proposed in Deleuze's theory of dialectical Ideas, so long as we are clear that it is not indexed onto the transcendental constitution of the human being.

I would now like to work through the Heideggerian line of thought that leads to this transcendental field. As its title indicates, the task of 'Vom Wesen der Wahrheit' is to articulate the *essence* of truth. Despite Heidegger's radical anti-essentialism when it comes to metaphysics, he maintains that when properly contextualised, 'in the concept of "essence" philosophy thinks being'.[56] There is a longer story about 'essence' that could be told here, but in short he uses it to mean 'Grund der Ermöglichung' ('ground of enabling') or, alternatively formulated, 'Grund der inneren Möglichkeit' ('ground of the inner possibility').[57] As in *Sein und Zeit*, the movement of thought in 'Vom Wesen der Wahrheit' proceeds from more derivative to less derivative or more essential forms of truth. In each stage, the progression is carried forward by an investigation into the ground that makes the form of truth with which it is concerned possible (a Heideggerian form of Kantian transcendental deduction). This brings about an evolution of the problematic of truth along a diagenic axis. As in *Sein und Zeit*, 'Vom Wesen der Wahrheit' begins its technical analysis with the traditional concept of truth as *adaequatio* (the correctness or accordance of a proposition or judgement with the matter it purports to be about). From this, the essay progresses by

> tracing the inner possibility of the correctness of a proposition [Aussage] back to the ek-sistent freedom of letting-be [Freiheit des Seinlassens] as its "ground," and likewise . . . pointing to the essential beginning of this ground in concealing and in errancy.[58]

With respect to the traditional concept of truth, 'Vom Wesen der Wahrheit' largely reiterates *Sein und Zeit*, with a few alterations stemming from a focus on the propositional, rather than cognitive, version of it. Heidegger briefly examines its medieval origins in the understanding of *veritas* as *adaequatio rei et intellectus*, focusing on Aquinas's position (without naming him), expressed well in *Quaestiones Disputatae de Veritate*. Then he turns to the way this becomes reformulated as the accordance or adequacy and correspondence of a proposition or statement with the matter it is about.

This presents a modified version of the problem of relationality explored above in section 1. If we take the example of a round coin lying on a table and the proposition 'this coin is round', the question is 'wherein are the thing and the proposition [Aussage] supposed to be in accordance, considering that the relata are manifestly different in their outward appearance?'[59] For, 'the coin is made of metal. The proposition is not material at all. The coin is round. The proposition has nothing at all spatial about it.'[60] Similarly to *Sein und Zeit*'s treatment of the adequation of a judgement's ideal content to the real thing it purports to be about, what is required is an analysis of 'the kind of relation that obtains between the proposition and the thing', particularly with respect to the 'essence' or ontological ground of that relation.[61] Also similar to that earlier text's phenomenological account, here this relation is described to be one in which the proposition 'presents' (*vor-stellt*) the thing 'and says of what is presented how, according to the particular perspective that guides it, it is disposed'.[62]

The structure of propositional presentation plays an important role in Heidegger's treatment of the problem of relationality in 'Vom Wesen der Wahrheit'. It prefigures structures of the ontological ground of truth and their relations, and, notably, replicates the basic structure of Dasein's disclosedness.

The relation by which a proposition presents an object such that it might be in accordance with the object is distinct from other relations of accordance, for instance between two objects. If two coins are on the table, an accordance between them might be said to hold insofar as both are round, metal, etc. But the presence of one coin has little to do with the presentation of the other. In contrast, in a proposition a relation is constituted to something else such that the other thing comes to be phenomenally presented (or, in Heidegger's preferred language, uncovered or unconcealed). In Heidegger's ontology, propositions, like thought, are not ontologically negligible or irreal but have a positive ontological status; in *Sein und Zeit*, for instance, this was grounded in Dasein's 'Rede' or 'discourse'. His approach to the relation between proposition and thing works at this basic ontological-structural level, not that of ontic or abstract categorial relations entailed in propositions.

To frame this in simple terms (setting aside the complexities of a proposition about itself or another proposition), we must explain the ontological structure of two essential characteristics of propositional presentation: its necessary difference from its object and its simultaneous correspondence with it. These might seem like rather mundane things to worry about, but they replicate in a new form the problem of access posed by representational thought discussed in Chapter 2. At stake are issues of ontological continuity and discontinuity, identity and difference, univocity and equivocity. In short, if one thing is absolutely different from another, how is any relation possible, other than perhaps one of pure exteriority? If not, what is the origin and constitution of their difference?

One might approach the problem by first entertaining two obviously faulty scenarios, one in which the proposition collapses into the identity of the object, the second in which the object is reduced to the proposition. Perhaps, according to the first, for the proposition to have an accordant correspondence, it must become something round and metal like the coin, or at the limit, identical to the coin itself. However, in that case the proposition ceases to be a proposition. Instead, the possibility of an accordance of proposition to coin requires that a difference hold between the two. In fact, insofar as a proposition about a coin can only be what it is in its difference from the coin, Heidegger can be seen to offer a proto-differential account of this relation; that is to say, the proposition's ontological constitution is partially differential in nature.

Inversely, from the 'object-pole' of the presentative relation, the difference of object from proposition is equally important. If, in the second scenario, the coin were to collapse into the proposition, the proposition would present nothing more than itself and there would be no meaningful accordance. To be a presentative proposition of the coin, the proposition must be informed by aspects of the coin that withhold from or withstand this or that phenomenal presentation. If the roundness of the coin were reduced to the 'roundness' expressed in the proposition and were not a characteristic of the coin that withstands such propositions (be they true or false), the proposition could not be in an accordance with what it is purportedly about. Heidegger capitalises on the terminology of *Gegenstand* (object) to emphasise this point, though he continues to disavow theories of consciousness, psychologies, and epistemologies that entail traditional *intellectus/res* dualism. 'To present', he writes, 'means to let the thing stand opposed [das Entgegenstehenlassen] as object [Gegenstand]'.[63] Lest the thing collapse into the proposition, it 'must maintain its stand as a thing and show itself as something withstanding [ein Ständiges]'.[64]

This difference is essential to and constitutive for propositional truth in the view Heidegger offers. However, it cannot be an absolute discontinuity, otherwise once again no presentation would occur. To be presented via a proposition, the object must inform it. In some sense the object must 'traverse an open field of opposedness [Entgegen]', which we can tentatively understand to be the field of difference between proposition and thing.[65] Inversely, the proposition must have a continuity with and insistence or co-inherence in the object, through which it accesses and comes to present it. Structurally speaking, then, the relation of accordance entails a simultaneous differentiation of and continuity between proposition and thing. Because of the simultaneity or reciprocal co-determination of such difference and continuity, I understand this to mean that there is a structural *tension* constitutive of this relation and thus of the possibility of accordance in propositional truth. This notion of tension will become important again in Chapter 5.

So, what is the nature of the constitutive open field of opposedness or tension? Does it tell us something about the ontological ground of propositional truth or is it simply a by-product of making propositions? It seems that the latter cannot be the case:

> the appearing of the thing in traversing a field of opposedness takes place within an open field [Offenen], the openness of which is not first created by the presenting but rather is only entered into and taken over as a domain of relatedness [Bezugsbereich].[66]

The claim here is that this open field renders presentational propositions, which can occupy it, possible. Justification for this is not well explicated in the text, but given what we know about Heidegger's fundamental ontology, the rationale is fairly evident. Presentational propositions don't just happen, they are made by Dasein. But Dasein's ability to thematise something in a proposition is grounded in its more originary pre-thematic openness to beings, that is, its 'disclosedness' via which it is able to comport itself among beings or 'be' being-in-the-world. Richardson translates this into the language of the proposition: here, as elsewhere, Heidegger maintains the 'thesis that the truth of judgments (therefore predicative) supposes a pre-predicative truth'; namely, 'the Open', which 'must be conceived as a matrix of relationships (*Verhältnis*) which constitute the sphere of potentialities of There-being [Dasein], one of which potentialities is exploited when an actual contact [with a being or object of a proposition] takes place'.[67] Stated concisely, the open field is what *Sein und Zeit* referred to as a 'world', while 'that which is opened up' in a world refers to the beings populating it. On this basis, the now familiar conclusion can be reiterated: the essence of truth is not the correctness, adequation, or accordance of the proposition with the thing, since these can be explained only by more originary structures entailed in pre-predicative, pre-thematic openness to a world. In other words, it must be grounded by 'the openness of comportment [Verhaltens]' – Dasein's disclosedness via which a world is phenomenally presented or unconcealed.[68]

It is tempting to allow this conclusion to close the enquiry into the essence of truth, for the position in *Sein und Zeit* seems to have been confirmed. However, a problem remains regarding the ontological status of the open field or world itself. As in *Sein und Zeit*, the first several sections of 'Vom Wesen der Wahrheit' maintain that a world or open field is held open by Dasein's disclosedness – that is, Dasein's openness to and insistence in the beings it encounters (which are in turn open to it) and its simultaneous difference or structural distance from them, which is both an ontic and ontological distance. We have examined the nature of propositional adequation with an eye to the structural conditions needed for such a thing to occur. More precisely, we have determined that the structure of openness or disclosedness attributed to Dasein is a necessary (though insufficient for a reason I will point out) ground for the possibility of such propositional adequation. But with this have we hit ontological bedrock? The problem is that such a picture might simply kick the can down the road: if explaining the open field of opposedness presupposed by propositional adequation required recourse to the diagenically prior field of Dasein's disclosedness, why shouldn't the latter require yet another explanation? Put differently, can Dasein's disclosedness sufficiently explain the openness in question? Or might Dasein's disclosedness force us back to the question of what, in turn, grounds it? Perhaps Dasein occupies a more originary structure of openness in a way similar to that in which a presentative statement occupies the 'open field of opposedness'. Ultimately, what we need is an explanation of the *origination* of the open region that Dasein has been suggested to ground, for this would mean explaining it on the basis of something not already opened. I think we only get part of this story in 'Vom Wesen der Wahrheit'. In Chapter 5 I will look at how the rest might be supplied by *Beiträge*.

To be certain, Heidegger does not pose the problem in this way and he does not construct the short argument I am about to make, which I will refer back to as 'the argument for the derivative character of Dasein's disclosedness'. Nonetheless, both are clearly entailed within the text and motivate its discourse. Appealing to Dasein's disclosedness to ground the open field occupied by propositions cannot be sufficient. A more originary ground is required precisely because Dasein is always already open; there is no Dasein that is not open, Dasein *is* its disclosedness. Dasein cannot explain the origination of the open realm, it presupposes it. If Dasein were the explanation, this would place what is originated in a position prior to its origination. Thus, explaining the open field requires explaining whatever is also responsible for the origination of *Dasein's* open character, and this must entail processes diagenically prior to Dasein. Now, answering to this challenge has two possibilities: the origination of the open field could either be (1) the same thing as the origination of Dasein (though not *grounded in* Dasein), in which case the open realm would be nothing beyond Dasein's disclosedness, or (2) the origination of a structure of openness that is itself diagenically prior to Dasein. In either case, Dasein's existence cannot be the *explanans*.

Heidegger's treatment of the status of the open field drives 'Vom Wesen der Wahrheit' to a new diagenic stage. He approaches it in different terms than I have just used, focusing on a distinct, but related, issue: the way that – via the open field – the object of a proposition can supply the standard according to which the proposition is either adequate or not. This parallels *Sein und Zeit*'s concern with the 'phenomenal context of demonstration'. 'Supplying a standard' is also tied closely to the 'withstanding' character of objects noted above and implies a distinctly ontic condition necessary for true propositions about such objects. Namely, the particular ontic characteristics of the object must inform the statement – hence the noted insufficiency of the ontological structure of disclosedness for propositional truth. Nonetheless, Heidegger's main interest is not in the ontic mechanics of the proposition *per se*, but rather the nature of the ontological ground that makes it possible for the object to supply a standard, that is, the pre-propositional open field. What prompts his ontology of truth to move to a new diagenic stage is 'the question . . . as to the ground of the inner possibility of the open comportment that pregives [vorgebenden] a standard'.[69]

What is interesting to me is that the need for this 'pregiving of a standard' tells us something about the structure of openness that grounds it. A proposition comes to accord with a thing by being informed or bound by it (Heidegger uses the verb 'binden'), not simply by occupying the open realm. Even though 'a proposition is invested with its correctness by the openness of comportment', it is so only insofar as 'through the latter' 'what is opened up [can] really become the standard for the presentative correspondence'.[70] This quietly sneaks in a point which at first seems unimportant given Heidegger's established account of being-in-the-world, but which has significant implications: Dasein's disclosedness is not isolated or one-sided, but co-constituted by the openness of the beings in which it insists or is enmeshed. Further, propositional accord requires that when Dasein makes a statement, the statement can be informed by the thing it is about. But what enables openness to be such that this kind of binding or informing can occur?

Heidegger's answer to this, and to the question of the ground of the openness of comportment, seems a bit strange: 'freedom'.[71] As noted earlier, 'freedom' has a technical sense here and does not mean 'human caprice', an 'absence of constraint with respect to what we can or cannot do', free will, or any other 'property of the human being'.[72] In short, this concept of freedom is not that of a human capacity for choosing. When the term is first presented in this text, it operates more or less as a place-holder. It designates whatever it is that enables the openness involved in Dasein's comportment to be bound or determined by beings, such that that comportment is directed in a pre-thematic, pre-predicative manner and might on that basis formulate thematic or predicative statements correctly presenting those beings. Freedom designates Dasein's ability to be informed by the world, not merely project upon it. In Heidegger's words, it is a 'freedom for what is opened up in an open field'.[73] But this is vague. What is this freedom more precisely?

According to Heidegger, freedom 'lets beings be the beings they are' and thus (tentatively) 'reveals itself as letting beings be [das Seinlassen von Seiendem]'.[74] Despite this rather off-putting turn of phrase, its meaning can be clarified by distinguishing two distinct senses of freedom as 'letting beings be'. I shall refer to them as 'freedom 1' and 'freedom 2'. Freedom 1 is a manner of comportment for Dasein. Freedom 2 is an ontological structure that enables beings to be.

Let us take the first first. Freedom 1 is a manner of comportment. As such, we might be tempted to think of it as something like an ability of Dasein to simply 'will' what is and what occurs in the world. However, this is not the idea. If it were, it would be meaningless to say that Dasein's comportment is bound, directed, or informed by beings. Rather, freedom 1 has to entail a reticence or restraint on Dasein's part that gives things room to be as they are: Dasein 'withdraws in the face of beings in order that they might reveal themselves with respect to what and how they are'.[75] Yet, this cannot be a disengagement from beings, for that would also preclude being informed by them and, consequently, preclude propositional adequation. Thus, to let beings be is 'to engage oneself with beings' in a particular way.[76] In Heidegger's use, we 'let beings be' by being attentive to the ontological ground that enables them to be, or, in temporally dynamic terms, to come into and recede from presence. Since beings are always distinctive and concrete, our attention cannot treat their ground as something abstract or disengaged from them. That is, it is an attention to this ground insofar as this or that distinctive set of beings is in fact in the process of being, and it preserves the presentation of those beings as so grounded. To capture the idea more concisely, freedom 1 is an attentiveness to the being of beings that tries neither to dominate nor disengage from them. Thus far, the nature of the ground involved has been described in terms of structural openness, and, in this regard, to let beings be is 'to engage oneself with the open field and its openness into which every being comes to stand, bringing that openness, as it were, along with itself'.[77] Likewise, in the terminology of truth, letting beings be is an engagement with the essence of truth that grounds the possibility of propositional adequation.

Freedom 2 is also a form of 'letting beings be', but here this designates an ontological structure, not a comportment by human existence. The claim governing freedom 2 is that any comportment by Dasein (including that of freedom 1) is possible only on the basis of an ontological openness more originary than that of Dasein. 'Freedom' in its second sense names this structure, which I will also refer to as 'originary openness' or 'originary disclosedness'. It names the way Dasein (a being) is let or enabled to be on the ground of such openness. It is only after the first few sections of 'Vom Wesen der Wahrheit' that Heidegger introduces the idea that freedom has this sort of ontological priority, writing that 'ek-sistent freedom [2] as the essence of truth is not a property of human beings; . . . on the contrary humans ek-sist and so become capable of history only as the property [Eigentum] of this freedom'.[78] His justification for this is sparse in the text. I can identify two lines of support.

The first is the implicit argument for the derivative character of Dasein's disclosedness discussed above. It eliminated the possibility that Dasein can sufficiently explain openness, that is, that Dasein is the ground whence openness is. This placed that ground in a position ontologically prior to Dasein and left the other two possibilities: either the openness generated is (1) simply the openness of Dasein or (2) also ontologically prior to Dasein.

The second argument eliminates possibility 1 and leaves us with possibility 2. It can be reconstructed like this: we know that Dasein's circumspective openness and understanding of beings enables it to track different paths – or possibilities of comportment – through the world via which it deals with whatever tasks it is concerned with. But those paths are constrained by the nature and range of beings that are actually disclosed at any given time, the same constraints that must bind Dasein's presentative statements. If I say 'That coin is pink' when it is in fact gold, my proposition fails to agree with its standard. If I aim to light a campfire, using a glass of water won't work; I need to find another route to accomplish the task. This sort of constraint, or the parameters of possible comportment it defines, cannot be reduced to features of the openness of Dasein's comportment (its disclosedness), since then they would not be *imposed* upon Dasein; the 'thrown' character of Dasein's finitude would dissolve and Heidegger's philosophy would be a vulgar form of idealism. Moreover, this imposition could not occur if the beings 'doing the imposing' were not themselves structurally or ontologically open, for then they would not be encounterable in a meaningful way at all. The specific and constrained openness of such beings shapes the field in which Dasein can encounter them. But this means that the openness of other beings is irreducible to that of Dasein's existence. Now, it might be tempting to conclude that openness *itself* is derived from the structure of beings (and thus that Heidegger offers merely an ontic realism). However, that would put the cart before the horse: just as Dasein's disclosedness presupposes an open field of relationality bound by those beings, the openness of those beings to anything else presupposes such a field. To be a being encounterable by anything else means to populate an open field of relationality. Though that field might exist only in forms given by these or those concrete beings, it cannot be reduced to a conglomeration of the structures of such beings, since no structurally open being could ever have come to be except by coming to populate such a field. While such a field cannot be abstracted from the concrete beings populating it, it nonetheless must be ontologically prior to them, that is, form part of the structure of the ground enabling them to be. Since Dasein is simply one of these beings, possibility 1 listed above is eliminated: originary openness is not simply the openness of Dasein, and its origination is not simply that of Dasein's openness. This ground is ontologically prior both to Dasein and to all other beings, though it is nonetheless immanently constitutive for them.

I can now refine some of the terms I have been using. 'Freedom' (2) or 'openness' (originary openness, the openness of the open field and not simply of beings) is Heidegger's name for this field of relationality. 'World' names this field as bound by concrete beings. In alternative terms, freedom 2 is the originary disclosedness Heidegger refers to as 'Da-sein'. Expanding on a passage cited above, he outlines an argument along these lines with respect to human existence as follows:

> If ek-sistent Da-sein, which lets beings be, sets the human free for his 'freedom' by first offering to his choice something possible (a being) and by imposing on him something necessary (a being), human caprice does not then have freedom at its disposal. The human being does not 'possess' [besitzt . . . nicht] freedom as a property [Eigenschaft]. At best, the converse holds: freedom, ek-sistent, disclosive Da-sein, possesses [besitzt] the human being – so originarily that only *it* secures for humanity that distinctive relatedness to beings as a whole as such which first founds all history.[79]

Freedom 2, originary openness, or Da-sein is the ground that enables both the openness of Dasein's comportment and the manifestation of beings in a world at all. In the account so far, it forms the essence of truth that enables propositional truth to function. Heidegger sometimes describes this ground as openness as such or 'the openness of the open field'.[80] In this picture, freedom 2 is 'the openness' on the basis of which the world *is*, and the 'open field' is that world: that 'into which every being comes to stand', in other words, 'τὰ ἀληθέα, the unconcealed'.[81] Freedom 2 grounds the disclosedness through which Dasein exists (stands outside of itself in a way absorbed in beings), that is, through which it is 'intrinsically' 'expos[ed] to the disclosedness of beings as such'.[82] Consequently, it is the basis on which Dasein engages the beings populating a world. Since freedom 2 is an ontological structure diagenically prior to Dasein and not dependent upon it, Heidegger's position here is not just a form of ontic, but of ontological realism. His ontology supports the view that at least some feature of being *is* regardless of whether human beings exist.

This also provides a basis for restating the nature of freedom 1 more precisely. Dasein's engagement with beings in a manner attentive to the ground whereby they are what they are is an attentiveness to originary openness as it is manifest in or bound by concrete beings and to the temporal process involved in their coming to presence and receding from presence in that openness (though I have left this latter qualification aside).

Clearly, 'Vom Wesen der Wahrheit' has now moved beyond *Sein und Zeit*. If freedom 2 is the openness of the open field, that is, the ground enabling beings to be, then human existence – that of a human being – cannot be identified with freedom. Originary openness is no longer grounded in human existence, as it was in *Sein und Zeit*. Heidegger's use of the term 'Da-sein' marks this shift. Da-sein grounds Dasein or makes the structure of human existence possible. Human existence and the world in which it exists are structured by freedom 2 or Da-sein.

In contrast to *Sein und Zeit*, the essence of truth can no longer be equated with Dasein's disclosure of beings, for that disclosure works only on the basis of freedom 2 or Da-sein. The human being is absorbed in the terrain of beings or meaning that articulates that freedom. If the world is τὰ ἀληθέα or the unconcealed, then 'ἀλήθεια' comes to signify unconcealment, where this is not simply the phenomenological disclosure of beings to Dasein, but the originary openness whereby beings are enabled to come into and recede from manifestation. Ἀλήθεια as part of the *essence* of truth is part of the ontological structure or ground whereby worlds of beings are enabled to be, while 'truth is disclosure of beings through which [that] openness essentially unfolds [west]'.[83] Thus, Heidegger's *a-lēthic* account of the essence of truth has decisively moved to a second stage, beyond the phenomenological stage in *Sein und Zeit*.

This leaves one important question: what of untruth or λήθη? In the phenomenological picture given in *Sein und Zeit*, λήθη was an equally essential and structurally correlated counterpart to ἀλήθεια. It was concealment, coveredness, or occlusion and the semblance involved in Dasein's fallenness. But what should we make of λήθη in light of the transformation found in 'Vom Wesen der Wahrheit'? In short, untruth is part of the essence of truth and since the latter now has a position diagenically prior to Dasein, so does the former. In fact, the way Heidegger treats untruth drives his ontology again to a more originary ground.

Freedom 2 or the disclosedness of Da-sein lets beings be, that is, it lets them become present in unconcealment. But Heidegger claims something strange about this: he suggests that this occurs only in a way oriented by a particular 'attuned' 'comportment'.[84] This is strange because he usually reserves the term 'comportment' to apply to Dasein (indeed, he also uses it in this sense in 'Vom Wesen der Wahrheit' without clearly noting the different use). What can this term mean in this new context and how can an ontological structure prior to Dasein be attuned? Answering this leads to an answer to the question about λήθη.

Clearly, freedom 1 is always attuned, like all of Dasein's comportment. By 'attunement' Heidegger means that the concrete meanings and possibilities offered by a world of beings to Dasein's comportment define or provide a distinct factical character to that comportment, and Dasein's futurally oriented circumspective concern is embedded in and guided by them. The factical possibilities of the kind of comportment described by freedom 1 are defined by the world of beings in which Dasein's existence insists or is absorbed. In such a world, there can be no such thing as a being that is completely open (whatever that would mean) because then it would not be delimited at all, it would not *be*. Openness is nothing without a limit. Λήθη names a concealing withdrawal which provides this delimitation and grounds the closedness belonging to beings. Without the finitude that closedness or concealment provides beings, Dasein's possibilities of comportment would evaporate. Thus, the closedness or concealment of λήθη is no less essential to a world than openness. How should we understand the character of λήθη more precisely?

At the level of freedom 2, Dasein's existence is structured or attuned by the originary openness enabling it to engage beings at all. In Heidegger's words, 'as letting beings be, freedom [2] is intrinsically the resolutely open bearing that does not close up in itself. All comportment is grounded in this bearing and receives from it directedness toward beings and disclosure of them.'[85] I take comportment at the level of freedom 2 to be the diagenic directionality that originary openness has to a concrete world of beings populating it. Indeed, openness always *is* in the contours of a concrete world of beings. Whence do the characteristics of those contours arise such that openness is openness of a factically concrete world? At one level – that of the distinct beings populating such a world – they are co-determined by the λήθη co-constitutive of the beings in question. At a more fundamental level – that of the ground enabling such beings to be – originary openness itself cannot be absolute or total, for then there would be no delimitation, no finitude at all. For the same reason, the closedness, concealment, or withdrawal co-constitutive of beings cannot be explained by originary openness alone. Ἀλήθεια, originary openness, originary unconcealment can gain delimitation only in correlation with what limits or makes openness finite: an originary closedness, concealment, withdrawal, or λήθη. This cannot be reduced to the λήθη belonging to beings as such for the same reason that openness cannot be reduced to the openness of beings: all beings are finite; finitude cannot be the result of beings, for they could not be without a delimitation ontologically prior to them. Thus, an originary form of λήθη correlates with originary ἀλήθεια, both of which are ontologically prior to worlds of beings, even if always existing only in their concrete contours.

Heidegger uses the concept of history to discuss the way originary λήθη delimits or configures a world in this or that factically distinctive manner. The epochal configurations discussed in Chapter 2 are distinctive instances of ontological withdrawal or concealment. I take Heidegger's notion of attunement at the level of Da-sein to designate the particular historical or epochal configuration determining the disclosure of a concrete, finite world of beings.

Such disclosure or unconcealment is always shaped in a finite, factical manner. This means unconcealment can never be total: no totality of being or beings can be disclosed. To disclose some concrete range of beings, 'beings as a whole' must withdraw into concealment.[86] The disclosure of a concrete range of beings is possible only on the basis of this withdrawal: only by the concealing withdrawal of beings-as-a-whole from disclosedness, that is, the concealment that refuses the possibility of total disclosure, is finite disclosure possible.

> Precisely because letting-be always lets beings be in a particular comportment that relates to them and thus discloses them, it conceals beings as a whole. Letting-be is intrinsically at the same time a concealing. In the ek-sistent freedom of Da-sein a concealing of beings as a whole comes to pass [ereignet sich].[87]

Heidegger's point is not that such concealment is an inevitable consequence of the unconcealment of beings, but that unconcealment is possible only on the basis of originary concealment. The finitude of concrete comportment enables that comportment to be at all. And that finitude is grounded precisely in a withdrawal from or refusal of openness. And this is originary, not derivative.[88]

> Considered with respect to truth as disclosedness, concealment is . . . the un-truth that is most proper to the essence of truth. The concealment of beings as a whole does not first show up subsequently as a consequence of

the fact that knowledge of beings is always fragmentary. The concealment of beings as a whole, un-truth proper, is older than every openness of this or that being. It is older than letting be itself.[89]

Λήθη or concealment is an irreducible structure of the essence of truth; indeed, the one most proper to it. As should be clear, it is not simply an epistemological limit, but an ontological structure co-constituting the essence of truth. Τὰ ἀληθέα is the articulated terrain of beings or meaning that is enabled by originary ἀλήθεια or openness and λήθη or conceal-ment. Since concealment is not merely semblance and occlusion but a dynamic structure in the heart of truth diagenically prior to beings and their meaningful disclosure, it holds no meaning.

It is worth pointing out that this account of the essence of truth under-mines Sheehan's phenomenological reading of Heidegger. In particular, Sheehan makes two claims that are incompatible with it. First, he suggests that for Heidegger *Sein* is really *Sinn* or meaning. Yet under the rubric of truth it is clear that a key feature of being – λήθη – is prior to and irre-ducible to meaning. In fact, it is distinctively devoid of meaning. Against Sheehan, this aligns Heidegger with Louis Althusser's late insistence on the 'non-anteriority of Meaning' with respect to the world; that is, the claim that there is no meaning inscribed in being prior to or guiding the advent of the world.[90] Since λήθη is the ground enabling the disclosure of any meaning, meaning itself cannot be attributed to originary λήθη. Otherwise, meaning would be ontologically prior to itself. From the per-spective of the world, λήθη figures a rupture or abyss in the terrain of meaning.

Second, Sheehan claims that being is always correlative with human existence. This clearly must be false. Ἀλήθεια and λήθη are what they are prior (on a diagenic axis) to the worlds of beings or meaning they enable to be. In fact, precisely because originary concealment is a refusal of dis-closure, it cannot have any relation of dependence upon that which is dis-closed. It (and perhaps even originary openness) is an ontological structure not dependent upon any relation to beings or meaning, while beings and meaning are dependent upon it. There is consequently a one-way direction of dependence which shows that Sheehan's rubric of reciprocity between being and human existence does not match up to Heidegger's account.

Heidegger explicates untruth further within the human context in terms of 'mystery' and 'errancy', which I can set aside for the purposes of this project. What will be important for Chapter 4 is having established the ontological-structural elements of the essence of truth in 'Vom Wesen der Wahrheit': (1) truth as the freedom, originary openness, or ἀλήθεια through which the movement of unconcealment, the disclosure of beings, or coming to be of a meaningful world are enabled, and (2) untruth as originary concealment, concealing withdrawal, the ground enabling unconcealment, or the λήθη of which ἀλήθεια is the alpha-privative. The essence of truth – or the Heideggerian transcendental field in 'Vom Wesen der Wahrheit' – is the ἀλήθεια/λήθη structure that grounds worlds of beings. In Heidegger's account of the essence of truth in *Beiträge*, ἀλήθεια and λήθη prefigure the structure of the event, and it is through a transformation of those concepts that a grounded account of beyng as event is developed. I shall return to this after some preliminary considerations in the next chapter.

Notes

1. GA65 56/46.
2. GA65 387/305. Cf. Richardson, *Heidegger: Through Phenomenology to Thought* 7.
3. GA65 348/275: 'Seyn . . . als Ereignis west als Wahrheit'.
4. Capobianco has a nice discussion of this in *HWB*, insisting that 'on this point, Heidegger drew his inspiration from Aristotle (not Husserl) and specifically from Aristotle's *Metaphysics*, *Theta* 10 at 1051b . . . where Aristotle states that "being" is spoken of not only in terms of the categories and with respect to the potentiality and actuality of these, but also *in the most proper sense* (reading *kyriotaton*) as the "true"' (*HWB* 12).
5. SZ 219/262; alternative translations cited from the Stambaugh translation of *SZ* 210.
6. For more on Heidegger's phenomenological conception of truth, particularly as it responds to Husserl, see Dahlstrom, *Heidegger's Concept of Truth* chapter II.
7. Dahlstrom recounts this well in *Heidegger's Concept of Truth* chapter I.
8. *WW* 188/144, 201/154.
9. *WW* 201/154.
10. For example, this leads Capobianco in *EH* to understand *Ereignis* and ἀλήθεια to provide equivalent accounts of being that merely use alternative terminologies.
11. *SZ* 226/269.
12. *SZ* 223/265, my italics.
13. *SZ* 212/256.
14. *SZ* 213/256, translation modified. Aristotle passages found at *Metaphysica aI*, 993b20 and Γ I, 1003a21.
15. *SZ* 214/257.
16. Ibid.
17. See Heidegger, *Being and Time* 257 translators' note 2.
18. *SZ* 214/257, inconsistencies in translators' use of quotation marks corrected.
19. Kant, *Kritik der reinen Vernunft* B82. Heidegger supports this point with citations from *Kritik der reinen Vernunft* B83 and B350.
20. *SZ* 215/258.
21. Ibid., italics removed.
22. *SZ* 215/258.
23. *SZ* 214/257, italics removed.
24. Ibid., italics removed.
25. Ibid., italics removed.
26. *SZ* 216/259.
27. Ibid.
28. *SZ* 217/259, 216/259.

29. *SZ* 216/259, italics removed.
30. *SZ* 217/260, italics removed; my italics on 'demonstration'. Dahlstrom discusses this at length in the context of Heidegger's appropriation of Husserl's phenomenological account of truth and evidence (*Heidegger's Concept of Truth*, chapter II).
31. *SZ* 218/260.
32. *SZ* 28/51, italics removed.
33. *SZ* 218/261, translation modified.
34. Ibid., translation modified.
35. *SZ* 219/262.
36. Ibid., italics removed.
37. *SZ* 213/256.
38. *SZ* 219/261, italics removed.
39. *SZ* 227/270, italics removed.
40. *SZ* 220/263.
41. Ibid.
42. *SZ* 223/265.
43. *SZ* 220–1/263.
44. *SZ* 133/171.
45. For a detailed discussion, see *EH* 87–122.
46. *SZ* 221/263.
47. *SZ* 221/263, 221/264.
48. Richardson, *Heidegger: Through Phenomenology to Thought* 47.
49. *SZ* 222/264, my italics.
50. *SZ* 222/264.
51. *SZ* 222/265, italics removed.
52. *SZ* 222/264, italics removed.
53. See *SZ* 222/265: "'Dasein ist in der Wahrheit' sagt gleichursprünglich mit: 'Dasein ist in der Unwahrheit'".
54. *WW* 201/153. For a more extensive reconstruction of *WW*, see Richardson, *Heidegger: Through Phenomenology to Thought* 211–54.
55. *WW* 177/136. See Kant, *Kritik der reinen Vernunft* A5/B8.
56. *WW* 200/153. I modify the translator's 'Being' to 'being' throughout my discussion of this text.
57. *WW* 177/136, 186/143.
58. *WW* 200/153, translation modified.
59. *WW* 183/140, translation modified.
60. Ibid., translation modified.
61. *WW* 183/141, translation modified.
62. *WW* 183–4/141.
63. Ibid.
64. Ibid.
65. Ibid.
66. Ibid., translation modified.
67. Richardson, *Heidegger: Through Phenomenology to Thought* 213, 214.
68. *WW* 186/142.
69. *WW* 185/142, translation modified.
70. *WW* 185/142.
71. *WW* 186/142.
72. *WW* 186/143, 189/145, 187/143.
73. *WW* 187/144, translation modified.
74. *WW* 188/144. For a later account of Heidegger's related concept of *Gelassenheit*, see GA77.
75. *WW* 188–9/144.
76. *WW* 188/144.

77. Ibid., translation modified.
78. *WW* 191/146.
79. *WW* 190/145–6.
80. *WW* 189/145, translation modified.
81. *WW* 188/144.
82. *WW* 189/144, 189/145.
83. *WW* 190/146.
84. *WW* 192/147.
85. *WW* 194/149.
86. *WW* 193/148.
87. Ibid.
88. This is a Heideggerian parallel to Markus Gabriel's argument for the impossibility of a domain of all domains, field of all fields of sense, or 'world'.
89. *WW* 193–4/148.
90. Althusser, 'The Underground Current of the Materialism of the Encounter', in *Philosophy of the Encounter* 169.

Chapter 4

Truth and Event in *Beiträge zur Philosophie (Vom Ereignis)*

In *Beiträge*, Heidegger argues that his treatment of the ontological problematic in earlier works like *Sein und Zeit* and 'Vom Wesen der Wahrheit' was ultimately inadequate. As I shall discuss, his claim is that his earlier positions remain determined by the conceptual framework of metaphysics, which he takes to prevent a sufficiently originary account of being. In an effort to rectify this, he recasts the most fundamental terms of his ontology. 'Being' he argues, must be rethought in terms of the event (*das Ereignis*). In other words, being – or rather, beyng (*Seyn*) – is evental in nature. A central task of *Beiträge*, then, is to work out what exactly the evental nature of beyng is. The problematic of the essence of truth plays a key role in this: not only must 'the question of the *essence of truth*' be 'posed radically as the question that is preliminary [Vorfrage] to the basic question [Grundfrage] of philosophy (How does beyng essentially occur [west]?)', but Heidegger will argue that 'beyng qua event essentially occurs [west] as truth'.[1]

This means that the way we understand truth in *Beiträge* has serious consequences for how we understand the event. Most commentators have understood *Beiträge* to remain within the basic framework of what I have called the second stage of Heidegger's *a-lēthic* concept of truth – that just discussed in the context of 'Vom Wesen der Wahrheit'.[2] However, as I have begun to suggest, I take this to be a mistake. *Beiträge* contains a new, differential concept of truth and this dramatically transforms the way we should understand the concept of event (in its ontological sense). Accessing this concept requires rethinking the problematic of truth in light of certain major ontological shifts that text proposes. In this chapter, I focus on these shifts in relation to truth, then in Chapter 5 I work out the differential concept of truth in relation to the event. By tracking the productive logic of *Grundlegung* from the phenomenological *a-lēthic* account of truth in *Sein und Zeit* to the quasi-transcendental *a-lēthic* account in 'Vom Wesen der Wahrheit' to the differential account in *Beiträge*, we see Heidegger's ontology evolve along a diagenic axis. The methodological progression through these stages performs the movement of *Er-gründung* via which alienated human existence endeavours to reground itself and consequently bring about the historical event.

To make sense of Heidegger's account of truth in *Beiträge*, I will begin by outlining the noted ontological shifts that text presents. First, I will examine in more detail a problem he identifies both in the history of ontology and in his own previous efforts at addressing the question of being; that of thinking being within the framework of *Seiendheit* or being-ness. In *Beiträge*, he aims to rectify this via a remarkable shift advancing the independence of being from beings. I will clarify this by looking at the shift of his focal term from *Sein* to *Seyn* and the correlated programmatic shift from what he calls the *Leitfrage* (guiding question) to the *Grundfrage* (basic question). This look at the problem of *Seiendheit* is necessary for making sense of a parallel shift he advances regarding the essence of truth: the essence of truth must be detached from or independent of what is true. With this frame, I then pick up the problematic of truth again and detail the first set of transformations it takes in *Beiträge*, paying special attention to the way it drives thought beyond the *a-lēthic* account. At the end of this chapter, I take a moment to engage two major alternative views on Heidegger's concept of event: the correlationist view advanced by Sheehan and Meillassoux and the view that 'event' is equivalent to *Anwesen*, ἀλήθεια, φύσις, or the giving of beings (*es gibt*) advanced by Capobianco.

I The problem of *Seiendheit* and the shift from *Sein* to *Seyn*

In *Beiträge*, Heidegger advances a major ontological shift that sets the stage for his account of the event in that text; namely, a shift in how he understands being with respect to beings. In *Sein und Zeit*, being was framed as 'the being of beings'.[3] There, Dasein or human existence – a being – can work towards developing an authentic understanding of being by developing an authentic understanding of its own existence. In other words, I can come to understand being on the basis of the relation being has to *a* being – Dasein, my own existence. In *Beiträge*, Heidegger makes a radical shift: he disassociates being from beings.[4] In other words, being is now to be thought independently of any relation it has to beings: 'beyng can no longer be thought on the basis of beings but must be inventively thought from itself.[5] This shift is signified terminologically by rewriting 'Sein' ('being') in the archaic form 'Seyn' ('beyng').[6] 'Sein' signifies being, understood as co-determined by a relation to beings. Its conceptual successor, 'Seyn', on the other hand, signifies being as thought independently of any relation it has to beings. The following passage crystallises Heidegger's point and indicates its implications for the related themes of metaphysics and the ontological difference. I will refer back to it again later.

> There is no immediate difference between beyng [Seyn] and beings, because there is altogether no immediate relation between them. Even though beings as such oscillate only in the appropriation [Ereignung], beyng remains abyssally far from all beings. The attempts to represent both together, already in the very manner of naming them, stem from metaphysics.[7]

As I hope to make clear, this independence does not mean beyng is transcendent or discrete from beings, but that beyng is not dependent upon beings or its relations to beings. Beyng is diagenically prior and, as Capobianco puts it, 'structurally prior' to beings.[8] Of course, Heidegger also details co-dependent or reciprocal relations between be*ing* and beings, as in the co-appropriation of Dasein and being that enables the constitution of meaningful worlds. Indeed, much of *Beiträge* is devoted to themes within this register. However, I take this to be a derivative relationship consequent upon the more originary, and independent, operations of beyng as event.

Though Heidegger's accounts of both the primal independence of beyng from beings and consequent relations of reciprocity between the two are quite complex, and I will not treat them fully here, I take his basic logic to be straightforward. It operates at a first order and then a second order level. At the first order level: as a child's existence is dependent upon the donors of its genetic material, beings are dependent upon beyng. 'If beings *are*, then beyng must occur essentially [wesen].'[9] But, as the donors are not dependent upon the child, beyng is not dependent upon beings. The child might cease to exist while the donors remain. This is a one-directional dependence. At the second order level, the donors might indeed become reciprocally determined by the child, but only insofar as they become *mother* or *father*. 'Mother' or 'father' is a secondary determination of the donor that only arises insofar as it enters into a certain correlation with the child and becomes partially defined in terms of that correlation. The primal independence and consequent correlation of beyng and beings is the same: beyng is independent of beings, while beings are dependent upon beyng. It is only insofar as worlds of beings are meaningfully disclosed by Dasein – a consequent structure – that beyng becomes reciprocally determined by beings (namely Dasein). Yet this remains at a second order level. The one-directional relation of dependence is consequently supplemented with a reciprocal co-determination.

The term 'Sein'/'being' applies in the register of this reciprocal co-determination, while the term 'Seyn'/'beyng' applies in the more originary register independent of it. Marking this distinction is essential to making sense of *Beiträge*. Without it, Heidegger's statements clarifying each become conflated and make a difficult text nonsensical. With it, seemingly enigmatic statements like the following become clear: 'The question of being is the question of the truth of beyng.'[10] For, truth is the determination of beyng in worlds of beings or meaning. Heidegger makes the point distinguishing being and beyng again, while also emphasising the difference of beyng from the metaphysical concepts of actuality and possibility, as follows:

> "Beyng" [Seyn] does not simply mean the actuality of the actual, and not simply the possibility of the possible, and in general not simply being [Sein] understood on the basis of particular beings; instead, it means beyng out of its original essential occurrence in the full fissure [Zerklüftung].[11]

The reason for Heidegger's shift is that thinking being on the basis of its relation to beings forces a determination of the concept of being on the basis of the concept of beings, that is, the conceptualisation of what beings are as beings (ὂν ᾗ ὄν), which Heidegger terms 'Seiendheit' ('beingness').[12] A series of related faults are involved with understanding being in the framework of *Seiendheit*. First, it leads to an abstract or generic account of being. Historically, a dominant procedure for deriving *Seiendheit* is examining a set of beings with an eye towards what is identical in all of them; in other words, deriving an essence by abstracting a universal from a set of particulars, which might be accomplished by a variety of *a priori* or *a posteriori* methods. In such cases, *Seiendheit* is that which most universally belongs to beings. For Heidegger, the paradigm case is Platonism's derivation of abstract universals or *ideas*.[13] The Aristotelian analogue is found in his account of 'οὐσία as the beingness of beings', which replicates the problem: 'despite [Aristotle's] denial that being has the character of a genus, nevertheless being (as beingness) is always and only meant as the κοινόν, the common and thus what is common to every being'.[14] A second problem is that within the framework of *Seiendheit*, 'nothing is said about the inner content of the essence of being'.[15] That is, the characterisation of being is donated only from the character of beings, not arrived at on the basis of being itself. In Heidegger's analysis, thinking being on the basis of beings prioritises beings over being by making the conceptualisation of beings as such determinative for the conceptualisation of being. Third, moreover, extant conceptions of beings as such are not 'innocent'. They are determined within faulty metaphysical historical and conceptual con-figurations. Characterisations of being drawn from beings carry this fault. Fourth, characteristics of beings are characteristics *of beings*, not being. Failing to register this means failing to register the ontological difference.[16]

It is tempting to understand the priority involved in beyng's inde-pendence in terms of a relation of conditionality. However, Heidegger is careful to point out that this would be mistaken. Showing why will help clarify the status of beyng's independence. In his view, if we take beyng as a condition for beings we continue to determine beyng on the basis of a relation between it and beings, that is, as *Seiendheit*.[17] The problem here is in the application of the very framework of conditionality to beyng. Concepts of condition must be distinguished from Heidegger's concepts of ground in *Beiträge*, which constitute an essential register of beyng itself as event: namely, 'Grund der Möglichkeit' ('ground of possibility') or the more developed ground as 'das Sichverbergen im tragenden Durchragen' ('self-concealing in a protruding that bears').[18] As I outlined in Chapter 2, this is differentiated into 'Er-gründung' ('fathoming the ground') and 'das ursprüngliche Gründen des Grundes' ('the original grounding of the ground') or simply the 'gründende Grund' ('grounding ground').[19] We can set aside the more derivative fathoming the ground here. Grounding ground is the originary grounding dynamic inherent to beyng itself as event. Grounding ground is necessary for beings to be but is not to be determined as a condition. Casting something as a condition always means understanding it as a condition *for* something: a condition *for* a being or *for* experience, for instance. The strange consequence Heidegger rec-ognises, in other words, is that casting something as a condition always subjects it to a co-determination by what it is a condition for, insofar as the condition is defined in terms of the relation it has to the conditioned. Although we *seem* to have good concepts for conditions that are independ-ent of what is conditioned, his point is that applying the very framework of conditionality to something means understanding it in terms of the relation of condition to conditioned, and vice versa. In this way, think-ing being as a condition for beings generates an account in which being is structurally conditioned by beings, not independent of them: 'If beyng is understood as a condition in any sense whatever, it is already degraded into something in the service of beings and supervenient to them.'[20] In *Beiträge*, on the other hand, grounding ground enables what is grounded on it to be, but is not itself essentially determined by what is grounded. In other words, it is conceived on the basis of the inherent grounding char-acter of the event, not the relation it has to what is grounded.[21] How this works can be seen in §242, where the originary structures or dynamics of ground – *Ab-grund, Ur-grund,* and *Un-grund* – are unfolded immanently as part of the originary dynamics of the event, not derived from what is consequent upon them.

It will be worth noting that in Heidegger's account, 'the original grounding of the ground . . . is the essential occurrence of the truth of beyng; truth is a *ground* in the original sense'.[22] This, as will be seen, means the essential occurrence of the truth of beyng must not be thought in terms of any relation to what is consequent upon it (beings), but likewise explicated immanently as part of the originary dynamics of the event.

These distinctions allow me to further clarify how I understand the structural and diagenic priority of beyng in *Beiträge*. It will be helpful to mark my agreement and disagreement with Capobianco's interpretation of this matter. As he writes: 'Heidegger's mature position, in my formulation of the matter, is that Being is *structurally* prior to and a condition of meaning. That is, only insofar as there is Being is there meaning.'[23] I take him to understand 'meaning' here as shorthand for 'the meaningful disclosure of a world of beings' or 'the disclosure of a world of beings in their meaningful relations with human existence'. I agree that without beyng, meaning or worlds of beings would be impossible. In contrast to Capobianco, though, my understanding is that, at least in *Beiträge*, being (as beyng, as *Ereignis*) is structurally and diagenically prior to, but not a condition of, meaning or worlds of beings. For, casting this priority in terms of conditionality inadvertently reinstitutes the dependence of beyng upon beings. In my view, to say beyng is structurally prior to meaning is to say beyng is prior on a diagenic axis or axis of ground, where 'ground' must not be conflated with 'condition'. This results in a different formulation: in *Beiträge*, beyng is structurally prior, prior on a diagenic axis, to meaning or beings.

Metaphysics, in *Beiträge*, is characterised by its essential orientation to think the beingness of beings: 'all metaphysics' is 'founded on the leading question [Leitfrage]: what are beings?' (cf. Aristotle's τί τὸ ὄν).[24] This is a central reason why it is insufficient for ontology. '"Metaphysics" asks about beingness on the basis of beings (within the inceptual – i.e., definitive – interpretation of φύσις) and necessarily leaves unasked the question of the *truth* of beingness and thus the question of the *truth* of beyng.'[25] Heidegger's shift to thinking beyng independently of beings aims to recast the problematic of being in a way liberated from metaphysical determination by the problematic of *Seiendheit*. This point allows a further clarification of his terminological distinction between 'Sein'/'being' and 'Seyn'/'beyng'. 'Sein'/'being' signifies being as understood within the framework of *Seiendheit*.

Being [Sein] is the condition for beings, which are thereby already established in advance as things [Dinge] (the objectively present at hand).
Being conditions [be-dingt] beings either as their cause [*summum ens* –
δημιουργός ('craftsman')] or as the ground of the objectivity of the thing
in representation (condition of the possibility of experience or in some way
as the 'earlier', which it is in virtue of its higher constancy and presence, as
accords with its generality).[26]

Hence, 'Sein'/'being' remains metaphysical in its signification.
'Seyn'/'beyng' does not. Recall the point made in the passage cited on
p. 133: 'The attempts to represent both [beyng and beings] together,
already in the very manner of naming them, stem from metaphysics.'[27]
Consequently, beyng cannot be 'the being of beings'. It must not be
understood on the basis of beings, in any way co-determined by a relation
to them as its counterpart. Importantly, however, Heidegger is not claiming beyng has *no* relation to beings, but that beyng has no *immediate* relation to beings. Beyng is related to beings *mediately* through what he calls
'the strife of world and earth'.[28]

2 The shift from the *Leitfrage* to the *Grundfrage*

As a consequence of these shifts, the *question* of beyng cannot be oriented
by that of the being of beings. The distinction between being and beyng
correlates with a distinction between two configurations of the question about being (or beyng): the 'Leitfrage' ('guiding question') and the
'Grundfrage' ('basic question').[29] The *Leitfrage* is governed by the question 'about beings as beings (ὂν ᾗ ὄν)'.[30] For Heidegger, Aristotle's 'τί
τὸ ὄν' ('What are beings?') renders its 'most general form'.[31] Since it has
this 'approach and directionality', when it comes to ask about being, it
asks 'the question of the being of beings'.[32] The meaning of the term
'Sein'/'being' ultimately remains determined by the framework of the
Leitfrage. Thus, Heidegger argues the *Leitfrage* must be supplanted. It is so
by the *Grundfrage*, for which 'the starting point is not beings, i.e., this or
that given being, nor is it beings as such and as a whole'.[33] It is 'the question of the essential occurrence [Wesung] of beyng', which interrogates
'the *openness for essential occurrence* [*Offenheit für Wesung*] as such, i.e.,
truth'.[34] Here, truth 'essentially occurs in advance [Voraus-wesende]' of –
that is, is diagenically prior to – the determination of (1) beings, (2) the
Leitfrage, and (3) the historical epoch of metaphysics.[35] In other words, the
Grundfrage enquires into the ground of these grounded terms, but not on
the basis of any relation this ground has to what is grounded. Rather, it
asks about this ground independently of any such relation.[36]

Expressing what I take to be a fundamental error in some scholarship on the question of metaphysics in Heidegger's work, Rae frames Heidegger's ontology as one defined by a 'wholesale abandonment' of metaphysics: 'For Heidegger, philosophy is so irreparably damaged by metaphysics that nothing other than its wholesale abandonment will rejuvenate thinking to being's becoming.'[37] Translated into the language I have just been using, this would mean that in the shift from the *Leitfrage* to the *Grundfrage*, the framework of the former is cast entirely to the flames. This is false and mischaracterises the structure of Heidegger's ontology. It fails to register the dimension of what I have described in terms of radical critique, which Heidegger recognises as essential to a sufficient ontology. If metaphysics constitutes a distorted ontology, a sufficient ontology must include an explanation, on more appropriate bases, of the genesis of that distortion. In other words, it must not abandon the framework of that distortion, but must offer the possibility to rethink it on proper grounds. Describing the shift here in terms of 'übergängliche Denken' or 'transitional thinking', Heidegger emphasises the point as follows:

> For transitional thinking, however, what matters is not an 'opposition' to 'metaphysics', since that would simply bring metaphysics back into play; rather, the task is an overcoming of metaphysics out of its ground . . . [T]ransitional thinking must not succumb to the temptation to simply leave behind what it grasped as the end and at the end; instead, this thinking must *put* behind itself what it has grasped, i.e., now for the first time comprehend it in its essence and allow it to be integrated in altered form into the truth of beyng.[38]

Heidegger's concern with this issue is seen clearly in the way he casts the transition from the *Leitfrage* to the *Grundfrage*. This transition is neither a simple switch from one orientation to another nor a seamless progression. The framework of the *Leitfrage* defines metaphysics, and its crystallisation by the ancient Greeks marks what Heidegger calls the 'first beginning' for thought. The shift towards the *Grundfrage* marks a shift towards an 'other beginning'. In this way, it is an essential part of what I have described as the event in the historical sense. But as argued in Chapter 2, that event would be impossible without an ontological element that drives or draws thought beyond the framework of the first beginning; namely, what Heidegger elaborates as the evental character of beyng (the event in the ontological sense). In the shift from the *Leitfrage* to the *Grundfrage*, we see part of this broader transformation taking place.

The overcoming of the first beginning and its *Leitfrage* cannot be accomplished by simple negation. It cannot be 'a *counter-movement*; for all counter-movements and counter-forces are essentially codetermined by that which they are counter to'.[39] Any attempt to overcome by way of a counter-movement remains reactionary or, as Heidegger puts it, 're-aktiv' (re-active).[40] 'A *counter*-movement never suffices for an *essential* transformation of history' – it never escapes the determinative force of that to which it is counter.[41] Rather, 'the task is an overcoming of metaphysics out of its ground'.[42]

Insofar as the historical and conceptual apparatus of the *Leitfrage* is grounded in the subject matter of the *Grundfrage*, even if this fact is obscured, the *Grundfrage* 'lies hidden in' the *Leitfrage*.[43] When the insufficiencies of the *Leitfrage* become apparent, so does the necessity of a rupture and another beginning for thought ('something utterly different must commence').[44] The conceptual apparatus of the *Leitfrage* can't establish this because of the determinative force of the historical and conceptual foundations defining it. Instead, a preparatory project that fractures or deconstructs those foundations is necessary (as found, for instance, in Heidegger's work from the 1920s and early 1930s). One can imagine, as much so-called 'Continental' philosophy did during the 1990s and early 2000s, that the deconstructive project might potentially be carried on indefinitely and come to define the project of philosophy. Ultimately, however, that would perpetuate the error belonging to the *Leitfrage*, since philosophy would be defined in relation to the *Leitfrage*'s remnant inscriptions. From a perspective within the horizon of this deconstructive project, then, resolving the *Leitfrage*'s error requires a rupture and radical shift – a so-called 'leap' – initiating another beginning. According to Heidegger, this can be accomplished via the problematic of truth: 'what is carried out is a leap into the *truth* (clearing and concealing) of beyng itself'.[45] In the language of the event, this means that an historical event must take place accomplishing a radical reconfiguration of the terrain of thought.

Nevertheless, the historical and conceptual configuration of the *Leitfrage* is not suddenly annihilated. Instead, the shift establishes the possibility that it be re-appropriated or grounded in a more originary way. 'Although no progression is ever possible from the guiding question [Leitfrage] to the basic question [Grundfrage], yet, conversely, the unfolding of the basic question does at the same time provide the ground for taking back up into a more original possession the entire history of the guiding question rather than simply repudiating it as something past and gone.'[46] Overcoming metaphysics out of its ground entails that the transition through the *Grundfrage* to another beginning 'free[s] up a creative ground' and offers the possibility of re-appropriating the apparatus of metaphysics and mobilising it in a non-reactive way.[47] This, however, would entail a fundamental transformation of the terms of the *Leitfrage*, of metaphysics, and of the way we understand the nature of beings. It should be emphasised, however, that Heidegger's primary concern was with rethinking the nature of being in terms of the event, not the re-appropriation of metaphysics.

The shift from being to its conceptual successor, beyng, also leads to an important shift in how Heidegger understands difference. I will simply point this out here and return to it in Chapter 5. In *Sein und Zeit*, the *Seinsfrage* was oriented by the ontological difference or difference between being and beings.[48] In *Beiträge*, the question of beyng cannot be oriented by the ontological difference because in that configuration being remains co-determined by the differential relation between it and its counterpart – beings. This shift is not meant to abandon or reject the ontological difference. Rather, Heidegger aims to give an account of the ground whence this very difference is possible. As I hope to show, through the problematic of the essence of truth in *Beiträge*, he shifts the key differential relationship from one between being and beings to a self-differential operation 'internal' to beyng itself. Recall the passage cited on p. 133 again, this time with respect to the ontological difference: 'There is no immediate difference between beyng and beings, because there is altogether no immediate relation between them. Even though beings as such oscillate only in the appropriation [Ereignung], beyng remains abyssally far from all beings.'[49]

3 The event and the essence of truth

With these programmatic and conceptual transformations in mind, let us return to the topic of truth and its role in explaining beyng as event. Heidegger's move to think beyng independently from beings has important consequences for this. As a point of emphasis, he treats the problematic of truth as an essentially ontological problematic: it forms a key register in which he articulates the nature of being (and now beyng), while epistemological and logical (formal) forms of truth are derivative in relation to that ground. In the ontology presented in *Beiträge*, the essence of truth constitutes certain structures of the event. Indeed, it is through the preliminary question (*Vorfrage*) of truth that the basic question (*Grundfrage*) of beyng gets addressed and a properly grounded account of beyng as event can be developed.[50]

Given the ontological status of truth for Heidegger, we would expect him to rethink truth in light of the transformations discussed above. This is just what we find: *Beiträge* contains an extensive effort to liberate the problem of the essence of truth from the framework of *Seiendheit*. This entails a move parallel to that advancing the independence of beyng from beings: the essence of truth is to be thought independently of what is true (*das Wahre*). Within this context, Heidegger provides a technical reformulation of the essence of truth as 'die Lichtung für das Sichverbergen' ('the clearing for self-concealing') or 'Lichtung des Sichverbergens' ('the clearing of self-concealing'), which I condense as 'the clearing for/of self-concealing'.[51] The connection of such truth with beyng is highlighted in an alternative formulation: the essence of truth is 'die lichtende Verbergung des Seyns' ('the clearing concealment of beyng').[52] Though these formulations are terminologically and conceptually related to the *a-lēthic* version found in 'Vom Wesen der Wahrheit', they in fact express a fundamental philosophical transformation. I will argue that 'the clearing for/of self-concealing' is a differential formulation, that is, it articulates the logic of difference that constitutes the essence of truth. To be clear, *Beiträge* contains no overt assertion that the essence of truth is differential. Rather, that it is so becomes evident by tracking the specifics of Heidegger's treatment of truth, which drive thought beyond the *a-lēthic* account into a differential account entailed in its logic and confirmed in his thinking of 'the decisional essence [Entscheidungswesen] of beyng'.[53] In this section I deal with the shifts in Heidegger's account of truth necessary for this new concept, then in Chapter 5 I connect it with his ontology of difference and develop the differential concept of truth in connection with the event.

The core discussion of truth in *Beiträge* (§§204–37) opens with an unusual formulation of the question of truth as one 'about *the truth of the truth*' ('nach der *Wahrheit der Wahrheit*')'.[54] Heidegger is well aware this is likely to draw a charge of circularity or 'vacuity'.[55] We can show that it escapes this charge by applying a diagenic distinction: 'truth' is used in two different senses, one of which signifies the ground or essence of the other. This distinction aligns Heidegger's analysis of truth with the *Sein/Seyn* and *Leitfrage/Grundfrage* shifts. 'Truth', here, signifies on the one hand 'die Wahrheit selbst' ('truth itself') and on the other 'das Wahre' ('what is true').[56] By 'what is true' he means not merely true propositions but everything grounded by the essence of truth; in other words, the world of disclosed beings or meaning, the domain of the 'Da', or the 'Entwurfsbereich' ('domain of projection').[57] 'Truth itself' is diagenically prior to what is true and is the essence of truth or the ground enabling what is true to be or come to presence. Truth itself 'is the original [ursprüngliche] truth of beyng (event)'.[58] The question of the truth of the truth enquires into truth itself, not what is true. Thus, we are no longer asking about the domain of projection itself as, for instance, in *Sein und Zeit*, where the existential analytic operated within the bounds of the horizon of temporality constituted by Dasein as thrown projection. Rather, 'what counts here is *the projection [den Wurf] of the very domain of projection [Entwurfsbereichs]*'.[59]

For Heidegger, the immediate upshot is that truth – that is, truth itself – is 'definitively detached [abgelöst] from all beings'.[60] Stated more poetically, 'truth is the great disdainer of all that is "true"'.[61] Truth itself is a feature of the event prior to and independent of that which it enables to become manifest. This is a diagenic and structural priority. As with the independence of beyng from beings, this independence is one-directional, for the manifestation of what is true is dependent upon truth itself. Conceptually separating these casts the disassociation of beyng from beings in terms of the problematic of truth.

Can we get a better picture of this independence? The following brief, and incomplete, line of reasoning is reconstructed primarily from Heidegger's analysis of 'Offenheit' or 'openness' in *Beiträge* §204–7. It employs some ideas absent from 'Vom Wesen der Wahrheit'. Heidegger initially situates that analysis in a critique of the confusion of truth with its derivative form, 'Richtigkeit' ('correctness').[62] Correctness takes the place of the *adaequatio* I discussed in Chapter 3 and operates at the level of a disclosed world of beings or meaning. Schematically, correctness is a syngenic equivalent to such a world, cast in a traditional, representational model of truth. In contrast, on a diagenic axis, correctness is consequent upon truth's essential structure of openness. Since openness is the ground enabling correctness, correctness always bears inherent constitutive reference to openness. Now, to give an account of openness itself – as part of an account of the essence of truth – it is tempting to do so in terms of its relation to correctness, that is, to understand openness 'as a condition' for correctness.[63] However, this would replicate the metaphysical folly of the *Leitfrage* and its orientation to *Seiendheit*. Instead, Heidegger recognises that if openness is an ontological structure diagenically antecedent to correctness, while correctness is produced only as consequent upon openness, then openness is not dependent on any relation it has to its consequent. To cast openness as a condition would be to misunderstand it on the basis of its relation to correctness and, in fact, to make it conditioned by correctness.

In contrast, to begin developing an account of openness as independent, Heidegger employs a very unusual idea: 'das wesentliche Ausmaß' ('the essential extent') of truth.[64] To make sense of this, we need to consider the logic of the essence of truth at one step farther than openness on a diagenic axis, that is, as diagenically prior to openness. This is the level that in 'Vom Wesen der Wahrheit' the diagenic enquiry into openness tacitly required but ultimately fell short of providing. At this level of Heidegger's ontology, there can be no openness or extended dimension whatsoever, since we are talking about the ground responsible for the very genesis of openness. From such a state, 'the essential extent of truth' names the onto-genesis of openness – the logical breaching open of openness – by a

ground that thus 'measures' openness in the sense of constituting its limits
or determinacy. Using Heidegger's term, this is a 'clearing' or opening
up of the structure of openness, where openness becomes determinate in
itself but is diagenically prior to determination with respect to any finite
world.[65] Insofar as openness does *consequently* become determined with
respect to a finite world, Heidegger sometimes refers to it as the 'amidst'
in which beings come to stand, that is, that is populated by beings.[66] As
he puts it, 'the essential extent itself determines the "place" (time-space) of
openness: the cleared "amidst" of beings'.[67] It is important to keep in mind
the role that λήθη, concealment, or concealing withdrawal plays relative to
openness (and now also to the essential extent of openness). I shall come
back to this shortly.

To return to the main point, since these structures and processes are
suggested to comprise the ground enabling the determination of any
world of beings, beings are dependent on truth itself but truth itself is
not dependent on beings, that is, what is true. There is, again, a one-
directional dependence. Truth itself must be thought as independent or
'detached' from any relation to beings. Vallega-Neu puts the point in
the register of beyng and its *lēthic* dimension as follows: 'there is no immediate relation between be-ing [Seyn] as enowning withdrawal and beings,
even if a being shelters the truth of be-ing [Seyn] . . .Why not? Because the
essential swaying [Wesen] of be-ing [Seyn] occurs in (but not only in) the
"not" of beings, because the withdrawal of be-ing [Seyn] is precisely what
withdraws in the concealing-sheltering [*ver*bergen] of truth.'[68]

The danger is that this independence of truth (and for that matter
of beyng) from beings might mean Heidegger reinstates a metaphysical
transcendence into his ontology, that is, a vertical arrangement of different levels of reality.[69] I don't think he does. I would like to suggest
truth itself, while diagenically prior to worlds of beings, is simultaneously
immanent to them, while enabling them to be. By 'immanent' here, I do
not mean that truth itself is on the same syngenic or equiprimordial plane
of ground as worlds of beings, which would render Heidegger's ontology
a thoroughly 'flat ontology'.[70] Rather, I mean truth itself (as the truth of
the event) is implicated within beings or worlds of beings, without any
sort of *real* distinction (Descartes) between them and without positing
any hierarchy of substantialised planes of reality that would make truth or
the event transcendent to this plane. This renders Heidegger's ontology a
'curved' ontology. He nicely allegorises the immanence of truth's dimension of openness, for instance, as follows:

> The open realm, which conceals itself at the same time that beings come to
> stand in it . . ., is . . . something like an inner recess [hohle Mitte], e.g., that

of a jug. Yet . . . the inner recess is not just a haphazard emptiness which arises purely on account of the surrounding walls and which happens not to be full of 'things'. It is just the opposite: the inner recess itself is what determines, shapes, and bears the walling action of the walls and of their surfaces. The walls and surfaces are merely what is radiated out by that original open realm which allows its openness to come into play by summoning up, round about itself and toward itself, such-and-such walls (the particular form of the vessel). That is how the essential occurrence of the open realm radiates back from and in the embracing walls.[71]

This allegory offers a way to reconcile the independence of truth itself with Heidegger's commitment that neither truth nor beyng is metaphysically transcendent. For Heidegger the essence of truth is not dependent upon any relation to beings, while remaining immanent to them. From the standpoint of beings, we can understand the openness of truth as structurally prior on a diagenic axis, and yet as an immanent structure through which the singular, finite contours of their being are determined and given the space to be differentiated from one another: 'Truth, as the event of what is true, is the abyssal fissure [abgründige Zerklüftung] in which beings are divided [zur Entzweiung kommt] and must stand in the strife.'[72] Truth itself, though, does not arise on account of beings. The openness of truth is a structure of the essence of truth; that is, it is a structure of the event as it occurs in and through truth.

Here, a partial outline of the structure of the event can begin to be discerned. The openness of truth is an aspect of the event that grounds worlds of beings, such that beings cannot be without it. Beyng as event 'summons up' beings, 'round about itself and toward itself', in the sense that beings bear a structural reference to the event which constitutes their ground, enables their manifestation, differentiation, temporality, and spatiality. Yet the event in its own right does not bear a constitutive structural reference to beings which would make it dependent upon them.

What, then, are we to make of Heidegger's formulation of the essence of truth as the clearing for/of self-concealing? To explain this, he follows the question of ground once again, radicalising the idea hinted at with the 'essential extent' and driving thought into a terrain more originary than that articulated by the *a-lēthic* account. If the major dimensions of the *a-lēthic* account are originary openness (ἀλήθεια, unconcealment, disclosedness) and concealment (λήθη, closedness, concealing withdrawal), which co-determine each other and operate in a dynamic that, while independent of any relation to beings, enables any world of beings to become manifest, the question Heidegger raises is: *whence and why concealment and openness?* That is, what is the origin of and ground explaining these two primordial moments of the essential structure of truth? This question marks a major development in Heidegger's ontology.

It is important to point out that Heidegger poses this question as: 'whence and why *concealment* and unconcealment?' ('woher und weshalb Verbergung und Entbergung?').[73] Though he uses the term 'Entbergung' here, he quickly makes it clear that the question at hand takes this neither in the derivative sense as the unconcealment of beings nor even as the more originary 'openness of beings as a whole'; it is to be understood in its essence, as 'the openness of self-concealing (being)', that is, the openness of the essence of truth.[74] This crucial question about the origin of the *a-lēthic* structures is easily overlooked. It is posed parenthetically in §207 and, though Heidegger returns to the task it poses in a number of places, the question itself is not emphasised prominently elsewhere in the text. However, it is key for making sense of the distinction drawn in *Beiträge* between truth as ἀλήθεια and truth as clearing for/of self-concealing: as Heidegger writes, 'truth as the clearing for concealment is . . . an essentially different projection [Entwurf] than is ἀλήθεια'.[75] Of central concern, he argues, is that the interpretation of concealment in terms of the *a-lēthic* framework is ultimately insufficient: 'Ἀ-λήθεια means un-concealment and the un-concealed itself', but in that case 'concealment itself is experienced only as what is to be *cleared away*, what is to be removed (*a-*)'.[76] Arguably, this definition of ἀλήθεια does not express the richest account of the concept in his work. Yet the point is that accounting for the structures of truth within the *a-lēthic* framework misses the important question: it 'does not address concealment itself and its ground'.[77] It consequently fails to rethink these structures within the framework of the *Grundfrage*, that is, on the basis of their immanent ground in the event rather than their role as ground for worlds of beings. Heidegger's point is not simply that concealment is neglected when we formulate truth as ἀ-λήθεια and that we need to rectify this neglect. Rather, it is that we must press beyond concealment on the diagenic axis, to a ground from out of which concealment and openness are themselves originated. Casting the essence of truth in terms of the *a-lēthic* framework fails to do this. The difference between the *a-lēthic* account of the essence of truth and the account as clearing for/of self-concealing is established precisely in the moment of asking about the originary ground of concealment and openness.[78] It is important to be clear what this does *not* mean: it does not mean Heidegger disavows his earlier accounts of truth as ἀλήθεια. Rather, the *a-lēthic* framework must be understood as grounded by a more originary essence of truth: the clearing for/of self-concealing.

In 'Vom Wesen der Wahrheit', the withdrawing action of originary concealment both opened up the primal open field (Da-sein as the ground

via which beings are disclosed) and refused the possibility of total disclosure, thus enabling the finite disclosure of a world of beings. In this
arrangement concealment is arguably more originary than openness on
the diagenic axis. Moreover, these were the most primordial ontological
structures thinkable – they formed the limit or horizon of thought's ability
to articulate the nature of truth, ground, and being.

In *Beiträge*, after disassociating the structures of originary concealment and openness from beings and affirming the consequent necessity of
rethinking them, their basic arrangement is reconfigured via the question
of the ground whence they are originated. Here, Heidegger rotates them
onto a syngenic, equiprimordial axis with respect to one another, then
questions along a diagenic axis into the ground enabling the origination
of these structures themselves. This is structurally akin to the post-Kantian
effort to reframe Kant by arguing that the very differentiation between the
phenomenal and noumenal is itself a moment in the absolute that requires
a genetic explanation.

We gain a sense of how radical this question is by isolating one dimension for a moment and asking: whence and why concealment? What is
the genesis or origin of concealment itself? Such a question was unthinkable in the conceptual landscape available in 'Vom Wesen der Wahrheit'
because its horizon was still determined by thinking the essence of truth as
that which enables the manifestation of beings. To ask 'whence and why
concealment?' is to investigate the origination of the most originary ontological structure thinkable in Heidegger's philosophy prior to this point.

Nevertheless, Heidegger's question is not just about concealment.
Concealment and openness are correlative; they always go hand in hand.
Concealment is a withdrawal from or refusal of openness and openness
is a breaching of concealment. Like the apparent 'two sides' of a Möbius
strip, they present themselves as irreconcilably conflictual or in strife, yet
an 'ursprüngliche Innigkeit' ('original intimacy') must hold for them to
correlate at all.[79] Otherwise, there would be a real or substantial distinction between them preventing any relation whatsoever. Thus, the question
'Whence and why concealment and openness?' enquires into the intimacy
that itself differentiates and generates these two, into the very fabric that
distends into them, or into the curve that traverses the difference between
them. This question asks how these very structures are originated.

The formulation 'the clearing for/of self-concealing' is meant to articulate the answer to this question. How, then, are we to understand this such
that it grounds and originates concealment and openness? The key, I think,
is in Heidegger's concept of decision, difference, or self-differentiation. It
is important to emphasise that how one understands Heidegger's account
of the essence of truth directly impacts how one understands his account

of the event. Understanding the former to be most fundamentally *a-lēthic* leads to an account of the latter in terms of the *a-lēthic* framework. That, however, is not the full picture. As I shall continue to argue, Heidegger's account of the essence of truth in *Beiträge* moves to a ground more originary than the *a-lēthic* framework. Namely, it moves to an account of originary difference constituting the essence of truth, the dynamics of which originate the *a-lēthic* structures. Thus, a differential account of the essence of truth establishes a more originary account of the event. After a short aside, I turn to this in the following chapter.

4 The correlationist interpretation of 'event' (Sheehan and Meillassoux)

I would like to briefly engage two dominant alternative interpretations of Heidegger's concept of event. The first claims the event is the mutual appropriation of human existence to being and being to human existence. In this view, this co-appropriation includes a necessary dependence upon human existence. Consequently, if human existence were annihilated, being as event would not occur. This is the interpretation advanced by Sheehan and Meillassoux. The second interpretation takes the event ('being itself') to be ἀλήθεια, φύσις, *anwesen*, *es gibt*, or other versions of what is suggested to be the same phenomenon. This position is represented by Capobianco. I take the first of these to be incorrect and the second incomplete.

Sheehan's account of *Ereignis* is framed by his discontent with the use of the terminology of *Sein* in Heidegger scholarship. In his words, 'the major obstacle in interpreting Heidegger today is the continued use of the ontological language of "being" and "beings"'.[80] Thus, Sheehan's position entails reinterpreting the most basic directive of Heidegger's thought: his 'core topic' – *die Sache selbst* – was never being, but rather meaning (*Sinn* or *Bedeutung*).[81] 'Scholars', he writes, 'must realize that throughout his texts the term "being" was only a provisional and ultimately misleading way of saying "meaning."'[82] If the word '*Sein*' can be taken to signify Heidegger's core topic, it is only because by '*Sein*' he meant '*Sinn*'. For Sheehan, *Sein* = *Sinn* = Heidegger's core topic, *die Sache selbst*. This thesis goes hand in hand with a second. Namely, because meaning 'occurs only in correlation with human understanding', Heidegger's problematic is contained entirely within the domain of the human being or Dasein as being-in-the-world.[83] Sheehan insists, 'Heidegger remained on one level only, that of the man-meaning conjunction, and everything in his corpus is about that . . . [H]e never got beyond human being, and never intended to.'[84] Sheehan maintains this to be true for both pre- and post-*Kehre* Heidegger.[85] Since 'Sein' is claimed to be synonymous with 'Sinn', that is, meaning correlative with human existence, this position can be distilled further: 'the *Da-sein/Sein* correlation is transformed into the *Da-sinn/Sinn* conjunction'.[86] I disagree with this view for a variety of reasons, some of which I have already given in previous chapters. My most straightforward contention is that Heidegger was a smart guy – if he had meant *Sinn* and not *Sein*, he would have said so. There is no reason he could not have simply used 'Sinn' in place of 'Sein' if that were what he intended.

Sheehan does affirm that the defining question of post-*Kehre* Heidegger – the 'basic question' (*Grundfrage*) – is the question of what *gives* meaning: 'getting to the *constituting source* of meaning as such'.[87] 'If meaning-giving (*Welt, Lichtung*) is responsible for things being meaningful, what is responsible for *Welt* and *Lichtung* as such?'[88] The answer, he agrees, comes in terms of *Ereignis*. However, Sheehan reabsorbs *Ereignis* into the framework of meaning: *Ereignis* is 'the appropriation of man to the meaning-giving process', that is, to being, world, *Lichtung*, or, using Sheehan's alternative term, 'mind'.[89] To be clear, he means 'mind' 'in the very specific Heideggerian sense of the structural condition for making intentional sense of anything'.[90] 'Mind in this sense is a priori "open" and meaning-giving. When things come to mind, they are disclosed."[91] But, according to Sheehan, this openness or disclosure only *is* insofar as it is held open by human existence. Thus, being/world/*Lichtung*/mind/meaning-giving is dependent on human existence, so the appropriation of human existence to the meaning-giving process is reciprocal – it is a co-appropriation.[92] This allows him to offer a fuller statement of his interpretation of *Ereignis*: '*Ereignis* is this hermeneutical circle of reciprocal need: human being's need of *Welt*/mind as meaning-giving, and *Welt*/mind's inability to subsist without human being.'[93]

I think this is an incorrect account of *Ereignis*. As we have seen, one of the decisive claims in *Beiträge* is that beyng as event – and even structures of the essence of truth – is not dependent on any relation with beings, let alone with human existence. Thus, the rubric of reciprocity does not match up to Heidegger's account. In fact, as I have suggested, an early version of this position is evident even in 'Vom Wesen der Wahrheit' with respect to λήθη or originary concealment. Furthermore, Sheehan's position steps into a philosophical trap: the correlationism critiqued by Meillassoux in *After Finitude*. Correlationism, for Meillassoux, is the position following upon Kant's critical philosophy that 'we only ever have access to the correlation between thinking and being, and never to either term considered apart from the other'.[94] To me such correlationism can be rendered both in epistemological and ontological registers, which in many cases overlap. In the former, whatever human existence aims to think or know – be it an object in itself, an unconditioned absolute, being, etc. – that thing is only accessible on the basis of its relation to us, that is, as something for us and never independently of any relation to us. A good example is Kant's transcendental philosophy and its phenomenon/noumenon distinction. In the ontological register, correlationist philosophies maintain that human existence always *is* in a correlation with being (or world or language or whatever primary ontological term one chooses) and, inversely, being always *is* only in a correlation with human existence. In other words, such philosophies would maintain that neither being nor any aspect of being can be accounted for as independent of human existence: no human existence, no being.

Meillassoux takes Heidegger to be a paradigm case of just such ontological correlationism, particularly with respect to the concept of event. He writes:

> On the one hand, for Heidegger, it is certainly a case of pinpointing the occlusion of being or presence inherent in every metaphysical conception of representation and the privileging of the present at-hand entity considered as an object. Yet on the other hand, to think such an occlusion at the heart of the unconcealment of the entity requires, for Heidegger, that one take into account the *co-propriation* (*Zusammengehörigkeit*) of man and being, which he calls *Ereignis*. Thus, the notion of *Ereignis*, which is central in the later Heidegger, remains faithful to the correlationist exigency inherited from Kant and continued in Husserlian phenomenology, for the 'co-propriation' which constitutes *Ereignis* means that neither being nor man can be posited as subsisting 'in-themselves', and subsequently entering into relation – on the contrary, both terms of the appropriation are originarily constituted through their reciprocal relation.[95]

In Meillassoux's account, Heidegger is a correlationist because he is able to think being only on the basis of a co-propriative relation between being and human existence. Moreover, Meillassoux takes *Ereignis* to be exactly this co-propriative relation. Sheehan's interpretation of Heidegger fits this model precisely. For Sheehan, because 'being' means 'meaning' and meaning is always correlative with human existence, being is always correlative with human existence. In fact, he terms this the 'human correlativity with meaning'.[96] Moreover, for Sheehan, 'Ereignis' names the hermeneutical circle of reciprocal need between human existence and that which gives meaning (world, openness, mind, etc. – what we are used to calling 'being').

His correlationist interpretation of Heidegger is further expressed in the following examples.

Example 1: 'Heidegger himself understood *Sein* phenomenologically, i.e., as *Sinn* (meaning) in correlation with the *Da* of *Sinn*, man as "where-meaning-appears."'[97]

Example 2: '*Ohne Da-sein, kein Sein; ohne Sein, kein Da-sein* (without human being, no being; without being, no human being).' In light of his thesis about meaning, Sheehan reformulates this to read '*Ohne Da-Sinn, kein Sinn; Ohne Sinn, kein Da-sinn.*'[98]

Example 3: According to Sheehan, in the phenomenological reduction 'from being to meaning, and from meaning to its constituting source – the outcomes are always a matter of correlation. In the first reduction the phenomenologist's focus is on the *intentional* correlation between understanding and the thing. In the second reduction, the phenomenological gaze focuses on one's *transcendence to meaning* (= one's a priori engagement with it), a correlation that *is* the source of meaning giving.'[99]

There are at least two different ways to argue against this sort of ontological correlationism, both depending on what we mean by 'being'. The first is to locate being as the being *of beings*, as Heidegger does in *Sein und Zeit*. In that case, one could argue that even in the absence of all human existence, beings would still *be*. Meillassoux begins his critique of correlationism with this idea, focusing on timeframes anterior to life on earth. Correlationist philosophies, he argues, cannot properly account for what he calls the 'ancestral', that is, 'any reality anterior to the emergence of the human species – or even anterior to every recognized form of life on earth'.[100] This includes things like 'the accretion of the earth (4.56 billion years ago)'.[101] In '*Facticity and* Ereignis', Sheehan entertains a version of this idea as an objection to his position: suppose a huge meteorite impacts Earth and extinguishes all life on the planet. It would seem that beings like the sun, black holes, and carbon atoms still would *be*. Thus, it would seem, 'when *Dasein* is gone, there still will be *Sein*'.[102] Disappointingly, Sheehan dismisses this critique with a circular line of reasoning. He simply reasserts his interpretation of being as meaning and meaning as dependent on human existence (beings have being insofar as they are made meaningful by human existence), which allows him to maintain that after the meteorite *Sein* will in fact not be. This is consistent with his broader interpretation of Heidegger. But as an argument *for* that interpretation and as a way out of the meteorite problem it simply fails by begging the question.

Whether or not the Heidegger of *Sein und Zeit* can answer to this sort of meteorite problem is something I will not address here. I am more interested in a second way of arguing against ontological correlationism. It takes a tack away from understanding being as the being of beings and argues that correlationism is false because being itself includes features that are not dependent on any relation with beings (notably, the human being). My analysis in this chapter of the transformations in Heidegger's ontology in *Beiträge* and their expression in the problematic of truth can serve as just such an argument. In Sheehan's account, Heidegger's post-*Kehre* programme is oriented by the question of what gives meaning, that is, what enables meaning to be at all. The answer is *Ereignis*, which Sheehan understands to be the reciprocal need human existence has for being and being has for human existence. In other words, *Ereignis* constitutes a strict ontological correlationism in which being only *is* in relation with human existence.

Both Meillassoux and Sheehan are wrong because, as I have shown, a central tenet of *Beiträge* is that being itself (as beyng) is dependent neither upon any relation with human existence nor any other beings. Rather, one of the core tasks set by Heidegger in the text is to think beyng in light of just this independence, which he does exactly in terms of *Ereignis*. By failing to recognise this shift, Sheehan and Meillassoux define Heidegger's project within the framework of the *Leitfrage* and reduce his core subject of enquiry to *Seiendheit*. Not only does Heidegger argue that there are features of being (as event) that are decisively independent of any relation with human existence, *Beiträge* also supplies specific examples of such features, including (among others that I will get to in the next chapter) the 'essential extent' and its operation of breaching open openness, originary openness itself, and concealing withdrawal. As further support, Heidegger's claim that the essence of truth is 'definitively detached [abgelöst] from all beings' straightforwardly invalidates both Sheehan's claim that *Sein* = *Sinn* = Heidegger's core topic and the correlationism that claim embodies in Sheehan's account of *Ereignis*.[103]

It is important that I be clear about my point to avoid a misunderstanding. Against my interpretation, it might be objected that several of Heidegger's texts after the 1930s do in fact argue that the disclosure of a world of meaning requires that being is locked into a co-dependent correlation with human existence – as in the account of *Ereignis* as a reciprocal need and mutual appropriation between human existence and being. How, then, could my point be correct? My response is that I agree with this . . . but only as far as it goes: insofar as Heidegger gives an account of *meaning* or of being *insofar as being is involved in the constitution of meaning*, that account involves a co-dependent correlation of being and human existence, or at the very least being and beings. Giving an account of meaning, however, is only one dimension of Heidegger's project: he addresses it *and more*. His account of meaning and the correlationism it involves takes place at a diagenically derivative level in comparison with his account of beyng as event in *Beiträge*. We simply have to be clear about the diagenic relation between these two levels in order to keep from conflating them. The correlationist interpretation makes just that error – it conflates these levels and thereby botches Heidegger's account.

5 The position that 'event' is equivalent to *Anwesen*, ἀλήθεια, φύσις, or the giving of what is given (Capobianco)

The second interpretation I wish to look at takes 'Ereignis' to be simply an alternative name for what is designated by 'anwesen' ('presencing') or 'das Anwesen des Anwesenden' ('the presencing of what is present'), 'ἀλήθεια', 'φύσις', 'es gibt', and number of other terms used by Heidegger.[104] This position is represented by Capobianco, for whom 'anwesen', 'ἀλήθεια', 'φύσις', and so on denote roughly the same thing: the manifestation of worlds of beings or meaning together with that which enables such manifestation. Similarly, Polt discusses this with a focus on 'the giving of the given' (cf. Heidegger's use of 'es gibt').[105] This view does not categorically excise the most fundamental dimensions of Heidegger's concept of event as Sheehan and Meillassoux's does, it just doesn't reach them. Thus, if the former view is incorrect, this one is merely incomplete (though I think there are some important problems with it that should be pointed out). Moreover, Capobianco has made a concerted effort to show that Heidegger's ontology supports a certain form of realism: in his interpretation, φύσις, ἀλήθεια, and so on occurs even if human existence is not around, for instance in the Proterozoic era (he describes this in terms of a 'structural primacy of Being in relation to the human being').[106] These concepts articulate ontological structures that are not dependent on human existence. I agree.

In *Engaging Heidegger*, Capobianco frames his interpretation of *Ereignis* by positioning himself against (1) those like Sheehan who reduce Heidegger's core question from one about being to one about meaning, and (2) those who claim 'Ereignis' names a fundamentally different matter for thought than 'being' did in Heidegger's earlier work. He insists 'Ereignis' is '(only) another name for Being itself': even though Heidegger used different core terms at different times, each designated the same 'fundamental matter'.[107] He makes this interpretive point as follows:

> [Heidegger] was clear and emphatic right to the end of his life that the single, defining concern of his path of thinking regarded the originary, fundamental, unifying meaning of Being, named by him over the many years as Beyng (*das Seyn*), Being itself (*das Sein selbst*), Being as such (*das Sein als solches*), and Being as Being (*das Sein als Sein*).[108]

And:

> The single, whole phenomenon – Being itself – that he named and renamed again over the course of his lifetime of thinking, and the abundant variety of names that he put into play succeeded in bringing into view the varied features of this one, simple phenomenon. So it is that we may also speak of the *unconcealing* of beings (*alētheia*), the *emerging* of beings (*physis*), the *laying out and gathering* of beings (*logos*), the *unifying, unfolding* of beings (*hen*), the *presencing* of beings (*Anwesen*), the *lighting/clearing* of beings (*Lichtung*), the *freeing* of beings (*das Freie*), the *letting* of beings (*Lassen*), the *giving* of beings (*Es gibt*), and the *appropriating or enowning* of beings (*Ereignis*). All of these names, and still others, say (*sagen*) and show (*zeigen*), in somewhat different ways, the primordial phenomenon. Or to put this in Heidegger's terms, all of these names are the Same (*das Selbe*), but not simply identical (*das Gleiche*) in an empty, purely formal, logical sense.[109]

Since this view holds that 'Ereignis' is only another name for 'Being itself', it also holds that 'Ereignis' should be given no special status in comparison with 'anwesen', 'ἀλήθεια', 'φύσις', and so on. Each contributes to the author's work of 'bringing into view the varied features of this one, simple phenomenon', Being itself.[110]

As my methodological considerations in Chapter 1 show, I agree that throughout Heidegger's career he had a unified focus on what he found to be the essential matter for thought. This was not meaning (*Sinn* or *Bedeutung*). Nor was there a break in which he abandoned an earlier project and began a new one inconsistent with the first. On the second of these points, Capobianco writes, 'Heidegger did not marginalize the *Seinsfrage* in favor of the thematization of *Ereignis* in the years following his burst of private *Ereignis*-writings.'[111] In other words, the turn to *Ereignis* was no dismissal of the core problematic in Heidegger's earlier thought. I agree with this claim, but not in the same sense or for the same reasons as Capobianco. Heidegger's turn to *Ereignis* in the 1930s was a continuation of his earlier work, but he was not merely rethinking his problematic in different terms, such that this might provide a better angle or greater clarity. His account of *Ereignis* in *Beiträge* was produced via the complex diagenic evolution of his ontology, pursuing the *Seinsfrage* to a ground more originary than those articulable by the concept of *Sein*. It recasts his problematic on this more originary basis. Heidegger's thematisation of *Ereignis* was a result of supplanting more derivative renditions of the ontological problematic, through which the *Seinsfrage* progressed in the methodo-logical evolution of his work. Capobianco makes an error here by taking the various accounts in which Heidegger addressed his core problematic (excluding the pre- to post-*Kehre* shift) to be syngenically equivalent. He does not register the diagenic relations that hold between some of them.

Consistent with his interpretation, Capobianco argues 'there is neither sufficient nor convincing textual evidence to maintain that [Heidegger] ever considered *Ereignis* as a *more* fundamental matter for thought than *das Sein*'.[112] I think this is false. Capobianco lists citations from *Beiträge* (GA65), GA66, GA67, GA69, and GA70 which rightly establish that for Heidegger *Ereignis* is *Seyn*, or *Seyn* is *Ereignis*.[113] This also rightly estab-lishes that the question of *Seyn* and the question of *Ereignis* are not two different or inconsistent philosophical questions, but one and the same. He then distinguishes *Seyn* from traditional metaphysical conceptions of *Sein*: 'the fundamental matter for thought, *das Seyn/das Seyn selbst* (Beyng/Beyng itself)' versus '*das Sein* as *die Seiendheit*, being as beingness, the proper concern of metaphysical thinking (*eidos*, *essentia*, essence, and all other forms of "perduring presence"'.[114] And he distinguishes Heidegger's own affirmative use of *Sein* in his sense (for instance in his pre-*Kehre* work) from that traditional metaphysical use. However, in relation to this Capobianco does not register the full weight of Heidegger's arguments in *Beiträge* according to which his own affirmative conception of *Sein* must be surpassed because, despite its best efforts, it, too, remained within the framework of *Seiendheit* (insofar as *Sein* is thought in one form or another as the coming to presence of beings – or even as the ground enabling the coming to presence of beings – it is understood in terms of its relation to beings and not independently). In Capobianco's analysis

> to think Being [Sein] in a non-metaphysical way is to think Being regarding its 'originating of presence' (*Wesensherkunft*) . . . Being [Sein], thought in a fundamental way, originates (gives, grants) beings (that is, what-is-present) in their beingness (that is, in their sheer presence or essence).[115]

In other words, Capobianco does not register the full significance of the programmatic evolution from the *Leitfrage* to the *Grundfrage* that Heidegger commits to in *Beiträge*.[116] The problem, then, is that by equat-ing *Ereignis* with *Seyn* and *Seyn* with *Sein* (as the Heideggerian coming to presence of beings – or ground thereof), Capobianco mistakenly equates *Ereignis* with *Sein*. Again, in his analysis: 'if Being [Sein] is thought "regarding its originating of presence," then indeed Being and *Ereignis* may be thought together . . . Being and *Ereignis*: the Same'.[117] Therein lies the (erroneous) foundation for his claim that '*Ereignis*' is just a different name for ἀλήθεια, φύσις, and so on, and that, in turn, '*Ereignis*' was not intended to name something more originary than being (*Sein*). On the contrary, 'Ereignis' was intended precisely to name something more originary than being, namely *Seyn* or beyng. My following remarks should help to clarify the core problem I see here and why it is significant.

If, for Capobianco, 'Ereignis' is (only) another name for being itself, what, more precisely, is 'being itself'? He understands this to be 'the temporal-spatial, finite and negatived, unconcealing of beings (*das Seiende*) in their beingness (*die Seiendheit*) as made manifest meaningfully by *Dasein* in language'.[118] As we have seen, this amounts to the claim that being as *Ereignis* is nothing other than *anwesen* or 'Being as *physis* as *alêtheia*'.[119] Importantly, he of course does not mean to suggest that *Ereignis* or being itself *is* presence, but that it is the dynamic process in which beings come into and go out of presence:

> Characterizing Being itself as the appearing or manifesting of beings does not in the first place refer to the sheer, abiding 'appearance' or 'presence' of beings (which came to be spoken of in the metaphysical tradition as *eidos, morphe, ousia, energeia, actualitas, essentia*), but rather to *anwesen selbst*, presencing itself, or to '*Bewegtheit*' (Heidegger's translation of Aristotle's *kinesis*), namely, the 'movedness' of all beings into and out of presence, which Heidegger meditated on at length, especially in his commentary on Aristotle's *Physics*, B, I.[120]

The following statements by Capobianco connect this idea directly with *Ereignis*:

- 'Being/*Ereignis* originates (gives, grants, lets, enables, allows) beings in their beingness.'[121]
- 'For Heidegger, then, *das Ereignis* "is" the Originating (*die Anfängnis*) "is" Beyng.'[122]
- 'Being/*Ereignis* is the "originating of presence."'[123]
- '*Ereignis* as *Es gibt* gives (grants, allows, enables) beingness; but *Ereignis* and Being itself: the Same.'[124]
- 'The word *Ereignis* makes manifest the Being-way by virtue of the three fundamental resonances of the word itself, namely, (1) the "event" or "happening" that is the efflorescence and effulgence of beings coming into (2) their "own" (the *eigen* of *ereignen*) and thereby (3) coming out into "full view" to Dasein (*ereignen* related to *eräugnen*, literally "to come before the eyes". . .).'[125]

In Capobianco's account, *Ereignis* is that which enables the manifestation or coming to presence and passing out of presence of beings. To be clear, Heidegger *does* deal extensively with this process in terms of *anwesen*, ἀλήθεια, φύσις, *es gibt*, and the other concepts listed in the citations above. And *Ereignis does* function as the ground enabling this process. However, this function *does not* reach the essential definition for *Ereignis*. So, Capobianco's position on this isn't entirely incorrect (indeed, it faithfully represents certain accounts of *Ereignis* given by Heidegger in some texts from the 1950s and 1960s). However, when it comes to *Beiträge*, and thus to the broader concept of *Ereignis* in Heidegger's work, it misses the mark.[126]

In my view, Capobianco tells only part of the story of *Ereignis*. That which enables the manifestation or coming to presence and passing out of presence of beings is a derivative dimension of *Ereignis* that Heidegger argues must be rethought on the basis of a more originary one. More specifically, the limits of this view can be seen in terms of two further problems that it runs into. First, it understands *Ereignis* on the basis of a relation to that which comes to presence, is unconcealed, or is given, that is, to beings. When it comes to Heidegger's ontology of events this makes the mistake of determining being in terms of characteristics of beings and thereby replicates the fatal flaw of metaphysics. This interpretation makes the same error that conceiving of being as a condition for beings makes. Even if aspects of ἀλήθεια, for instance, are taken to be structurally prior to beings or meaning, so long as ἀλήθεια is defined in terms of the unconcealment *of beings* or *of meaning*, that definition is derived in terms of a relation to them. Likewise, if beyng as *Ereignis* is understood as the giving of the given, it is conceptually defined in terms of a relation to what is given. Consequently, this view remains within the bounds of the *Leitfrage* and its orientation to *Seiendheit*. The second problem this view runs into is that it cannot account for features of the event that exceed ἀλήθεια, φύσις, *anwesen*, etc. However, as I will continue to argue in the next chapter, there are indeed such features in Heidegger's account. This is clear, for example, in his move to enquire into the ground originary of the very structures of ἀ-λήθεια. As an extension of this, I shall argue that there are features of the event beyond even the logic of appropriation and expropriation.

Notes

1. GA65 387/305, 348/275.
2. As a general statement of such a position: 'For Heidegger, the essence of truth is always understood in terms of unconcealment' (Wrathall, 'Unconcealment' 337).
3. *SZ* 6/26.
4. In *Beiträge*, Heidegger defines what counts as a being very broadly: '"Beings" – this term names *not* only the actual (and certainly not if this is taken as the present at hand and the latter merely as the object of knowledge), not only the actual of any sort, but

at the same time the possible, the necessary, and the accidental, everything that stands in beyng in any way whatever, even including negativity [Nichtige] and nothingness [Nichts]' (GA65 74/59).

5. GA65 7/8.
6. It should be noted, though, that Heidegger is not entirely consistent with the use of this convention in *Beiträge*.
7. GA65 477/375.
8. *HWB* 11.
9. GA65 7/8. Though this analogy uses a relation of efficient causality, which is a decisively ontic relation, I do not mean to suggest beyng is a cause of beings. Rather, I mean to illustrate that there is a relation of dependence, where, if beyng did not 'occur essentially', beings would not be. Thus, this is a structural analogy, not an example.
10. GA65 6/8.
11. GA65 75/60.
12. Ibid. For more on Heidegger's understanding of *Seiendheit*, see Polt, *EB* 55–6 and 63–4.
13. Heidegger makes this point well in *Nietzsche* volume IV. 'Plato interpreted the being-ness of beings as *idea*' (Heidegger, *Nietzsche* volume IVe 194). 'In the question "What is the being as such?" we are thinking of being, and specifically of the being of beings, that is to say, of what beings are. What they are – namely, the beings – is answered by their what-being [Was-sein], *to ti estin*. Plato defines the whatness of a being as *idea* (see *Plato's Doctrine of Truth*). The whatness of being, the *essentia* of *ens*, we also call "the essence"' (Heidegger, *Nietzsche* volume IVe 206). Heidegger's essay, 'Plato's Doctrine of Truth', is found in GA9. For more of Heidegger's related comments on Aristotle, Kant, and Nietzsche, see *Nietzsche* volume IV 41.
14. GA65 75/60.
15. Heidegger, *Nietzsche* volume IV 156.
16. While Heidegger critiques the ontological difference in *Beiträge*, attaining the conceptual and methodological position from which that critique can be made is itself dependent upon having previously marked the ontological difference and worked through the ontological problematic it opens.
17. For instance (keeping attentive to the distinction between *Sein* and *Seyn*), see the passage from GA65 478/376 block-quoted below. Similarly, in GA66 Heidegger writes: 'Das Seyn als Er-eignis des ab-gründigen Austrags der Kreuzung von Entgegnung und Streit ist weder vom Seienden her als dessen Abhub und Nachtrag, noch auf das Seiende zu als dessen Ursache und Bedingung er-dacht' (GA66 93/78).
18. GA65 297/234, 379/300.
19. GA65 307/243.
20. GA65 479/377.
21. Ground is also that which is most proper to what is grounded; it bears the gravity of essence. In *WW* 'essence' was provisionally understood to mean 'ground of enabling' or 'ground of the inner possibility' (*WW* 177/136, 186/143).
22. GA65 307/243.
23. Capobianco, 'Coda on Being is (not) Meaning', Heidegger Circle Forum Post, 30 August 2013. Again: 'Being *qua* manifestation is structurally prior to, and the ontological condition of, any "constitution" of meaning' (*HWB* 11).
24. GA65 12/12.
25. GA65 297/235, my italics on 'truth'.
26. GA65 478/376.
27. GA65 477/375.
28. Ibid. Again: 'As a consequence of its solitude, beyng essentially occurs in relation to "beings" always only mediately, through the strife of world and earth' (GA65 471/371).

29. GA65 75–6/60.
30. GA65 75/60.
31. Ibid.
32. Ibid.
33. GA65 75–6/60.
34. GA65 76/60.
35. Ibid.
36. For more on the *Grundfrage* versus the *Leitfrage* see GA65 §§85, 91, and 172.
37. Rae, *Ontology in Heidegger and Deleuze* 3.
38. GA65 172–3/136.
39. GA65 186/146.
40. GA65 173/136, italics modified.
41. GA65 186/146.
42. GA65 173/136.
43. GA65 76/60.
44. GA65 186/146.
45. GA65 76/60.
46. GA65 77/61.
47. GA65 186/146. For more of Heidegger's comments on the non-reactive nature of this shift see §§85 and 92.
48. For a more detailed discussion of the ontological difference and the ambivalent meanings of the Greek 'ὄν', see Richardson, *Heidegger: Through Phenomenology to Thought* 10–15.
49. GA65 477/375.
50. In a reformulation of the idea cited at the beginning of this chapter, Heidegger writes, 'the precursory question [Vor-frage] of truth is simultaneously the basic question [Grund-frage] of beyng; and beyng qua event essentially occurs [west] as truth' (GA65 348/275).
51. GA65 348/275, italics removed, 329/261. The connection of this with beyng is highlighted again in the alternative formulation: the essence of truth is 'die lichtende Verbergung des Seyns' ('the clearing concealment of beyng') (GA65 380/300).
52. GA65 380/300.
53. GA65 455/359, italics removed.
54. GA65 327/259.
55. Ibid.
56. GA65 345/273.
57. GA65 327/259.
58. GA65 329/261.
59. GA65 327/259, my italics.
60. GA65 329/261.
61. GA65 331/262.
62. GA65 327/259, italics removed.
63. GA65 328/260.
64. GA65 329/261.
65. It would be mistaken to take this to mean truth is originally *infinite*. There is no infinite–finite dichotomy at play here, according to which truth could fall on the side opposed to the finite. Rather, the originary clearing or breaching of openness arises from the differential operation constituting the essence of truth, where that differential operation is precisely the mechanism of the event's self-coagulation or intensification, distension, and elaboration in the more derivative *a-lēthic* structures of truth.
66. GA65 329/261.
67. Ibid.
68. *HCP* 112.
69. See GA65 §152. For some of Heidegger's comments on transcendence, see GA65 §7

and §227. For another short discussion on the non-transcendent nature of beyng, see Brogan, 'Da-sein and the Leap of Being' 176–8.
70. Cf. DeLanda, *Intensive Science and Virtual Philosophy*.
71. GA65 338–9/268.
72. GA65 331/262.
73. GA65 330/261, translation modified.
74. GA65 335/266.
75. GA65 350/277. For more, see GA65 §226.
76. GA65 350/277.
77. Ibid.
78. Ibid.
79. GA65 345/273. Möbius strips have only one side.
80. *FE* 42.
81. *FE* 43.
82. *FE* 42.
83. In Sheehan's words, 'Heidegger's extensive corpus from beginning to end remained a hermeneutics of Dasein or an analytic of human existence' (Sheehan, 'Astonishing!' 3).
84. Sheehan, 'Astonishing!' 4.
85. *FE* 43.
86. Sheehan, 'Astonishing!' 3.
87. *FE* 54, 51.
88. *FE* 51. Or again: 'Heidegger's sights were ultimately set not on that which is meaningful (in traditional language, *das Seiende*) not even on what gives it meaning (traditionally, *das Sein*) but rather on the *source* of meaning (*das Wesen/die Wahrheit des Seins*)' (*FE* 51).
89. *FE* 53, italics removed, 56.
90. *FE* 56, italics removed.
91. *FE* 56. See Sheehan's text here for more on his concept of mind.
92. For more detail on Sheehan's understanding of *Ereignis* as reciprocity, see *FE* 57 and 59–60.
93. *FE* 56–7.
94. Meillassoux, *After Finitude* 5.
95. Meillassoux, *After Finitude* 8.
96. *FE* 48.
97. *FE* 49.
98. *FE* 47–8.
99. *FE* 45.
100. Meillassoux, *After Finitude* 10.
101. Meillassoux, *After Finitude* 9.
102. *FE* 48.
103. GA65 329/261.
104. For more on Heidegger's use of 'anwesen', see *EH* 27–8. In short, 'anwesen' names the ontological process of presencing (Capobianco translates it with that gerund) and is distinguished from *das Anwesende* ('that which appears or is present') and *Anwesenheit* (presence), as in, 'what is present in its sheer "presence" (*Anwesenheit*)'. The latter express metaphysical definitions of the beingness of beings (*EH* 27).
105. *EB* 24. For more on Polt's interpretation of 'the giving of the given', see *EB* 24–33.
106. *HWB* 41–2.
107. *EH* 35, 34.
108. *EH* 34.
109. *EH* 4.
110. Ibid.

111. *EH* 36. Capobianco means between the years 1944–56 here. Of course, as he points out, *Ereignis* did move back to a focal role for Heidegger in the late 1950s and 1960s.
112. *EH* 34.
113. *EH* 39–43.
114. *EH* 44.
115. *EH* 47.
116. *EH* 44.
117. *EH* 47.
118. *EH* 34.
119. *HWB* 50.
120. *HWB* 25.
121. *EH* 47.
122. *EH* 43. For Capobianco's helpful comments on 'die Anfängnis', see *EH* 42–3.
123. *EH* 47.
124. *EH* 49.
125. *HWB* 21.
126. For Polt, similarly to Capobianco, *Ereignis* is 'the "happening" through which being "takes place" in the "there" of being-there' (*EB* 29n3). (Here, Polt is affirming his agreement with Walter Pratt that this is a good account of *Ereignis*.) This means beyng (*Seyn*) 'is best interpreted as the giving of being, that is, as the event in which beings as such and as a whole are enabled to make a difference to us' (*EB* 28–9). We must be careful not to conflate being (*Sein*) and beyng (*Seyn*) here. For Polt, *Sein* 'is the givenness of beings as such and as a whole – that is, not the "mere fact" that something is given, but the background meaning that enables us to *recognize* anything as given' (*EB* 28). *Seyn*, in distinction, is the giving of that givenness.

Chapter 5

Difference, Truth, and Event

In Heidegger's *Beiträge*, the question of the essence of truth provides the methodological path for grounding thought in the logic of beyng as event. In Chapter 4 I argued that this path moves beyond the *a-lēthic* framework by enquiring into the ground enabling and originating the ἀλήθεια/λήθη distinction. In Chapter 5, I shall argue that in their most diagenically advanced moments, *Beiträge* and the related private manuscripts maintain that beyng as event is difference or a process (which I call a logic) of differentiation. The central terms Heidegger uses for this are *Unterschied* (difference) and in a very specific sense *Entscheidung* (decision), to each of which a variety of cognates are bound. I argue that the ground of the ἀλήθεια/λήθη distinction is such difference and that Heidegger's core formulation of the essence of truth in *Beiträge* – that it is 'the clearing for/ of self-concealing' ('die Lichtung für das Sichverbergen' or 'Lichtung des Sichverbergens') – is a differential formulation. Within the context of his broader ontology of difference, we can begin to unfold his logic of beyng as event by asking and answering the question, 'What would the logic of difference have to be like in order to explain the origination of ἀλήθεια and λήθη?' In other words, the question of the essence of truth offers thought a first stance grounded in the logic of difference that is beyng as event.

On this basis, that logic can be further unfolded and eventually move beyond the terms of truth. Doing so provides a way to explain a variety of Heidegger's other evental concepts via their 'originary' or genetic ground in the differential logic (for instance, 'appropriation', 'expropriation', and 'time-space'). To be clear, though Heidegger presents numerous fragments of the differential logic of the event, he does not work it out in a systematically unified way. Yet, his concept of difference is poised to do just that. My claim moving forward is this: the logic of difference that I propose underwrites or is expressed in the ontology presented in *Beiträge*; it is what is necessary to hold the rest of that text's ontology together. Without this logic, the text's concepts become disconnected, arbitrary, or a matter of authorial fiat rather than parts of a philosophically consistent, and thus coherent, picture. My view on this is no doubt heterodox. But I have seen no other viable explanation that does not rely outrightly on conceptual vagueness or mysticism.

1 Heidegger's ontology of difference

Heidegger's account of difference undergoes a major reconfiguration in *Beiträge*. Under the headings of *Unterschied* and *Entscheidung*, we see a concept of originary difference or self-differentiation being developed that constitutes an essential operation of beyng as event. We can develop this idea via two more local tacks: one oriented by the problematic of the 'ontological difference' (*ontologischen Differenz*) and the other by the problematic of historical 'decision' (*Entscheidung*).[1]

1.1 The ontological difference

The ontological difference is the difference between being and beings so crucial to Heidegger's pre-*Kehre* work. In *Beiträge*, this is seen as a transitional concept to be replaced by an account of the more originary ground enabling that difference to be conceived at all. This is necessary because the concept of the ontological difference is insufficient for the programme of enquiring into the nature of beyng as event – it remains structured by the problematic of the *Leitfrage* and thus carries the error of metaphysics. More precisely, in the frame of the ontological difference: (1) being is understood through its *difference from*, and thus in a way co-determined *by*, its counterpart – beings, (2) being is understood as the being *of* beings, and thus (3) the question of being is oriented by the question of the being of beings. Each of these are elements of the *Leitfrage* explored in Chapter 4, sections 1 and 2. Consequently, Heidegger writes:

> as necessary as the distinction [between being and beings] is and even if it must be thought in terms of the tradition in order to create a very first horizon for the question of beyng, it is just as fatal – since it indeed arises precisely from an inquiry into beings as such (beingness [Seiendheit]).[2]

This does not mean that the concept of the ontological difference is simply discarded. Rather, 'the question of beyng, as the basic question [Grundfrage]', is 'driven immediately to the question of the *origin* [*Ursprung*] of the "ontological difference."'³ Through this second question Heidegger arrives at a more originary concept of difference that is consistent with the programme of the *Grundfrage* and that operates at the heart of the essence of truth and, in turn, beyng as event.

The conceptual difference between being and beings is possible, he argues, only because beyng is of such a nature that it '*sets itself off in relief* [*abhebt*] over and against beings'.⁴ 'Setting itself off in relief' is not a function of human experience, for instance in the forms discussed by Gestalt psychology, but the structural feature of beyng by which it is inclined to become conceptualised in the difference between being and beings. Setting itself off in relief 'can originate only in the *essential occurrence* [*Wesung*] of beyng'.⁵ Why, then, is beyng inclined towards this? In Heidegger's words, it is because:

> Beyng, as the 'between' which clears, moves itself into this clearing and therefore, though never recognized or surmised as appropriation [Ereignung], is for representational thinking something generally differentiable, and differentiated, as being. This applies already to the way beyng essentially occurs in the first beginning, namely, as φύσις, which comes forth as ἀλήθεια but which is at once forgotten in favor of beings (ones that are perceivable as such only in virtue of ἀλήθεια) and is reinterpreted as a being that *is* most eminently, i.e., as a mode of being and specifically the highest mode.⁶

In other words, because beyng brings itself to determination (in part) in the operation of truth, the possibility is established for thought to account for beyng in terms of that determinate dimension and to distinguish that dimension in terms of a co-determinate differential relation with beings. Certainly, one might deny (as Heidegger does in *Sein und Zeit*) that being, thus differentiated from beings, must be 'a being' that 'is' most eminently. But this is not the real issue. The real issue is that the ontological difference remains structurally determined as a difference *between* two 'things'. Framing the problematic of beyng in terms of the ontological difference 'captures' beyng in this differential relation with beings. It casts beyng in terms of a difference from beings. But this replicates the framework of metaphysics found in the *Leitfrage*.

The crucial point Heidegger recognises in *Beiträge* is that the difference between being and beings points to an aspect of beyng more originary than itself. The ontological mechanism required for determining the ontological difference at all must be prior to that difference. For Heidegger, here, the ontological difference is 'the merely metaphysically conceived, and thus already misinterpreted, foreground [Vordergrund] of a de-cision [Ent-scheidung] which is beyng itself'.⁷ This decision is referred to alternatively in the terminology of the 'Lichtung' or 'clearing' belonging to the essential occurrence of beyng as event and first accessed as the essence of truth. The clearing operation is precisely a de-cision or differentiation – which is not a difference between two beings, but, rather, is difference itself. That is, this clearing or decision is an operation of self-differentiation that enables things that have differences between them to be, but it is not to be understood on the basis of those things or their differences. It is more originary. In part, the heart of beyng as event is this self-differentiation. 'The event of ap-propriation includes the *de-cision*: the fact that freedom, as the abyssal ground, lets arise a need out of which, as the excess of the ground, the gods and humans come forth in their separateness.'[8] This originary self-differential operation of the event Heidegger calls the '*Entscheidung*wesen des Seyns' ('*decisional* essence of beyng').[9] I shall return to it in just a moment.

Beistegui's *Truth and Genesis* provides one of the few available sustained examinations of difference in *Beiträge*. He rightly recognises that difference plays a key role in Heidegger's shift to thinking beyng as event and shows this has important implications for how we understand his ontology. As he writes, for Heidegger 'the sense of being . . . with which being comes to be identified, is that of difference. But . . . the sense of difference itself has shifted, and radically so, freeing being of ontotautology altogether.'[10] I do, however, find that Beistegui's analysis misses the mark when it comes to showing the extent to which Heidegger rethinks difference. It does not register the move to a concept of difference more originary than the ontological difference. Just when he is on the brink of Heidegger's concept of originary difference and the logic of self-differentiation it entails, he slips back into the vestiges of the framework of *Seiendheit*, suggesting that 'by difference, we must now understand the originary event in the unfolding of which the world takes place. The sense of being that is at issue here is entirely contained within the space of the ontological difference.'[11] And again, 'being is only in and through its difference from beings'.[12] The crucial distinction that Beistegui misses is the diagenic distinction between the ontological difference and the differential ground making it possible. By conflating these, his conception of Heidegger's event is stuck within the domain of the *Leitfrage*, prevented from making the key diagenic move necessary for defining the ontological concept of event in the domain of the *Grundfrage*.

1.2 Decision

Heidegger articulates the originary clearing or self-differential operation of the event early in *Beiträge* as the ground of historical 'decision' (*Entscheidung*) or 'de-cision' (*Ent-scheidung*).[13] The notion of decision is that of separating or, as Vallega-Neu describes, 'partedness' or 'part*ing*'.[14] As a reader, it is tempting to understand 'decision' here as the type of thing done by humans who deliberate about different possible actions, for instance, and choose one. However, this is not the primary sense of Heidegger's concept. Decision is not 'a human act', 'choice, resolution, the preferring of one thing and the setting aside of another'.[15] Taking it as such would fall into what he calls 'the "existentiell" misinterpretation of "decision"', which is in fact an 'existentiell-*anthropological*' misinterpretation: it takes the human being as a subject making this decision, whereas the human being is subject *to* or structured *by* originary decision and the ontological features it generates, for instance, the *a-lēthic* structures of the essence of truth.[16]

To be clear, by distinguishing between the originary and existentiell versions of decision, I do not mean that Heidegger's concept excludes a secondary sense pertaining to the human being. It certainly also has this: the notion of decision comes into play in his account of history and the role of the human being in establishing another beginning for thought (see GA65 §43–9). But in that context, 'decision' has to do with consequent structures based on this antecedent, more primal ground: 'what is here called de-cision . . . proceeds to the innermost center of the essence of beyng itself'.[17] McNeill nicely calls this the 'event of differentiation'.[18] Vallega-Neu understands it as 'a differencing which occurs within the essential swaying [Wesung] of be-ing [Seyn]'.[19] I maintain that in the current context decision should be understood as such a separating, differentiation, or differencing occurring in the essence of truth, that is, it should be understood as the event insofar as the event occurs in and through the essence of truth. This is confirmed when the text states that 'de-cision refers to the sundering [Auseinandertreten] itself, which separates [scheidet] and in separating lets come into play for the first time the ap-propriation [Er-eignung] of precisely this sundered *open realm* [*Offenen*] as the clearing for the self-concealing'.[20]

Heidegger's movement towards an account with a differential operation at the heart of beyng as event is further verified by GA71 *Das Ereignis*, where he addresses 'der Unterschied als das Sichunterscheiden (Ereignis)' ['the difference as self-differentiating (event)'].[21] I cite the following passages to support this key point:

- 'Inasmuch as nothingness is beyng, beyng is essentially the difference [Unterschied] as the inceptually concealed and refused departure [Ab-schied].'[22]
- 'The difference is a matter of the event (the resonating of the turning).'[23]
- 'The difference . . . which first allows beings to arise as beings, and

separates [scheidet] them to themselves, is the ground of all separations [Scheidungen] in which beings can first "be" these respective individuals.'[24]

- 'Beyng as the difference – essentially occurring as the departure [Abschied].'[25]

- 'The difference, as beyng itself, appropriates [er-eignet] the differentiation [Unterscheidung] in which at any time obedience is involved.'[26]

- 'The difference [Unterscheidung] as the essential occurrence of beyng itself, which differentiates *itself* [*sich* unterscheidet] and in that way lets beings arise in emergence [Aufgang]. The differentiation is inceptually the difference [Die Unterscheidung ist anfänglich der Unterschied].'[27]

- 'Without having experienced the truth of beyng as event, we will be unable to know the difference and, thereby, the differentiation.'[28]

- 'The difference, in which the differentiation essentially occurs, is the departure as the downgoing of the event into the beginning.'[29]

The essence of beyng – the most originary element of the eventual structure – is difference or differentiation. To emphasise: this is not a difference relegated to marking a distinction or relation between two 'things' of any sort (including 'being' and 'beings'). That would make the error of placing the things distinguished prior to the differential process that is purported to ground the possibility for there to be any things whatsoever. As an extension of this idea, such difference can in no way be dependent upon any form of identity prior to it, which it would differentiate (as, for instance, in the case of Aristotle's specific difference, which can be marked only on the basis of the identity of a common genus).

This has an important methodological consequence: Heidegger's concept of originary difference cannot be defined by derivative or external terms. Doing so would make a mistake in the order of onto-genesis proposed. This leaves only one other option. Since difference holds the most diagenically originary position in his ontology, it must be explained using solely its own terms. So, how can we begin to provide such an explanation? How can we understand such difference? Well, what does difference do? Difference *differs* or *differentiates*; it is not identical. What can difference differ from or differentiate? At this level of the logic of Heidegger's ontology, the answer can be nothing other than difference 'itself'. Hypothesising something else which difference is applied to or differs from would, again, use something generated by difference to define it – that is, it would make the same mistake regarding the order of onto-genesis. Instead, it must be pure self-differentiation, that is, *difference differing from itself*. Given these conditions, the logic of self-differentiation cannot be clarified by empirical or phenomenological examples since it is logically prior to anything of which such an example could be composed. This makes for a rather abstract-sounding account of it, but one necessarily so.

I will suggest that we should understand self-differentiation to be the operation of beyng as event by which it self-coagulates or intensifies, distends, and becomes elaborated in distinct structures and dynamics; that is, it is the onto-genesis or origination of a logic of determinacy or of the 'Da' expressed in the term 'Da-sein'. In *Beiträge*, the concept of truth (along with those of ground and time-space) articulates just this elaboration. This means that the essence of truth must be differential; 'the clearing for/ of self-concealing' must be defined by a differential logic, part of which it conceptually grasps. We have already begun to see how this will work by connecting Heidegger's concept of 'clearing' to the decision or self-differentiation of difference. But what is the logic of this difference? How does it unfold? And returning to my earlier question, how must it be, such that it originates the *a-lēthic* structures of truth?

With these questions we run up against a limit of Heidegger's ability to articulate his problematic. He claims that difference or self-differentiation must be the originary character of beyng as event; he grasps this character in terms of evental structures originated by difference (truth, ground, time-space); but he is unable to present explicitly a unified logic of difference explaining the origination of these structures and thereby rigorously defining them. Nonetheless, such a logic must underwrite or be expressed in them and constitute their consistency. In what follows, I construct a few moments of this logic that I take to perform this function. I go beyond Heidegger's text by extrapolating this logic, but I maintain that it is not only consistent with but required by and entailed in his ontology. To be clear, by 'logic', I do not mean the formal relations of propositions, but the structure of beyng, how parts of that structure relate, and how some lead into others. The logic of difference is the dynamics of difference insofar as it constitutes and generates the structures of beyng or the event.

2 Heidegger's differential concept of truth

In this section I treat Heidegger's concept of the essence of truth in its relation to difference. As indicated, I hold that the formulation for the essence of truth used in *Beiträge* – 'the clearing for/of self-concealing' – is differential in the sense I have been discussing. What exactly this means has yet to be worked out. To do this, we need to frame the topic with reference to the major diagenic move Heidegger makes in his account of truth in *Beiträge*. This is the move I emphasised at the end of Chapter 4 section 3. Namely, after Heidegger integrates the shift from the *Leitfrage* to the *Grundfrage* into his approach to truth, he drives his ontology to a new diagenic stage by asking: whence and why concealment and openness (the originary forms of λήθη and ἀλήθεια)? This question enquires into the ground of the most originary ontological structures thinkable by Heidegger up to that point. The answer – the essence of truth – is 'the clearing for/of self-concealing', which captures the logic of the event in the language of truth. Consequently, the first task we are posed with is to work out how 'the clearing for/of self-concealing' articulates the logic of difference and, on this basis, provides a genetic explanation for the *a-lēthic* structures. So, how does this work?

As noted, Heidegger stops short of a full account of the operations through which originary difference generates the *a-lēthic* structures. Nevertheless, the resources for doing so are present in the text, even if its author might not have recognised this. A moment ago, when discussing the origin of the ontological difference between being and beings, we looked at Heidegger's claim that this results from the way beyng 'moves itself into the clearing'. We know that in this account the clearing or *Lichtung* cannot be something pre-existing that beyng then moves itself into; rather, it must be a genetic operation by beyng whereby beyng constitutes a cleared field (openness). The mechanics of this were left rather vague. But we can now say that the operation by which beyng performs this clearing is self-differentiation. In other words, clearing is the self-differentiation of difference. In the register of truth, this is the story of the genesis of openness and concealment. 'The clearing for/of self-concealing' articulates the event's differential self-intensification or distension in the terms of the register of truth. Heidegger puts the idea about this genetic process characterising truth as follows:

> Inasmuch as truth essentially occurs, *comes to be* [*wird*], the event becomes [*wird*] truth. The event eventuates [*das Ereignis ereignet*], which means nothing else but that it and only it *becomes* truth, becomes that which belongs to the event, so that truth is precisely and essentially the truth of beyng.[30]

Insofar as the event 'becomes' truth, it elaborates itself in the *a-lēthic* structures of openness and concealment.

It is worth taking a brief aside to point out a methodological principle connected to a defining feature of the relation between these structures. According to Heidegger, each is in a relationship of simultaneous strife and intimacy with the other. This means that any account of the origination of openness and concealment should be able to explain these relations. Giving this explanation is not my primary focus, but I will return to it in a moment as a partial gauge of the success of my account.

Coming back to the main topic, on the basis of Heidegger's terms we can begin to work out a genetic account of the essential structures of truth – concealment and openness. As indicated, if beyng as event is originary difference or the differentiation of difference from itself, then derivative terms cannot be imported to describe this without first defining them in differential terms. It also means that the genesis of openness and concealment must be explained in terms of originary difference, even if they methodologically prefigure its logic. But how? Answering this makes for a linguistically painful exercise, but one nonetheless systematically necessary.

Originary difference can differ only from itself. Yet precisely in so doing, a determination must occur, that is, a set of correlated structures must be generated. On the one hand, insofar as difference is differentiated from itself it constitutes what could be called a 'field' of difference. By 'field' here I mean the structural distance generated between (1) difference insofar as it differs from itself and (2) difference insofar as it is what is differed from. I take this to be the most basic form of *a-lēthic* openness. On the other hand, a second structure must arise simultaneously in the very same operation, namely, a correlated structure of difference determined in its differentiation from the open field it originates. If it is difference differing from itself that originates this field, that means that difference is irreducible to the field originated. More precisely, by the very same action by which difference generates the field, it differentiates itself from the field generated. In relation to the field, such difference gains a determination: it becomes determined by distinguishing itself *from* that field, that is, from what it originates. If it is difference differing from itself that originates the open field, it does so by withdrawing, refusing, or *differentiating itself from it*. I take the most basic form of *a-lēthic* concealment to be just this 'withdrawal' or 'refusal' of difference from itself, the refusal of difference to be identical with itself and with that which it originates.[31]

Now, originary differentiation cannot occur in any ontologically prior medium, but only through difference itself. This means that the aspects of difference that are differentiated – the field of openness and the difference differing or withdrawing from that field – bear structural reference to one another. Both are constituted by precisely the same operation and each has its determination by its contrast or difference from the other. In other words, these features are simultaneously constituted by their difference from and structural reference to one another. Because of this, I take them to constitute a field of ontological tension: the differentiation of difference from itself entails the generation of an immanent field of tension, that is, entails the self-intensification of beyng. But since difference and difference alone accomplishes this, it can equally be called self-distension, or just distension.

We can bring together these ideas about the onto-genesis of openness and concealment to synthesise a more precise differential, genetic definition of the essence of truth. Using a geometric analogy helps to picture the logic involved. The core of this definition is as follows: Concealment and openness *are* or rather essentially occur (*wesen*) in their differentiation from one another. In the way that a point is extended into a line, openness is generated or breached as the distention of differentiation differing from itself. As the limits of a line recede, drawing it out, difference refuses to be that which it generates; concealment is or essentially occurs as this refusal, generated as differentiation differing from itself.

Since what we are after at the moment is a differential explanation of Heidegger's formulation of the essence of truth as 'the clearing for/ of self-concealing' ('die Lichtung für das Sichverbergen' or 'Lichtung des Sichverbergens'), we should be able to use this definition to provide this. In turn, this amounts to an elaboration of seeds of the logic of difference just described. I will highlight each of the terms comprised by this formulation on its own: (1) the *clearing* for/of self-concealing, (2) the clearing *for*/of self-*concealing*, (3) the clearing for/*of* self-*concealing*, and (4) the clearing for/of *self*-concealing.

First, the *clearing* for/of self-concealing: We have already established that the famous clearing or *Lichtung* in Heidegger's formulation is the basic operation of the self-differentiation of difference, that is, the *clearing* for/of self-concealing is originary differentiation. This can now be given more detail. Heidegger uses the term 'Lichtung' or 'clearing' in the sense of a distancing or a 'sundering' ('Auseinandertreten').[32] This distancing or sundering occurs immanently to difference and what is sundered are the differential structures of openness and concealment. Openness and concealment cannot pre-exist their sundering, but rather must be generated and constituted by it, that is, by the differentiation whereby each becomes distinguished from the other. In this genetic process, as two passing ships are said to 'clear' one another, concealment clears openness and openness clears concealment. Since this sundering originates and grounds openness and concealment, which in turn ground worlds of beings, it cannot be defined as taking place between two already established 'things' of any order. Clearing is an operation of self-differentiation prior to and originary of any such things and the differences between them.

More precisely, clearing is difference differing from itself such that a sundering of openness and concealment is originated. Yet openness and concealment remain correlative, for this sundering or distancing is itself the breaching open of openness, the breaching of the 'essential extent' (the most originary extended dimension or place) that I discussed in Chapter 4. Clearing is the breaching of a space 'between' or, rather, a distension

that itself constitutes openness and concealment by constituting their difference. In this sense, with respect to concealment Heidegger writes: 'that
a clearing might ground what is self-concealing – that is the meaning of
the dictum that truth is primarily clearing-concealment'.[33] In this picture
the clearing for/of self-concealing cannot be one *or* the other, concealment
or openness. For, as Heidegger points out, to think the essence of truth is
to think that which originates concealment *and* openness; namely, pure
difference.[34]

It is worth pointing out that this conception of clearing demonstrates
an error in a common interpretation of Heidegger. According to this interpretation, the essence of truth and, in turn, the event are the same thing as
self-concealment, the concealing withdrawal of being, or originary λήθη.
However, they are not. This mistake misses the critical question: whence
and why concealment and openness? It thus misses the diagenic move to
the ground of the *a-lēthic* structures. Self-concealment is indeed a moment
of the evental dynamic. But the essence of truth is difference differing
from itself, self-distending in the manner of clearing for/of self-concealing.
Concealment is derived from difference and is therefore *not* the prime
feature of Heidegger's ontology.

Second, the clearing *for*/of *self-concealing*: The differential essence of
truth is clearing *for* self-*concealing* because it does something 'in the service
of' the concealing operation of beyng, so to speak. This does not mean
difference is telos-driven or 'intends', but simply that it generates concealment and clears or sunders it from openness. Concealment owes its
distinctness from openness to clearing (differentiation), without which it
could not occur at all. That is, the differentiation of difference from itself
enables concealment to occur – where concealment is difference's refusal
to be the openness or distension it generates – while that very operation of
differentiation is also the sundering of concealment from openness.

Third, the clearing for/*of* self-*concealing*: The differential essence of
truth is a clearing *of* self-*concealing* in both the objective and subjective
genitive senses. Concealment (1) gets cleared in the generation of openness and (2) itself takes part in generating openness. With respect to the
former, we have seen that clearing is a genetic differentiating or sundering
of concealment from openness and openness from concealment. With
respect to the latter, concealment plays a constitutive role in the originary
determination of openness: without concealment, the differentiation or
clearing of concealment from openness could not occur. Openness would
be granted no determinateness and no distinctness from concealment, that
is, it would not occur at all.

Finally, the clearing for/of *self*-concealing: The differential essence
of truth involves *self*-concealing because it is differentiation itself that

withdraws from its own clearing: concealment is the self-refusal enacted by differentiation.

It is important to emphasise that in this picture openness and concealment must be originated *simultaneously* by the differentiation of difference from itself. That is, the same operation constitutes the two by constituting their difference. It cannot be the case that one is logically prior to the other because each gains structural determination only in its correlation with the other. For the same reason, it also cannot be that they are ultimately discrete. In that case, they would have no correlation. Using my earlier geometric imagery, that would amount to placing concealment at one end of a line and openness at the other, with the line marking their absolute divorce. Rather, the account of originary difference allows us to understand (1) openness as the distension of difference differing from itself, that is, in the position of the line itself, and (2) concealment as the self-refusal simultaneously enacted by difference differing from itself, that is, in the place of the receding limit by which the line is drawn out.

Let us now return to the question of evaluation. As a criterion of success for this differential account, it should be able to ground what Heidegger calls the simultaneous strife and originary intimacy that characterise the structural relation between openness and concealment, and it should be able to explain the logic of these relations in a conceptually precise way. I think it can. As an initial point, there can be no such thing as strife without intimacy or intimacy without strife. That which is in strife must simultaneously have an intimacy because without intimacy there could be no relation. Likewise, that which is intimate must be characterised by a simultaneous strife, since it must be distinguished from that to which it is related (otherwise intimacy would simply be identity). The challenge is to provide an account of the simultaneous strife and intimacy of openness and concealment rather than simply asserting it (as Heidegger sometimes seems to do).

In what way can an intimacy hold between openness and concealment? In the *a-lēthic* picture given in 'Vom Wesen der Wahrheit', the two seemed to share nothing in common. Despite openness gaining its constitutive limit from concealing withdrawal, the two were presented as irreducibly distinct features of being. In *Beiträge*, the two are not irreducibly distinct, they can be reduced to one and the same operation of differentiation. To put it better, openness and concealment are each grounded in and originated by precisely the same operation of originary difference: the differentiation of difference from itself. At a first level, this constitutes a diagenic intimacy between each counterposed moment via their shared genetic ground. In terms of the logic of the event, difference differs from itself, simultaneously drawing itself out or breaching open openness and differing from or refusing to be that openness, that is, originating concealment. Though openness and concealment are thus 'sundered', each is constituted by the same differential operation and bears a structural reference to that operation. At a second, syngenic level, there is an intimacy between openness and concealment insofar as the structure of the one is co-extensive with that of the other, that is, insofar as each constitutes the limit providing the other's determinacy.

What then of strife? Openness and concealment are originated by the differential operation precisely insofar as it originates their difference. Their strife consists in the clearing or sundering of each from the other whereby each gains structural determination. This again works at two levels. At the primary, diagenic level, this strife is the differentiation of difference from itself by which it simultaneously draws itself out (breaching openness) and withdraws from that openness (originating concealment). At the secondary, syngenic level, openness and concealment each require the contradistinction this establishes from the other. Openness is structurally determined by its contrast with concealment and concealment by its contrast with openness. Their strife lies in both this constitutive contradistinction and the differentiation by which it is originated.

The structures of openness and concealment each bear a constitutive reference to the other, both at the syngenic level of contradistinction and the diagenic level of originary difference. Within this frame, the logic of difference satisfies the evaluative criterion in a rather elegant way. It shows the specific manner in which intimacy is structurally implied in strife and strife in intimacy, providing a genetic ground for both. Since the intimacy and strife involved in the structures of the essence of truth are simultaneously generated by one and the same differential operation and each is constitutively entailed in the other, I take this account to imply that Heidegger's terminology of intimacy and strife is one of ontological intensity. The differential logic at the heart of Heidegger's understanding of beyng as event and the essence of truth, generating the determinateness required for anything to be, entails that his ontology is an intensive ontology.

2.1 Two points of clarification

It is worth taking a pause to make two points clarifying this account. The first has to do with its relation to the overarching argument I have been making since Chapter 3 regarding the status of Heidegger's concept of truth; the second has to do with the ontological status of difference.

First, we have seen that the problematic of the essence of truth has a special importance in *Beiträge* because it provides the methodological pathway to an account of beyng as event. That is, thought first gains a properly grounded stance within the event by way of the problematic of truth. We can now say that it accomplishes this by opening up access to the logic of difference defining both the essence of truth and the 'decisional essence of beyng', that is, the event. 'The clearing for/of self-concealing' articulates the logic of difference in the register of truth. It allows us to unfold this logic using the terms of that register: clearing, concealing, openness, and so on. Exactly this provides the foothold needed. Even if Heidegger insufficiently elaborates originary differentiation, it is the genetic ground of the *a-lēthic* structures of truth. Thus, his account of the essence of truth in *Beiträge* is primarily differential, not *a-lēthic*. Interpretations of truth in *Beiträge* which remain within the *a-lēthic* framework are unable to access the differential logic and consequently botch Heidegger's account of the event.

Second, we can add a bit of clarity about the ontological status of originary difference by relating it to Heidegger's concepts of ground and time-space. As I've said, along with truth, ground and time-space are registers in terms of which he works out an account of beyng as event. The same logic of difference must generate the structures of all three. This means that we must not mistake originary difference to be within time or space, since it is originary of time-space. Likewise, it is not consequent upon the structures of ground, because it is originary of those very structures. It would be equally inaccurate to take difference to be eternal or to be transcendent to the domain of ground. No dichotomies according to which difference could fall on the side of metaphysical eternality or transcendence are at play here. Rather, time-space and the structures of ground arise from the operation of originary differentiation, which is immanent to them.

3 Heidegger's differential concept of event

Within the framework of Heidegger's ontology, the problematic of the essence of truth has provided a first properly grounded stance for thought in the evental structure of beyng, that is, in the logic of difference at the heart of the event. Beyng as event is the differentiation of difference from itself together with the ontological structures of the essence of truth, ground, and time-space thereby generated. The origination of these structures is the generation of the Da. Da-sein is the event's self-determination in those structures.

Even though the problematic of truth provides a grounding in the logic of the event, the event is not simply the clearing for/of self-concealing; 'truth' is only one of its registers (albeit methodologically distinctive). Nonetheless, the stance it provides in the logic of difference makes it possible to elaborate and define the structure of the event in the terminology of the event itself. Namely, the following modulations of the term 'Ereignis' are especially important: 'Er-eignis' (appropriating-event) or 'Er-eignung' (appropriating eventuation or ap-propriation) and 'Enteignis' (expropriation) or cognates thereof. These must be defined by the logic of difference. In part, they articulate the same movement of intensification and distension seen in the clearing for/of self-concealing, but they allow us to further elaborate the logic of difference in ways irreducible to the register of truth.

To define these terms, it is first necessary to make a few remarks about the role of *Enteignis* in *Beiträge*. In other texts from Heidegger's later period (the 1969 *Zur Sache des Denkens*, for example) the word 'Enteignis' appears as an essential correlate of 'Ereignis'. In *Beiträge* the term does not appear in its substantive form, but only the verbal cognate 'enteignet', and that quite rarely.[35] Rojcewicz and Vallega-Neu translate 'enteignet' as 'disappropriated'. Stambaugh translates 'Enteignis' as 'expropriation', which would suggest rendering 'enteignet' as 'expropriated'. I prefer the latter because it better conveys the 'out of' sense of the German prefix 'ent-' and because the alternative, 'disappropriation', more strongly suggests that what it describes was previously proper, belonged as proper, or was first appropriated before being 'disappropriated'. This would make *Enteignis* secondary to or derivative of *Ereignis* (or more accurately, *Er-eignis*), which is a problem because in Heidegger's account, appropriation and expropriation are equiprimordial features of the logic of the event.

In *Beiträge*, both uses of 'enteignet' describe the forgottenness or abandonment of beyng characteristic of human existence and the historical framework of metaphysics. Yet, as I began to explore in Chapter 2, this human or historical errancy is a derivative configuration of the ontological distortion at work in the event's operations of appropriation and expropriation. Heidegger addresses this distortion in terms of 'Un-wahrheit' or 'un-truth', the 'Un-wesen' or 'distorted essence' of truth, and the 'Unwesen des Seyns' or 'distorted essence of beyng'.[36] It is this *Unwesen* that sets the stage for human or historical errancy. Despite the rarity of the term 'enteignet' in *Beiträge*, my elaboration of the event will give it a central role. This is because the structure Heidegger elsewhere describes in terms of 'Enteignis' is very much present in *Beiträge*, but simply in other terms: along with *Unwesen*, *Vergessenheit* (forgottenness), and *Verlassenheit* (abandonment) are, for example, 'Weg-sein' (being-away), 'Befremdung' (alienation), 'Un-grund' (distorted ground), self-concealing, and so on.[37] Using 'Enteignis' or 'expropriation' allows me to keep the focus on the most originary sense of what these describe. 'Expropriation' designates constitutive alienation from propriety, which I will explain momentarily.

Beyng is *Ereignis*, the event, which at the most originary level occurs essentially (*west*) as the differentiation of difference from itself. As seen in terms of the essence of truth, the logic of difference entails the event's self-determination or intensification, which is precisely the origination of the Da, the structural distension captured in the term 'Da-sein'. In the language of the event, Heidegger describes this intensification as an appropriation accomplished by beyng: 'the "there" is appropriated [ereignet] by beyng itself'.[38] In contrast to earlier texts like 'Vom Wesen der Wahrheit' that understood Da-sein in relation to human existence, in *Beiträge*

> Da-sein moves (though not localizable anywhere) away from the relation to the human being and reveals itself as the 'between' [Zwischen] which is developed [entfaltet] by beyng itself so as to become the open domain for beings that protrude into it.[39]

For Heidegger, the intensification of the event or origination of the Da is an appropriation, and one occurring at the most originary level of beyng. But what sense can there be in calling this an appropriation? It is not the case that one pre-existing thing takes over another to make it its own. Rather, according to Heidegger what occurs is the origination of 'das Eigentum' – the 'domain of what is proper' or 'structure of propriety' – that I began to discuss in Chapter 2. *Das Eigentum* is the most basic form of ontological determinateness described in *Beiträge*. As he puts it,

> Da-sein is the axis [Wendungspunkt] in the turning of the event, the self-opening center of the counterplay between call [Zuruf] and belonging [Zugehörigkeit]. Da-sein is the 'domain of what is proper' [Eigentum], understood in analogy with the 'domain of a prince' [Fürsten-tum], the sovereign center of the appropriating eventuation [Er-eignung] as the assignment [Zueignung], of the ones who belong [Zu-gehörigen], to the event and at the same time to themselves: becoming a self.[40]

We know already from Chapter 2 that for Heidegger 'becoming a self' at this level of the ontology is not the origination of a cogito, human self, or any other self ascribed to a being ('selfhood is more originary than any I or thou or we').[41] Rather, what is at stake is the generation of the ontological structures without which beings could not be at all, the origination of finitude. This is nothing like a production from the infinite, but rather the self-intensification of the structurally self-problematising differential logic of the event. Appropriation is an operation of the event whereby an ontological structure of propriety is originated, a structure such that all that falls within its range (*die Zu-gehörigen*) bears an assignment (*Zueignung*) to that structure or, in the case of that structure itself, to that whereby propriety is originated. And this is all that 'becoming a self' refers to at this level. Though Heidegger is vague about what he means by 'Zueignung' or 'assignment', I take it to designate a structural reference constitutive of all that falls within the range of propriety, including the basic structure of propriety itself. To be precise, then, propriety at this level is an ontological structure such that all its aspects are constituted by structural reference to some other aspect, namely, to that ontological operation whereby they are originated.

Similarly, all that is secondarily constituted on the basis of propriety (that is, beings) bears such reference both to that structure and, in turn, to the ontological operation of appropriation. To help make sense of this point, it can be translated into the terminology of truth by recalling that beings like humans, pine trees, and rocks are constituted on the basis of openness (together with concealment), while openness is constituted on the basis of the differential operation of clearing. Thus, such beings bear constitutive structural reference both to openness and in turn to clearing. The three are arranged along a diagenic axis.

For the sake of clarity, it will be useful to answer the following question: at the most fundamental level of the event, what is required for there to be a domain of propriety at all? On the one hand, a structural distension of the event must occur. Without a distension differentiating one part from another, there could be no constitutive reference, but only simple identity, or, since Heidegger's ontology does not maintain an ontological priority of identity, utter indeterminateness or lack of finitude. On the other hand, the parts differentiated in distension must bear a constitutive reference or assignment to the operation of the event whereby distension is enabled to occur, that is, whereby appropriation is accomplished. These two characteristics – distension and constitutive reference – are genetically inseparable and articulate the most basic determinateness of beyng. Their origination marks the logical transition of indeterminate difference to determinate difference.

I would like to make two quick asides here on the basis of these requirements. First, if there is no structure of constitutive reference ontologically prior to appropriation while at the same time an operation of the event originates such a structure, this means that that operation is liminal – it is simultaneously intrinsic to and in excess of appropriation. That is, an operation of the event is ontologically prior to, irreducible to, and yet constitutive for appropriation. I return in a moment to a more precise account of the excess involved here.

Second, regarding Heidegger's concepts of essence and ground, recall that he understands essence to be that which is most proper to something or which enables it to be whatever it is, that is, its ontologically constitutive ground. For the terminology of essence to make sense, there has to be a distension or disjoint inherent to whatever it is applied to whereby more essential aspects are differentiated from less essential or more derivative ones. This is seen, for example, in the relation discussed in Chapter 4 between 'that which is true' and 'the essence of truth'. Accordingly, the framework of essence can be established only through the origination of something (1) differentiated from the operation whereby it was originated, but (2) bearing constitutive reference to that operation (to that which enables it to be). Likewise, recall that Heidegger understands something's ground to be the ontological structures enabling it to be. The relation between ground and that which is grounded can be established only in the same manner as the framework of essence. This means that as an articulation of the origination of constitutive structural distension and reference, Heidegger's concept of appropriation describes the origination of the very frameworks of essence and ground.

Returning to Heidegger's concept of appropriation, it is one thing to state that it is an operation of the event whereby propriety is originated and it is another to explain how this occurs, that is, to give a genetic account. So, how does appropriation occur? Just as should be expected given the differential conception of beyng, Heidegger claims that as event, 'the essence of beyng essentially occurs in the ap-propriation [Er-eignung] of de-cision [Ent-scheidung]'.[42] That is, appropriation is accomplished by and as decision – the differentiation of difference from itself. As Vallega-Neu puts it, this operation is 'the differencing, i.e., the de-cision in which en-owning [Er-eignis/appropriating event] occurs'.[43]

Without the differential logic, this claim seems rather mysterious. But with it, we can make good sense of what Heidegger means. Beyng as event is the differentiation of difference from itself. Difference refuses to become identical with itself, that is, it differs from itself. By differing from itself, difference distends. In the register of truth, this differentiation is called 'clearing'. The distension it generates is the origination of a field such that some aspect of difference is differentiated from some other aspect. That is, rather than pure indeterminateness, difference generates determinateness or finitude by generating aspects of itself defined in their difference from one another: *this* distended dimension of difference is difference that comes to be defined via the origination of contrast from *that* difference that refuses to be it. But with this we find exactly the structural elements just listed that go into a domain of propriety: we have (1) distension or the distinction of aspects of a structure, namely, the aspects of difference that are distinguished from one another, and (2) structural reference constitutive of each of those aspects. Put another way, we have the generation of an aspect of difference that is distended from another aspect of difference, while that generative process is exactly the self-differentiation of each aspect from 'itself' and in turn from the other. Thus, each aspect is determined by the other such that it bears a structural, constitutive reference to the other, that is, to that which enables it to be.

This provides a genetic explanation of the domain of propriety based on the logic of difference. In this account, the differentiation of difference from itself can be said to enact appropriation in two essentially correlated senses: (1) it is the origination of a domain of propriety, and (2) since that domain is constituted by nothing other than determinate difference, it is the appropriation – in the sense of taking over – of difference in a determinate, intensive structure. Taking these senses together, appropriation is the self-determination of beyng. It will be worth keeping in mind that this is the same movement that the problematic of truth described. In terms of truth, the structure of distension is the field of openness and the event's self-appropriation or origination of a domain of propriety is the origination of that openness.

What, then, of *Enteignis* or expropriation – the event's origination of a structural alienation from propriety? To make sense (genetically) of this, we can begin by looking at the form it takes in the register of truth. In terms of truth, openness is correlative with concealment. Not only are openness and concealment generated by the same operation of the event, but each is structurally dependent upon the other, from which it gains contrast. We can see this by looking at each in turn. On the one hand, *concealment* is the event's self-refusal from the openness it originates and therefore it is defined in contradistinction from openness. On the other, *openness* is the field of the event's distension, but it is originated by the event's concealing withdrawal or refusal, in contradistinction from which openness gains determinacy. In terms of truth, if openness is a domain of propriety, then concealment (the event's refusal or withdrawal from that propriety) is expropriation – the genesis of a constitutive alienation from propriety. In this case, the event's self-appropriation as openness entails its simultaneous self-expropriation as concealment. In other words, precisely the same operation by which the event self-determines in the structure of appropriation/openness entails the self-determination of the event in the structure of expropriation/concealment. Each is genetically bound to the other.

But beyng as event is not reducible to the framework of truth; expropriation, like appropriation, must be given a systematic definition in terms of the logic of difference, not simply cast as concealment. How? Beyng as event is self-differentiation – the differentiation of difference from itself. By differing from itself, difference distends. This distension is the origination of a domain of propriety, that is, distension is appropriation.

But appropriation is accomplished only by the refusal or withdrawal of difference from itself. Expropriation is exactly this differentiation of difference *from* itself (as appropriation). But in expropriation, that dimension of difference that differs from appropriation becomes determined: it becomes endowed with a structural reference to appropriation, namely, one precisely of alienation from or of *not* being proper to appropriation. Expropriation is difference that repels or withdraws from the appropriation of the domain of propriety, thereby enacting the distension of difference that constitutes that appropriation, but also gaining a determinateness of its own, namely as bearing a constitutive reference to that which it refuses to be (propriety). Expropriation is the origination of structural alienation from propriety.

Defining the concepts of appropriation and expropriation by the logic of difference gives us an account of the basic structure of the event in Heidegger's ontology. In particular, it explains how the event self-intensifies or originates determinateness, finitude, or the Da of Da-sein. Taken together, the genesis of appropriation and expropriation is the genesis of the logic of determinateness or logic of the world in Heidegger's ontology. But the event has another important feature. Earlier in Chapter 2, I emphasised that the event's differential logic must include an aspect irreducible to or in excess over the logic of appropriation and expropriation and that this renders evental differentiation liminal in character. In *Beiträge*, Heidegger refers to this excess in the terminology of the *Ab-grund* or abyss, which I return to in Chapter 6. For now, it is sufficient to show why this excess is necessary and how it fits into the logic already seen. I will again make the point first in the terminology of truth where it is more easily recognisable and then in the terminology of the event itself.

Above, I looked at appropriation and expropriation sequentially. Yet, to make sense of the excess involved in the event it is necessary to keep in mind that they are structurally equiprimordial. Appropriation and expropriation are generated simultaneously by the very same operation of difference, each forming a portion of the logic that unfolds. Each is partially defined in contradistinction from the other and thus is constitutively co-dependent upon it. This means that appropriation and expropriation are structurally continuous with one another; the logic of one can be traced seamlessly to that of the other. And this is so via both their constitutive co-dependence and shared genesis.

In terms of the problematic of truth, the shared genesis of appropriation and expropriation is the clearing for/of self-concealing. The clearing for/of self-concealing is evental differentiation insofar as it originates the *a-lēthic* structures of openness and concealment. But since these structures are generated by pure difference, it is necessary that such difference is ontologically prior and irreducible to them. It is only as a consequence of difference differing from itself that the clearing for/of self-concealing is enacted at all. As prior, this primal difference can have no character of openness or concealment.[44] The origination of determinateness in those structures relies upon difference that differs from or is deferred beyond even its own logic of self-determination, that is, difference that is necessarily in excess over the clearing for/of self-concealing.

We can now translate this into the terminology of the event. In it, the differentiation of difference from itself is the shared genesis of appropriation and expropriation. But this genesis is possible only because beyng as event, at its most primal level, is pure difference or differentiation. The operation by which the event self-determines is consequent upon difference that is ontologically prior to that operation and that must exceed it for it to occur. In expropriation, for instance, the determination of difference in a structural contrast from propriety is dependent upon the fact that beyng is *difference*. Only because beyng is difference does it self-differ from propriety. Such difference, ontologically prior to determination in appropriation and expropriation, can have none of the determinate structures characteristic of them (distension and constitutive reference). The origination of determinateness in those structures relies upon difference that differs or is deferred beyond even its own logic of self-determination, that is, difference that is necessarily in excess over the logic of appropriation and expropriation.

Thus, even though appropriation and expropriation are essential dimensions of the event, the event appropriates and expropriates only by a differing of difference that is in excess over those very processes. The event's origination of a logic of determinateness entails an emission of difference from that logic. For terminological clarity, I will call this excess 'primal difference'. Since primal difference is not the property of the logic of determinateness (the reverse being the case), I will call the differentiation characteristic of primal difference anterior to that logic 'primal expropriation'. Particularly after *Beiträge*, this is what I take Heidegger to designate with the term 'Abschied'. Primal difference and primal expropriation should be distinguished from what I have called 'originary' difference and 'originary' expropriation' or just 'expropriation'. These refer to the most primordial aspects of difference or the event insofar as it is involved in the *origination* of the logic of determinateness, that is, of the Da. As noted, the interminable, inexhaustible primal expropriation of difference can alternatively be called 'the abyss'. The event, then, must be said to include not only the logic of appropriation and expropriation, but also the abyss of differentiation exceeding even the structures it differentiates and thereby generating them.

4 The genesis of distortion in the structure of the event: the *Un-wesen* of truth

With the basic differential logic of the event outlined, we can now turn to the theory of ontological distortion in Heidegger's *Beiträge*. In Chapter 2, I discussed ways that distortion and alienation are active at the historical level of his ontology, especially in the forms of machination, representation, and lived experience. Those forms contribute to the historical framework of metaphysics that the historical event would undermine. If historical distortion and alienation are the types of things that can in principle be resolved (even if only incrementally), ontological distortion cannot. It is an ineliminable structure of beyng or the event. As noted, Heidegger addresses this in terms of 'Un-wahrheit' or 'un-truth', the 'Un-wesen' or 'distorted essence' of truth, and the 'Unwesen des Seyns' or 'distorted essence of beyng'.[45] Each addresses the same form of distortion in the structure of beyng.

Ontological distortion is the ground enabling the historical, existential, and conceptual distortion entailed in the framework of metaphysics. Because of this, a full explanation of ontological distortion would offer the ground for a Heideggerian radical critique of metaphysics in the sense I defined in Chapter 2. I will not do this here; my goal is simply to establish the basic form of ontological distortion, since it is an essential element in Heidegger's ontological concept of event. In Chapter 2, I also defined distortion as the process by which something constitutes a self-obfuscation or, in cases where two things are in a diagenic relation, the process by which one obfuscates the other. We can now see how this works at the level of beyng as event. In this context, distortion is the curvature of beyng that makes Heidegger's ontology a curved ontology, not a flat one nor one vertically organised by metaphysical transcendence. It is an ineliminable curvature generated in the event whereby certain parts of the logic of the event are obfuscated from other parts. I will approach this in terms of the distorted essence of truth.

In Heidegger's account, the distorted essence of truth is manifested in originary 'Verstellung' (distortion), 'Irre' (errancy), or 'Anschein' (semblance) and forms the basic structure on which human and historical errancy take hold.[46] While the latter are generally undesirable and often harmful, ontological distortion is not a failure of beyng and must not be taken in a pejorative sense. It need not and cannot be eradicated or excised. Distortion is a structurally essential aspect of the event and is 'proper' to its logic of determinateness. In Heidegger's words, 'the *distorted essence* belongs intrinsically to the essence [of truth]'.[47] How so?

Heidegger offers little direct explanation of this ontological distortion, but a good account can be pieced together. If the distorted essence belongs intrinsically to the essence of truth, this means that the essence of truth entails its own distortion; that distortion must arise as a constitutive aspect of the essence of truth, not as a result of extrinsic factors. The essence of truth is the event articulated in the register of truth, that is, the logic of difference elaborated in the clearing for/of self-concealing. Since its structures are generated through the eventual logic of difference, the same logic must simultaneously generate ontological distortion. To emphasise, since the structures in question are ontologically prior to representation and even to beings that think, ontological distortion is not an error in representation, judgement, or any other epistemological function. Moreover, since it is prior to worlds of beings, it cannot be reduced to distortion arising from the relations of beings. Ontological distortion characterises beyng or the essence of truth itself, the differential clearing for/of self-concealing.

Heidegger associates the distorted essence of truth with the 'negativity [Nichtigkeit] of being' or, more precisely, the 'negativity [Nichtung] of the "*there*" [*Da*]', since truth is beyng insofar as beyng is determined or projected into the 'there' or 'Da'.[48] It is common in Heidegger scholarship to understand being (and beyng) to have an irreducibly negative dimension and to understand that negativity in terms of λήθη, refusal, lack, or concealing withdrawal. If beyng as event is interpreted within the *a-lēthic* framework rather than the differential one, that makes good sense. For, in that view λήθη is an irreducible character of beyng (perhaps even the most originary one). Since λήθη presents itself in seemingly negative forms it would appear that beyng has an essentially negative character.

However, if, as I have argued, the *a-lēthic* structures are grounded by the logic of difference, negativity cannot be an irreducible character of beyng; it can only be a derived one. Indeed, Heidegger makes an important claim that is consistent with just such a view: the negativity involved in the distorted essence of truth is 'by no means as a sheer lack' but a 'resistance' ('Widerständiges').[49] I take this to challenge the common view about Heidegger just mentioned. Heidegger's position here is strikingly similar to one Deleuze takes in his own attempt to develop an affirmative concept of difference in itself in *Différence et répétition*. Namely, Deleuze argues that 'difference implies the negative, and allows itself to lead to contradiction, only to the extent that its subordination to the identical is maintained'.[50] In this context, Deleuze is addressing Hegel, but the point stands with respect to Heidegger. Heidegger's conception of difference can be cast in terms of the negative only if it is considered within the framework of his dyadic oppositional concepts like ἀλήθεια and λήθη, openness and concealment, or appropriation and expropriation, that is, insofar as it is understood in terms of an already-established identity of these terms that are defined in contradistinction from one another. In that case, one can play the role of the positive and the other the negative. In contrast, if difference is posited as diagenically anterior to and generative of these distinctions themselves, its ontological status is outside the domain of the positive-negative dichotomy. This is precisely what we find in Heidegger's move beyond the *a-lēthic* framework.

Indeed, this shift is evident even at the more derivative, historical level of alienation. In Heidegger's view, the abandonment by being that is to be remedied by the historical event 'has arisen from the distorted essence of beyng [Unwesen des Seyns] through machination'.[51] When he asks, 'whence this distorted essence?', he answers, 'hardly from the fact that beyng is permeated with negativity; on the contrary!'[52] The different modes of the abandonment by being 'are merely emanations [Ausstrahlungen] from an intricate and obdurate dissimulation [Verstellung] of the essence of beyng, especially of its fissure [Zerklüftung]'.[53] At the level of historical alienation, this describes the obfuscation and 'forgetting' of the inherently self-problematising logic of the event.

Heidegger's association of ontological distortion with negativity thus does not entail that distortion results from a primal negativity of beyng, but that negativity is a form of resistance generated by distortion. Ontological distortion is a feature of the logic of the event that generates, but is irreducible to, the λήθη often interpreted to mean that beyng is essentially negative.

What, then, is the nature of this distortion? For the reasons just given, it must be defined in terms of the logic of the event. We will also need to elaborate on the notion of expropriation a bit. In the logic of the event, each moment of the structural dyads produced – appropriation and expropriation or openness and concealment – entails a constitutive contrast from the other. Put genetically, the origination of one entails the dynamic expulsion of the other. More precisely, this is an expropriation of the difference composing the contrasting dyadic structure – an expulsion of whatever difference differs from the structure generated. This form of expropriation can be clarified by looking at it from the perspective of each 'side' of the structural dyads. First, let's take the perspective of the domain of propriety or openness. From its perspective, its own origination is dependent upon an expulsion or expropriation of difference: openness gains no determinacy without the difference differing from it which it comes to be counterposed against; the same goes for the domain of propriety. In each case, the difference expropriated is not simply indeterminate, for it is difference that differs *from* the openness or propriety generated. In other words, the difference expropriated gains a distinctive determination exactly insofar as it is as a structure of alienation from propriety. Second, let's take the perspective of the domain of concealment or of 'alienation from propriety'. From its perspective, its own origination is equally dependent upon an expulsion or expropriation of difference, but here the difference expropriated is nothing other than that determined in the structure of propriety or openness.

The important point here is that the domains of propriety and alienation from propriety are equiprimordial; the logic of one should not be given priority relative to the other: they are generated by precisely the same differential operation. The domain of alienation from propriety is no more consequent upon propriety than propriety upon it. In fact, from the perspective of each side of the structural dyad, it itself is a domain of propriety and the other is a domain of alienation from propriety. Since the structural elements of the domain of alienation from propriety are *proper to it*, the domain of alienation has a certain propriety in its own terms. It is the 'alienated' side of the structural dyad only insofar as it is defined from the perspective of the other one. Nonetheless, expropriation or the genesis of the domain of alienation from propriety (in its own propriety) entails the expulsion of that difference that is determined in the form of openness or as the domain of propriety; that is, it entails an expropriation of just such difference. Thus, in the event's origination of the logic of determinateness, that is, its appropriation and expropriation, each of these structures becomes what it is by way of an expropriation of the other. Stated in terms of truth, the generation of openness entails an expropriation of concealment and the generation of concealment entails an expropriation of openness. Stated in terms of the logic of difference, originary difference self-appropriates as each moment – openness and concealment – in a way co-determined by the expropriation of the other.

How, though, does this help explain distortion? The answer is that each side of the dyadic structures entails the structural obfuscation of the other; it constitutes a form of distortion or semblance. From its own perspective, the logic of the one *seems* to exclude the logic of the other and vice versa. In terms of truth, neither openness nor concealment is adequate to the essence of truth; each entails a blind spot with respect to the other. But this is exactly the constitution of a structural distortion: from any point within the logic of determinateness some aspect of that logic is obfuscated. This obfuscation or distortion is an inescapable aspect of the constitution of each moment of that logic, since each moment gains its structural determinateness through an expropriation of difference in the form of the other.

However, exactly because each 'side' of these dyads is essentially correlated with the other (bearing a constitutive structural reference to the other) and because they are generated by one and the same logic of difference, there is, in fact, continuity throughout their logics: together appropriation or openness and expropriation or concealment form a continuous logic of determinateness. Yet each obfuscates not only the other but, by that very fact, aspects of the logic of difference whereby it itself is originated. This means that structural distortion is proper or essential to the logic of determinateness. The logic of determinateness cannot be generated except in such a way that entails distortion. *This* is how we should understand Heidegger's claim that the distorted essence of truth belongs intrinsically to the essence of truth.

Another interesting conclusion follows from this. Namely, the genesis of the logic of determinateness by the evental logic of difference entails that all aspects of the determinateness generated bear a structural alienation from evental difference, that is, from what enables them to be, their essence, or their ground. The genesis of the logic of determinateness is the genesis of the very distinction between the more essential and the less essential or between the grounding and the grounded. This distinction arises exactly with ontological distortion, that is, with the distorted essence of truth or of beyng. It supports the entire diagenic programme of Heidegger's ontology up to the point of articulating beyng as event. His philosophy at every diagenic level is an effort to grapple with the ontological conundrum that distortion is essential to being.

Finally, resistance: if Heidegger claims that the essential negativity of beyng is resistance, I take resistance to be nothing other than the tension held in the logic of determinateness, the tension held between moments of appropriation and expropriation, simultaneously consistent and inconsistent with one another, or what he refers to as the 'intimately conflictual essence of truth'.[54] For Heidegger, negativity is not an *irreducible* character of beyng, it is produced by the excess of difference. This, I maintain, places him closer to Spinoza and Deleuze and farther from Hegel, Derrida, and 'deconstructive' Heideggerians. The famous negativity characterising Heidegger's thought is ultimately derived from an excess in the differential logic of the event.

By way of concluding this chapter, let me review the argument that it has brought to a head. Most interpreters take Heidegger's concept of truth in *Beiträge* to remain within the framework of the second stage of the *a-lēthic* account that I described in Chapter 3. Since it is by way of the problematic of the essence of truth that an account of beyng as event is to be developed, this leads to an understanding of the event within the *a-lēthic* framework. That, however, is a mistake which results in disjointed or mystical accounts of the ontology Heidegger presents. In contrast, as I have argued, he pushes his ontology to a new diagenic stage by enquiring into the ground whence the *a-lēthic* structures of truth are generated. This ground is originary difference or the differentiation of difference from itself. 'The clearing for/of self-concealing' articulates the logic of difference insofar as difference originates the *a-lēthic* structures. Consequently, Heidegger's account of the essence of truth in *Beiträge* is not primarily *a-lēthic* but differential. By pursuing the problematic of truth, thought gains a grounded stance in the differential logic of the event, which enables an elaboration of that logic, first in the terminology of truth and then in that of the event.

According to the logic of difference underwriting or expressed in Heidegger's ontology in *Beiträge*, beyng as event is the differentiation of difference from itself, together with the logic of determinateness this generates. The logic of determinateness is the logic of beyng's self-intensification, distension, and elaboration, that is, the origination of the Da in 'Da-sein'. This logic is articulated not only in terms of truth, but also in the properly evental terminology of appropriation and expropriation. Yet the logic of the event includes an excess of difference over the logic of determinateness, which makes the event liminal with respect to determination. As such, beyng as event is irreducible to appropriation and expropriation. Additionally, the event's self-determination entails an essential structural distortion, which is the basis for human and historical errancy, the metaphysical regime of representation, and the famous 'forgetting' of beyng that these involve.

Notes

1. GA65 465/366, 87/70.
2. GA65 250/197. Or again: 'The "ontological difference" is a passageway which becomes unavoidable if the necessity of asking the basic question is to be made visible on the basis of the guiding question' (GA65 467/367).
3. GA65 465/366.
4. Ibid.
5. Ibid.
6. GA65 466/366–7.
7. GA65 474/373.
8. GA65 470/370.
9. GA65 455/359. Beistegui's use of 'being' here is not meant in the technical sense I distinguished from 'beyng', but simply that of the central topic of Heidegger's enquiry.
10. Beistegui, *Truth and Genesis* 109.
11. Ibid.
12. Beistegui, *Truth and Genesis* 111.
13. GA65 87/69.
14. *HCP* 109.
15. GA65 87/69.
16. GA65 88, 87/70, my italics.
17. GA65 88/70.
18. McNeill, 'The Time of *Contributions to Philosophy*' 138.

19. *HCP* 111.
20. GA65 88/70.
21. GA71 122/104.
22. GA71 124/106.
23. GA71 123/105.
24. GA71 125/106, italics removed.
25. GA71 126/107.
26. GA71 126/108.
27. GA71 127/108.
28. GA71 129/109, italics removed.
29. Ibid., italics removed.
30. GA65 349/276.
31. 'Refusal' is not used in a voluntaristic sense here. In the context of the relation of concealment to openness, I use 'refusal' to describe the fact that what withdraws from openness is inherently not open: it 'refuses' to be assimilated to openness. This should be explained in terms of originary difference. In that context, 'refusal' should be understood to describe the movement of difference insofar as difference *differs* or repels from itself (if it did not do this, it would not be originary difference of the type Heidegger suggests at all).
32. GA65 88/70.
33. GA65 342/271.
34. Such difference is the Heideggerian version of what Meillassoux refers to as 'hyper-Chaos' in *After Finitude*. Likewise, the origination of the structures of truth articulates the origination of what Meillassoux refers to as 'contingency'.
35. It is found once at the end of §57 and again at the end of §118.
36. GA65 345/273, 347/274, 107/85.
37. GA65 324/256, 347/275, 380/300.
38. GA65 299/236.
39. Ibid.
40. GA65 311/246–7, italics removed.
41. GA65 320/253, italics removed.
42. GA65 95/75.
43. *HCP* 113.
44. This primal difference in Heidegger's ontology takes a similar logical position to the pure or immemorial past in Deleuze's three syntheses of time.
45. GA65 345/273, 347/274, 107/85.
46. GA65 347/274–5.
47. GA65 347/274.
48. GA65 347/274, 348/275, correction of translators' omission of italics on 'there'.
49. GA65 356/281.
50. Deleuze, *Différence et répétition* 1/xix.
51. GA65 107/85.
52. Ibid.
53. GA65 118/94.
54. GA65 348/275.

Chapter 6

Event, Ground, and Time-Space

Time-space is the abyss [Abgrund] of the ground – i.e., the abyss of the truth of being.[1]

Truth, ground, and time-space are three key registers in terms of which Heidegger works out the nature of beyng as event in *Beiträge*, that is, the ontological sense of 'event'. They overlap one another in important ways, yet none is reducible to the others. The heart of the event is pure difference – difference that is prior to and forms the genetic ground of any determinate 'things' that have differences between them. Indeed, it is diagenically prior to the very ontological difference between being and beings. As I argued in the previous chapter, the event is the differentiation of pure difference from itself together with the ontological structures originated thereby and the primal difference that exceeds those structures. I have described the origination of these structures as the origination of a 'logic of determinateness'. In the terminology of the event, the logic of determinateness is that of originary appropriation and expropriation, which can be described alternatively in terms of truth, ground, and time-space. The event's self-determination in this logic is the generation of the 'Da' expressed in the term 'Da-sein'. In other words, it is the event's self-intensification or distension and elaboration, forming the basic ontological structures enabling worlds of beings to be.

In this chapter I build upon my reconstruction of Heidegger's ontological concept of event vis-à-vis its connection to ground and time-space. The problematics of ground and time-space articulate the event in a way structurally parallel to that of truth, providing additional registers for elaborating the logic of the event. The origin of ground and time-space is the event's logic of difference, which is immanent to them. Like truth, they form aspects of the event's logic of determinateness. To put it another way, ground and time-space are 'grounded' in the differential logic of the event, while that logic is elaborated in terms of them. Heidegger's accounts of ground and (*especially*) time-space are extraordinarily dense and often opaque, employing a number of unusual terms. Explaining the two will require a highly technical analysis of some of the passages in which he presents them, particularly when it comes to time-space.

As we've seen, there are two main senses of 'ground' in *Beiträge*: (1) 'Er-gründung' or 'fathoming the ground' which describes the ways alienated human existence regrounds itself in beyng or the event, and (2) 'gründender Grund' or 'grounding ground', which describes the inherent grounding character of the event. In Chapter 2, I dealt with the former; in this chapter I focus on the latter, *gründender Grund*, which has three main modalities: 'Ab-grund' or 'abyssal ground', 'Ur-grund' or 'primordial ground', and 'Un-grund' or 'distorted ground'. I then turn to time-space. When treating this topic, I first look at a problem Heidegger locates in traditional representations of time and space, which prompts his analysis of time-space. I then provide a basic definition of time-space in terms of the differential logic of the event. This enables me to reconstruct the cryptic technical terms he uses to describe time-space, ultimately leading to an account of what he calls 'Entrückung' or 'transporting' and 'Berückung' or 'captivation', which are terms for the event's origination of temporality and spatiality.

I The event and ground

> The more originarily we master the essence of truth, the more pressing the problem of ground must become.[2]

In *Beiträge*, 'ground' is one of the essential registers of the event. The structures and operations of ground compose structures and operations of the event. Sometimes Heidegger makes this point by saying that, as with truth, the event essentially occurs (*west*) as ground. In fact, some structures of the essence of truth double as structures of ground – 'ground' and 'truth' both articulate the event, but in different conceptual registers. Heidegger does not always keep these registers strictly parsed. Sometimes he describes grounding characteristics of truth and sometimes aspects of the essence of truth that belong to ground. The overarching reason is that at the level of the logic of the event, both articulate the event's origination of the Da or the logic of determinateness and certain structures of that logic. The same is the case with time-space. One reason I find Heidegger's concept of ground so fascinating is its role in the logic of determinateness: not only is 'ground' a concept used to explain how one thing supports, leads to, or constitutes another, but in a broader sense he also uses it to explain why beyng is such that it enables the resistance, thickness, or viscosity of the world. In terms I used in Chapter 5, the concept of ground contributes to the Heideggerian account of the event's self-intensification or coagulation and distension.

At a cursory level, the relation between the structures of the essence of truth (those comprised by the formulation 'the clearing for/of self-concealing') and those of ground can be specified in three ways. (1) The essence of truth grounds what is true: 'truth itself is that wherein what is true has its ground'.[3] In other words, the essence of truth serves as a ground enabling worlds of beings to be. (2) Consequently, an aspect of the essence of truth is a ground. That is, the character of grounding is proper to the essence of truth. Or, stated in terms of ground, part of the structure of ground involves or is co-extensive with the structure of the essence of truth. (3) Even though truth and ground are what they are (partially) in and through each other, neither is a subset of the other. Truth has its character of ground on the basis of 'that whereby the ground is a ground, i.e. . . . the event', not on the basis of ground itself.[4] Ground and truth are partially co-extensive because they are both originated through the same operations of the event. Moreover, just as 'truth' entails a variety of structures that work at different diagenic levels, so does 'ground'.

As mentioned, despite Heidegger's widespread use of the concept of ground, some scholars are hesitant to associate it too closely with his ontology. The fear seems to be that the terminology of ground is metaphysical and thus cannot properly be used in Heidegger's core problematic. It is sometimes suggested that his discussions of ground are either restricted to historical commentary (on Leibniz, for example) or to deconstructive analysis. As I have argued, this is quite mistaken. It will be useful, though, to summarise briefly what ground is *not* for Heidegger, that is, how his concept is distinguished from a metaphysical one. First, for Heidegger the grounding character of beyng is neither a ὑπόθεσις nor a condition of possibility, and thus neither κοινόν nor ὑποκείμενον.[5] Ground is not a fully determinate substratum, foundation, substance, or principle conceived on the basis of the time determination of presence. I discussed the reasons why ground is not a condition of possibility in Chapter 4, section 1: defining ground as a condition would limit it to the relation between condition and conditioned (where beings are the conditioned), thus defining ground within the framework of *Seiendheit* and rendering it metaphysical.

The two main registers of ground in *Beiträge* mirror two major movements coursing through the text.[6] The first, *Er-gründung* or fathoming

the ground, correlates with the movement of regrounding human existence insofar as it has become alienated from beyng. Methodologically
speaking, this is the movement of *Grundlegung* involved in radical science. In Chapter 2, I defined Heidegger's historical concept of event in
terms of the transformative rupture in the historical framework of metaphysics that this movement holds the promise to accomplish. The text's
second major movement aims to work out the nature of beyng as event
independently of any relation it has to beings. In other words, it aims
to think the event on its own terms (the ontological concept of event).
'Das ursprüngliche Gründen des Grundes' ('the original grounding of the
ground') or the 'gründende Grund' ('grounding ground') correlates with
this second movement.[7] In this context, Heidegger develops a technical
formulation for grounding ground as 'das Sichverbergen im tragenden
Durchragen' ('self-concealing in a protruding that bears').[8] Determining
what this means will rest upon clarifying the different modalities of *gründender Grund*: *Ab-grund*, *Ur-grund*, and *Un-grund*.

The different modes of *Er-gründung* or fathoming the ground that I
have discussed are enabled by the structures of ground essential to the
event. That is, the modes of *Er-gründung* are themselves grounded in the
more originary *gründende Grund*. Preliminarily, Heidegger understands
gründender Grund to be that which enables what is grounded on it to be.
Recall that in 'Vom Wesen der Wahrheit' he casts ground as 'Grund der
Ermöglichung' (ground of enabling); in *Beiträge*, this is sometimes carried
over in the tentative formulation, 'Grund der Möglichkeit' (ground of
possibility).[9] However, in *Beiträge*, *Grund der Möglichkeit* is understood
within the framework of the *Grundfrage* (How does beyng essentially
occur?), while in 'Vom Wesen der Wahrheit' *Grund der Ermöglichung*
was still tied to the *Leitfrage* (What is the being of beings?) and thus
defined on the basis of its relation to beings. Although Heidegger holds
that 'ground of possibility' 'is still a metaphysical *expression*', he modifies
it such that 'it is *thought* out of the abyssal and steadfast *belongingness*
[*Zugehörigkeit*]' characteristic of beyng.[10] In Chapter 5, I showed that
Heidegger's 'Zugehörigkeit' ('belongingness') is defined in terms of the
way the event generates a domain of propriety (*Eigentum*) such that all
that falls within the range of that domain bears a constitutive structural
reference or assignment (*Zueignung*) to that domain. Or, in the case of
the structures of the domain of propriety itself, belongingness describes
the constitutive structural reference they bear to that whereby propriety is
originated (the evental logic of difference). In other words, 'ground of possibility' is conceived on the basis of the genetic logic of structural reference
or the inherent grounding character of the event, and not derived on the
basis of a relation between that character and what is grounded.

Nonetheless, it is true that this kind of ground is also that which is most proper to what is grounded. In this sense, ground is tied to Heidegger's notion of essence (in 'Vom Wesen der Wahrheit', 'essence' meant 'ground of enabling' or 'ground of the inner possibility'). The essence of something is the ontological ground enabling it to be. This is not to resort to a circular definition of ground in terms of essence and essence in terms of ground, but to indicate that the terminologies of 'ground' and 'essence' are both used to describe aspects of the same thing. As I argued in Chapter 5, section 3, this same thing is the relation whereby one thing is generated by and bears constitutive structural reference to another thing, while this type of relation is established by the event's structure of propriety.

In *Beiträge*, the technical formulation of ground as 'self-concealing in a protruding that bears' applies at the level of *gründender Grund*. 'Ab-grund' ('abyssal ground'), 'Ur-grund' ('primordial ground'), and 'Un-grund' ('distorted ground') are the three main modes of this register of ground, and they articulate different structures of the event and its essential unfolding via the structures of truth and time-space.[11] In the core discussion of these terms (which closely ties them to time-space), Heidegger provides a condensed statement of the relations between these modes of ground and also of their relation to truth:

> *Truth grounds as the truth of the event.* The event, grasped from the perspective of truth as ground, is therefore the *primordial ground.* The primordial ground opens itself up, as what is self-concealing, only in the *abyssal ground.* Yet the abyss is completely disguised through the *distorted ground.*[12]

In what follows, I unpack these terms and relations, defining them via the differential logic of the event. I begin with *Ab-grund*, then turn to *Ur-grund*, and finally move to *Un-grund*. In brief, Heidegger characterises *Ab-grund* as the 'the staying away [Weg-bleiben] of ground', which gives rise to *Ur-grund*.[13] *Ur-grund* is ground insofar as it is determinate and thus able to 'bear' or function as a support (that is, as 'ein Tragen').[14] *Un-grund* is *Ur-grund* that manifests distortion by obfuscating *Ab-grund*.

1.1 Ab-grund

Heidegger defines *Ab-grund* or abyssal ground as 'the originary essential occurrence of the ground [ursprüngliche Wesung des Grundes]'.[15] As 'originary', *Ab-grund* is the most primal of the three modes of *gründender Grund*; it is that dimension of the event whence the other modes of ground are originated and gain their grounding characteristics. For Heidegger, 'the ground [Grund] is the essence of truth' – the clearing for/of self-concealing.[16] Describing ground as the essence of truth makes sense because the structures of the essence of truth manifest tension or resistance capable of bearing things that are more derivative. In Chapter 5, I showed that the clearing for/of self-concealing is the event, insofar at the event originates the structures of truth (clearing, concealing, openness, and so on). I also argued that the event is the differentiation of pure difference from itself, together with the logic of determinateness this originates, and that 'the clearing for/of self-concealing' articulates this logic of determinateness in the register of truth. In terms of the logic of the event, difference differs from itself, simultaneously drawing itself out or breaching open openness and differing from or refusing to be that openness, that is, originating concealment. The origination of the determinate logic of openness and concealment can be defined alternatively as the origination of domains of propriety (appropriation) and alienation from propriety (expropriation). Together these form a seamless (though structurally distorted) logic of determinateness. For Heidegger, to say that 'abyssal ground is . . . the originary essence of the ground, of its grounding' means that *Ab-grund* is the originary essence 'of the essence of truth'.[17] In other words, *Ab-grund* is that which originates the structures of the essence of truth. As such, *Ab-grund* can be defined in terms of the event.

Ab-grund has two main aspects. If it is that which originates the essential structures of truth, one is originary difference, insofar as originary difference differs from itself (breaching open openness) and simultaneously differs from or withdraws from openness (originating concealment). In this aspect, *Ab-grund* is the track of evental difference differing from itself, specifically insofar as this difference withdraws from the structures of the essence of truth that it originates. Heidegger describes this as follows: 'the abyssal ground, as the staying away of the ground . . . is the first clearing of the open as "emptiness" [Lichtung des Offenen als der "Leere"]'.[18] He then specifies that emptiness here should not be taken

> in the sense that space and time, as forms of ordering and as frameworks for calculable and objectively present things, are simply vacant, i.e., not in the sense of the sheer absence of such things therein, but, rather, in the sense of a temporal-spatial emptiness, an originary yawning open in hesitant self-withholding.[19]

I understand this to mean that 'emptiness' describes the field of originary openness as this is generated by the evental dynamics of difference.[20]

Yet *Ab-grund* cannot be defined solely in terms of difference's role in originating the logic of determinateness: the logic of determinateness is originated because beyng as event is at its heart pure difference. This difference differs from itself and thereby distends into that logic. This entails that an aspect of beyng as difference is prior to and in excess over the logic of determinateness. I've called this excess 'primal difference', as opposed to 'originary difference', which I use to designate difference insofar as it is involved in the origination of the logic of determinateness. *Ab-grund* in its first aspect as originary difference is originary *by reason of* primal difference. Consequently, *Ab-grund* is most primordially the event's excess of primal difference: difference that exceeds the logic of determinateness. Said differently, this second part of *Ab-grund* is the event's primal self-expropriation or the excess of difference differing from itself; it is the abyss of the event's self-differentiation.

Though Heidegger does a poor job of distinguishing these two aspects, *Ab-grund* must include both: primal difference and originary difference. *Ab-grund* is the event insofar as the event is primal difference and primal difference gives rise to the originary differentiation of the determinate structures of propriety, alienation from propriety, truth, and ground. If the origination of the logic of determinateness is the event's self-intensification, *Ab-grund* is the curve between the intensive structures originated and the difference that differs from them, where this curve tends towards primal difference, which has an intensity of zero.

Ground, insofar as it is determinate and thus able to 'bear' or function as a supportive ground, is *Ur-grund* (primordial ground). In contrast to the bearing character of *Ur-grund*, Heidegger claims that the 'mode of grounding' belonging to *Ab-grund* is the staying away (*Weg-bleiben*) of ground. Yet he also insists that the abyssal staying away of ground 'is not sheer self-withholding in the sense of simple withdrawal and going away' or absence of ground: 'the *lack* of the ground is the lack of the *ground*' ('der *Ab*-grund ist Ab-*grund*').[21] Though Heidegger's limited explanation of these claims is unsatisfying, our explanation of *Ab-grund* in terms of the differential logic of the event can illuminate them. *Ab-grund* is the *staying away* or *lack* of ground because it is that dimension of eventual difference that withdraws from the logic of determinateness (and thereby from *Ur-grund*). 'Ab-grund' designates the event's self-concealing or withdrawal from openness and, exceeding even this, designates the event's dimension of primal difference. But it is precisely these aspects of *Ab-grund* that give rise to grounding. Thus, the *Ab-grund*'s mode of *grounding* is the staying away of ground. As Heidegger puts it, to say that *Ab-grund* is a staying away of ground means that it is:

> ground in self-concealing, as self-concealing in the mode of the withholding of the ground. Yet withholding is not nothing; instead, it is a preeminent and originary kind of leaving unfulfilled, leaving empty. It is thereby a preeminent kind of opening up.[22]

Ab-grund originates or grounds *Ur-grund*, but it does so precisely insofar as it is an abyss of difference.

At the same time, from the perspective of *Ur-grund*, *Ab-grund* is the lack *of the ground*, that is, it is the lack of ground inherent to ground. *Ur-grund* bears an inherent structural reference to this lack or staying away. It does so because *Ab-grund* is that whence *Ur-grund* is originated. *Ab-grund* enables *Ur-grund* to be a ground.

Before moving on to discuss *Ur-grund* more precisely, a final characteristic of *Ab-grund* must be defined. Heidegger uses an opaque term for it: 'Zögerung' or 'hesitancy'.[23] *Ab-grund* 'abides in hesitancy', he says.[24] The notion of hesitancy is important in his account of time-space, so it will be helpful to define it here in terms of ground. He offers a limited explanation of hesitancy as follows: 'inasmuch as the ground, even and precisely as abyss, still grounds and yet does not properly ground, it abides in hesitancy'.[25] This sounds rather mysterious when read outside of the context of the differential account of the event that I have argued for. However, I believe that that account can provide 'hesitancy' with a good definition. I take the *Ab-grund*'s hesitancy to be its simultaneous inclination to stay away from ground and to ground. In other words, the *Ab-grund* is hesitant because it is both primal and originary difference. In the register of ground, hesitancy describes the *liminal* character of the event with respect to primal difference and originary difference involved in the logic of determinateness.

1.2 Ur-grund and Un-grund

The second mode of grounding ground is *Ur-grund* or primordial ground. If *Ab-grund* is the event's abyss of difference or the staying away of the ground, then *Ur-grund* grounds. In and through *Ur-grund* the event becomes able to bear (*tragen*) what it bears; namely, more derivative ontological structures, worlds of beings, and human existence. *Ur-grund* is the Da of Seyn, or, more precisely, the most originary structures of Da-sein. Heidegger elaborates this in terms of the essence of truth and time-space; I discuss the former here and take up its relation to time-space in section 2.

In Heidegger's account, 'the primordial ground [Ur-grund], the one that grounds, is *beyng*, but in each case *as* essentially occurring in its truth'.[26] That is, *Ur-grund* is the event insofar as the event self-intensifies, self-determines, or self-appropriates through the clearing for/of self-concealing, unfolding the structures of truth. This definition enables us to reconstruct the concept of *Ur-grund* in terms of the logic of the event, particularly with respect to the origination of the logic of determinateness in the essence of truth. This reconstruction requires two things: first, a genetic definition of *Ur-grund*, that is, an explanation of its origination in terms of the logic of the event; second, an explanation of the basic mechanism of bearing or grounding that characterises *Ur-grund*.

A genetic definition of *Ur-grund* can be given fairly straightforwardly, since Chapter 5 worked this out in terms of the event's origination of truth and the domains of propriety and alienation from propriety. Stated in terms of truth, evental difference differs from itself (abyssally), simultaneously drawing itself out or breaching open openness and differing from or refusing to be that openness, that is, originating concealment. As I have shown, Heidegger incorporates the terminology of *Ab-grund* in his explanation of the origination of *Ur-grund* in a way that fits this genetic definition. In this sense, the staying away of *Ab-grund* (the event's abyss of difference) originates the *Ur-grund* (in the guise of the structures of truth):

> The staying away of ground – is that not the *absence* of truth? Yet the hesitant self-withholding [of the Ab-grund] is precisely the clearing for concealment and is thus the presencing of truth. Certainly, 'presencing', but not in the way something objectively present has come to presence; instead, the essential occurrence of what first founds [begründet] the presence and absence of beings.[27]

'Ur-grund' names 'what first founds the presence and absence of beings', which Heidegger frequently explains in terms of truth. This defines an essential aspect of the event: 'the event, grasped from the perspective of truth as ground, is . . . the primordial ground [Ur-grund]'.[28]

While these passages define *Ur-grund* in the terminology of truth, *Ur-grund* can also be given a genetic definition in terms of the event's operations of appropriation and expropriation. In the logic of the event, difference differs from itself and by doing so distends. This distension is the origination of a field such that some aspect of difference is differentiated from some other aspect. Rather than there being pure indeterminateness, difference generates determinateness or finitude by generating aspects of itself defined in their difference from one another: *this* distended dimension of difference is difference that comes to be defined via the origination of contrast from *that* difference that refuses to be it. This distension is the origination of both a domain of propriety (appropriation) and a domain of alienation from propriety (expropriation). A domain of propriety is originated because (1) in the distension of difference, aspects of difference become structurally distinguished or determinate, and (2) those aspects bear constitutive reference to the operation of the event whereby distension is enabled to occur, that is, whereby appropriation is accomplished. It should be added that each aspect is also determined by the other, and so each also bears a structural, constitutive reference to the other. The distension of difference whereby a domain of propriety is originated simultaneously originates a domain of alienation from propriety, for appropriation is accomplished only by the refusal or withdrawal of difference from itself. Expropriation is this differentiation of difference from itself (as appropriation). In expropriation, that dimension of difference that differs from appropriation becomes determined since it becomes endowed with a structural reference to appropriation, namely, one of alienation from or *not* being proper to appropriation. Expropriation is difference that repels or withdraws from the appropriation of the domain of propriety, thereby enacting the distension of difference that constitutes that appropriation, but also gaining a determinateness of its own, namely as bearing a constitutive reference to that which it refuses to be (propriety). The event self-intensifies through the dynamics of appropriation and expropriation. In other words, the event originates the Da expressed in the term 'Da-sein'. *Ur-grund* is constituted by the evental structures of propriety and alienation from propriety.

The second task required for reconstructing Heidegger's concept of *Ur-grund* is to explain the basic mechanism of bearing or grounding that characterises it. This, in turn entails explaining the third mode of *gründender Grund*: *Un-grund* (distorted ground). At one level, *Ur-grund* is a ground that bears in the same sense that openness and concealment ground worlds of beings. I discussed this in Chapters 3 and 4 and will not return to it here since there is a more originary sense of bearing at stake in *Ur-grund*.

At this more originary level, *Ur-grund* is a ground that bears because it manifests the distinction of ontological structures from each other, where those structures are endowed with constitutive reference both to their counterpart and to the *Ab-grund* whence they are originated. The origination of these structures is the differentiation between something grounded and something serving as the ground enabling it to be or bearing it. The domain of propriety, for instance, is borne by the domain of alienation from propriety together with the abyss of difference. The domain of alienation is borne by that of propriety and the abyss of difference. In the register of truth, openness is borne by originary concealment and the abyss of difference, while originary concealment is born by openness and the abyss of difference. And as described in terms of the *Ab-grund*, the whole logic of determinateness that these structures comprise is originated by the abyss of difference.

My hypothesis is that *Ur-grund* is able to bear derivative ontological structures, properties, and beings because in it is constituted the structural tension or resistance described in Chapter 5, sections 2 to 4. In both structural couplings, 'openness and concealment' and 'propriety and alienation from propriety', each term is constitutively bound to its counterpart, while also being what it is only by being differentiated from that counterpart. I described this in terms of what Heidegger calls the simultaneous 'strife' and 'intimacy' characterising openness and concealment, which, I argued, constitutes a structural tension. The origination of the structures involved in strife and intimacy is the event's self-intensification or coagulation, that is, the projection of the Da.

This intensification also involves the origination of structural distortion, described by Heidegger in terms of the distorted essence of truth, the distorted essence of beyng, and, now, the *distorted ground* or *Un-grund*. *Un-grund* is the grounding character of the event insofar as the event constitutes distortion. As with the distorted essence of truth discussed in Chapter 5, the distortion at stake at this level of the event is structural and not to be taken in a pejorative sense. Yet it is the ground enabling historical and human errancy, which *are* to be taken in a pejorative sense. In historical and human errancy, distortion is manifested in the framework of metaphysics, the forgottenness of being, representation, calculation, machination, and so on. Though *Un-grund* is not the same thing as these distortions, it is the ground enabling both them and the broader tendency of human existence to become estranged from *gründender Grund*. *Un-grund* thus leads to the need for *Er-gründung* or fathoming the ground.

The distortion involved here is the curvature of the event whereby the abyssal logic of difference is eclipsed. Vallega-Neu describes this as follows: 'When the truth of be-ing [Seyn] remains hidden in its occurrence as abyss and in its occurrence as enowning [Ereignis], be-ing refuses its essential occurrence and, therefore, sways as unessential ground [Un-grund].'[29] My earlier analysis of the structural distortion belonging to the essence of truth should help to explain this evental distortion. *Un-grund* involves two closely related senses of structural obscuration: as defined in Chapter 5, each term of the couplings 'openness and concealment' and 'propriety and alienation from propriety' entails (1) the obscuration of the other and (2) the obscuration of aspects of the evental logic of difference whereby the term is originated. From its own perspective, the logic of each term in each coupling *seems* to exclude the logic of the other and vice versa. In terms of truth, neither openness nor concealment is adequate to the essence of truth; each entails a blind spot with respect to the other. This constitutes a structural distortion: from any point within the logic of determinateness some aspect of that logic is obscured. Yet because appropriation/openness and expropriation/concealment are generated by one and the same logic of difference, there is, in fact, continuity throughout their logics: together they form a continuous logic of determinateness. Additionally, because each term entails a structural obscuration of the other, from any position within the logic of determinateness aspects of the event whereby the terms of that logic are originated are obscured. That is, from within the logic of determinateness aspects of the logic of difference that are essential to the event are obscured. These two aspects of structural obscuration constitute what Heidegger calls 'resistance' (*Widerstand*), which he understands to be the most basic negativity belonging to beyng as event. A consequence is that the genesis of the logic of determinateness entails that all aspects of the determinateness generated bear a structural alienation from evental difference, that is, from what enables them to be: the *Ab-grund*.

The tension and resistance constituted in *Ur-grund* and *Un-grund* enable beyng as event to bear (that is, to support) more derivative structures and, ultimately, worlds of beings. Such tension and resistance constitute an ontological viscosity or Heideggerian version of inertia. The derivative structures borne are folds and complications of this tension. Their genesis should in principle be traceable from out of the logic of the event. It is in this sense that Heidegger describes the grounding character of ground as a protruding (*Durchragen*): 'And what is the ground? It is that which veils itself and also takes up [Sichverhüllende-Aufnehmen], because it bears [weil ein Tragen] and does so as the protruding [Durchragen] of what is to be grounded.'[30] This protruding is the self-intensification of the event, a crystal growing out of pure difference. The grounding function of the event, that is, the way it enables some more derivative structure to be, is the track of the logic of tension whereby that thing is generated. Since that tension is itself partially generated by the event's dimension of self-concealing and also essentially includes structural distortion, *gründender Grund* essentially includes modes of self-concealing. Thus, in Heidegger's condensed technical formulation, ground is 'das Sichverbergen im tragenden Durchragen' or 'self-concealing in a protruding that bears'.[31]

2 The event and time-space

As is well known, Heidegger consistently argues that the problematic of time is essential to the problematic of being.[32] In *Beiträge* he posits that space is equiprimordial to time and that both are originated by an ontological process that is neither properly temporal nor spatial. He designates this process 'Zeit-Raum' or 'time-space'.[33] As I have argued, the prominent components of Heidegger's ontology in *Beiträge* are underwritten by the differential logic of the event. Truth and ground are two of the three core registers in terms of which the ontological structures originated by that logic are articulated. Time-space is the third. The structures composing truth, ground, and time-space are all originated by the same evental factor: the abyss of difference or the differentiation of difference from itself. Stated more precisely, the essence of these ontological structures *is* the abyss of difference, particularly insofar as that difference originates the logic of determinateness or the Da expressed in the term 'Da-sein'. In the register of truth, this essence is named 'Lichtung' or 'clearing', in that of ground, it is named 'Ab-grund' or 'abyssal ground', and in that of temporality and spatiality, it is named 'Zeit-Raum' or 'time-space'.

Heidegger's discussion of time-space is framed by a condensed summary of failings he finds in the historical treatment of time and space. This summary is discontinuous, incomplete, and contains many statements that are not well explained. For my purposes of explicating time-space in relation to the event, these shortcomings of the text are not detrimental. To move to Heidegger's direct treatment of time-space, it is sufficient to summarise the problem he sees in traditional accounts of time and space and establish how time-space is grounded in the structure of the event.

In *Beiträge*, Heidegger sees the central problem with the historical treatment of space and time to be the way they are *represented* as categorically distinct schemata or forms of order. Such a representation, he argues, rests upon certain mistaken historical and metaphysical presuppositions. To elaborate, he engages several canonical figures, but comments most extensively on three: Aristotle, Descartes (under the rubric of 'the modern era' as a whole), and Kant. In brief, these presuppositions are rooted in Aristotle's interpretation of being as οὐσία and thereby in terms of the time determination of presence. Here, 'posited along with presence is the πέρας ["limit"], the περιέχον ["that which encloses"]'.[34] The result, Heidegger states, is that 'for Aristotle . . . the ποῦ ["where"] and the ποτέ ["when"] are categories, determinations of beingness, of οὐσία'.[35] In the modern era, space and time become represented as schemata for mathematical calculation. This is exemplified by the Cartesian coordinate system used for plotting mathematical points in three-dimensional space. Adding a fourth, temporal dimension adds another order, one in which changes in position or changes in the values of a function can be plotted over time. With Kant, the positions of space and time shift: they become part of the subject's cognitive apparatus – the forms of outer and inner intuition – rather than an objective milieu within which the subject is located. According to Heidegger, all three of these examples share the conviction that time and space are entirely distinct forms of order.

The representation of space and time as categorically distinct forms of order fails in each instance, Heidegger suggests, because in such a representation the concept of space entails *temporal* determinations and the concept of time entails *spatial* determinations. In other words, the absolute categorical distinction can never be established because spatiality and temporality are intrinsically intertwined. The temporal order is represented in one way or another as a 'space of time' (*Zeitraum*): the span between T_1 and T_2, for instance.[36] Likewise, space, having no duration in itself, is purely *present*. As Heidegger makes the point, 'in a particular respect, space can be represented as an *ordo* and as the sphere for things conjointly at hand, which indicates that space, as so represented, is representable in terms of a presencing (a determinate mode of temporality)'.[37] In fact, Heidegger emphasises, 'space and time . . . [have been] thought together since antiquity'.[38] Despite the best efforts of the tradition to represent space and time as purely distinct orders, this co-determination remains and indicates to Heidegger that the two are ontologically entwined in some manner.

This does not mean that Heidegger collapses space and time into one order. He does not hold, for example, that time-space is a four-dimensional fabric of reality. Instead, he maintains that time and space are radically distinct, but that their distinction is generated by a shared process of origination. Their entwinement is found in this origin.

> Space and time are not only different in the number of 'dimensions' they are ordinarily thought to possess but are also radically different, different in their most proper essence, and only in virtue of this extreme difference do they point back to their origin, time-space. The more purely the proper essence of each is preserved and the deeper their origin is placed, so much more readily is their essence grasped as time-space in its belonging to the essence of truth as clearing ground for concealment.[39]

The question, then, becomes how to understand spatiality and temporality, both with respect to their radical distinctness and their entwinement in a shared ontological origin. For when we enquire into the essence of either space or time, the concept of the one implies the other; yet space and time are not one and the same thing. Obviously, Heidegger put a great deal of effort into rethinking the nature of time and space in the years prior to *Beiträge*. In *Beiträge* he advances his account to a position on the diagenic axis more originary than, for example, the one given in *Sein und Zeit*: rather than understanding time to be the ecstatic structure of Dasein's existence and the horizon for the understanding of being, time and space are grounded in time-space, which is a process of the event and as such is diagenically prior to human existence and the constitution of worlds of beings. It is important to emphasise that this undermines the tradition's representations of time and space because it undermines the whole machinery of representation. It does so by moving to a ground that is more originary than representation: 'the issue here is not at all the mere modification of representation and of the directionality of representation;

rather, what is called for is a dislodging of the essence of the human being into Da-sein'.[40] Heidegger rethinks temporality and spatiality on the basis of time-space, defining them with the technical terms 'Entrückung' or 'transporting' and 'Berückung' or 'captivation'. I return to these terms shortly.

2.1 Preliminary clarification of time-space

Heidegger writes, 'time and space, as belonging to the essence of truth, are originally united in time-space and are the abyssal grounding of the "there"; through the "there," selfhood and what is true of beings first come to be grounded'.[41] In the remainder of this chapter, I use my earlier reconstruction of Heidegger's account of the event, truth, and ground to sort out his understanding of time-space. This, in turn, will offer a more detailed picture of the structure of the event.

First, a few preliminary clarifications and terminological distinctions must be made. As indicated, in Heidegger's account time-space is not the same as time and space. It is the ground enabling time and space to be. Time and space are generated by or unfold from time-space: 'space and time, each represented for itself and in their usual conjunction, arise out of time-space, which is more originary than they themselves and than their calculatively represented conjunction'.[42] In *Beiträge* §§238–42, Heidegger's use of the terms 'space' and 'time' often signify the spatial and temporal dimensions of the event insofar as these dimensions are governed by the historical determination and conceptual structure of metaphysics. For the sake of consistency in my analysis, I will reserve this sense for the terms 'space' and 'time'. In contrast, the terms 'spatiality' and 'temporality' will designate the spatial and temporal dimensions generated by the event and understood on the basis of the event. These terms designate space and time as properly grounded, not metaphysically represented. Within this context, 'Räumung' or 'spatialisation' and 'Zeitigung' or 'temporalisation' name the operations *of time-space* by which the event becomes spatial and temporal, that is, generates spatiality and temporality. 'Time-space' designates the operation of the *event* by which the event spatialises and temporalises itself, together with that spatialisation and temporalisation. My main goal will be to reconstruct Heidegger's account of time-space, its processes of temporalisation and spatialisation, and the connection of all this to the event.

Heidegger begins his account of time-space proper by relating it to the essence of truth and the event. In one sense, time-space belongs to the essence of truth: 'time-space belongs to truth in the sense of the originating essential occurrence of being as event'.[43] In another sense, a full understanding of truth requires elaborating truth in terms of time-space: 'what truth itself is cannot be immediately and sufficiently said in itself, but only in grasping time-space'.[44] That is, explaining time-space offers a more detailed account of the essence of truth and the event. 'The question', though, 'is how and in what guise time-space belongs to truth'.[45] I take the basic answer to be that truth is a primary conceptual register for articulating the Da in 'Da-sein', and that time-space does the same thing in a different register. Working out the nature of time-space provides greater elaboration of the ontological origination and structure of the Da. Heidegger makes this point as follows: we must understand 'time-space as arising out of, and belonging to, the essence of truth and as the thereby grounded structure (joining) of the "there," a structure of transport-captivation [Entrückungs-Berückungsgefüge]'.[46] Here, the concept of 'transport' designates the structure of temporalisation, while the concept of 'captivation' does the same for spatialisation. Temporality and spatiality are two structures of the Da.

2.2 Time-space, temporality, spatiality, and the logic of the event

Heidegger offers two working definitions of time-space, the first focused on a notion of 'Erklüftung' or 'sundering' and the second on 'sammelnde Umhalt' or 'gathering embrace':

> Time-space is the appropriated sundering [Erklüftung] of the turning paths [Kehrungsbahnen] of the event, the sundering of the turning between belonging [Zugehörigkeit] and call [Zuruf], between abandonment by being [Seinsverlassenheit] and beckoning intimation [Erwinkung].[47]

> Time-space is the gathering embrace [sammelnde Umhalt] that captivates and transports at once; it is the abyssal ground which is structured [gefügte] in this way, which disposes [stimmende] accordingly, and whose essential occurrence becomes historical [geschichtlich] in the grounding of the 'there' by Da-*sein* (by its essential paths of sheltering [Bergung] the truth).[48]

While these passages exemplify Heidegger's off-putting cryptic terminology, the text offers a key for deciphering them:

> Even in their unity, space and time have nothing in common; instead, what unifies them, what allows them to emerge *in* [an] . . . inseparable referentiality [Gewiesenheit], is time-space, the abyssal grounding of the ground: the essential occurrence of truth. This e-mergence [Ent-springen], however, is not a tearing off [Losriß]; just the opposite: time-space is merely the unfolding of the essence of the essential occurrence of truth [Wesensentfaltung der Wesung der Wahrheit].[49]

This allows us to see that time-space is the abyssal grounding of the ground. It is the essential occurrence of truth or, rather, the unfolding of the essence of the essence of truth. Our previous analysis of these aspects of the event and the differential logic defining them provides a basis for defining the terminology in these passages and reconstructing Heidegger's account of time-space itself. In the differential logic of the event, the abyss is originary difference together with the track of primal difference that exceeds the logic of determination. In the register of truth, the abyssal differentiation of difference from itself is the clearing or sundering whereby openness and concealment are originated. The 'unfolding of the essence of the essence of truth' is the clearing or sundering of difference into the co-determinate structures of openness and concealment. In the register of ground, the 'abyssal grounding of the ground' is the liminal differentiation of difference from itself, or the staying away of ground whereby *Ur-grund* and *Un-grund* are originated. In terms of the event itself, the genetic operation described is that by which the event self-determines (appropriates and expropriates) in structures of propriety and alienation from propriety, while this operation is enabled by the primal expropriation of difference that exceeds those structures. Consequently, given Heidegger's definitions, time-space is at root this same evental process, the abyssal differentiation of difference from itself whereby the event originates a logic of determinateness. But here, that logic of determinateness is the logic of temporality and spatiality. Time-space is the event insofar as the event temporalises and spatialises itself (that is, originates temporality and spatiality) by the abyssal differentiation of difference from itself. It is the operation of the event by which the event becomes temporal and spatial.

Even if all this is accepted, a major question is still on the table: how, exactly, does the event's differential logic temporalise and spatialise? Answering this requires defining the key terms used in the passages cited above, as well as a few additional terms. This will ultimately lead to a definition of transporting or temporalisation and captivation or spatialisation as structures unfolded from the event.

To begin, I return to the partial definition of time-space in the first passage just cited (the 'sundering' definition) and its claim that 'time-space is the appropriated sundering of the turning paths of the event'. Good sense can be made of this strange statement because these terms have been defined already in the terminologies of truth and the event itself. 'Sundering' occurs at two essentially related levels here. At the first, in terms of truth, the sundering of the turning paths of the event is the clearing of openness from concealment and concealment from openness, that is, the differentiation of difference from itself such that it simultaneously modulates into these counterposed but co-determinative structures.

Likewise, in terms of the event itself, the sundering is the twisting apart or splitting accomplished in difference's simultaneous self-appropriation and self-expropriation in the structures of propriety and alienation from propriety. At the second, most fundamental level, sundering must also refer to the simultaneous, dual inclinations of the event towards the logic of determinateness and towards the abyss of primal difference. In both the terminology of truth and that of the event itself, the 'turning paths of the event' are the tracks of the event's self-determination into the counterposed moments of the logic of determinateness and, more fundamentally, the tracks of the event insofar as it inclines towards both determinateness and the abyss. Consequently, if time-space is the appropriated sundering of the turning paths of the event, this should be taken to mean that time-space is the evental differentiation of difference from itself insofar as this originates (or appropriates itself in) a logic of determinateness comprised of counterposed structures of spatiality and temporality. The turning paths here are the event's logics of spatialisation and temporalisation.

We shouldn't be thrown off by Heidegger's specification of the sundering involved in time-space as a 'sundering of the turning between belonging [Zugehörigkeit] and call [Zuruf], between abandonment by being [Seinsverlassenheit] and beckoning intimation [Erwinkung]'.[50] Rather, this confirms the account I have just given. Within the context of the event, belonging or *Zugehörigkeit* is exactly the constitutive structural reference that (together with the differentiation of distinct aspects of a structure) defines the domain of propriety (see Chapter 5, section 3). Call or *Zuruf* is the constitutive structural reference characterising the domain of *alienation* from propriety insofar as that reference is one by which that domain is defined in its withdrawal or contrast from the domain of propriety, that is, from that from which it is alienated. The structural reference to the domain of propriety which is inscribed in the domain of alienation constitutes a drag within or 'call' to the domain of alienation. Likewise, at the more fundamental level, *Erwinkung* or beckoning intimation is the recession of the abyss of difference insofar as this draws the event into determinate structures like openness and concealment, propriety and alienation from propriety. When it comes to the *Seinsverlassenheit* or abandonment by being, we've seen that Heidegger often uses this term to describe the state of human existence and its alienation from being. In its use here, however, at the level of the event, the abandonment by being cannot be defined in terms of human existence, since what is at stake is the ground enabling human beings to be at all. Instead it must describe a structural aspect of the event. At the level of the event, the abandonment by being is the alienation from the event's abyssal dimension that is necessarily constituted in the logic of determinateness insofar as that logic entails structural distortion (in the distorted essence of truth, distorted ground, and so on). In other words, and for that reason, the logic of determinateness is characterised by an abandonment by being. What remains to be seen is how these characteristics become manifested by the spatialisation and temporalisation of the event.

Before turning to the terminology presented in the second definition of time-space quoted (the one focused on 'gathering embrace'), it is necessary to elaborate on some of the terms I have just defined. This will allow a set of additional terms that are needed to make sense of the 'gathering embrace' definition to be explained. I return first to intimation. 'Intimation' is a term Heidegger uses to describe an aspect of the event's genetic operation. It plays an important role in his explanation of transporting and captivation. He writes:

> The intimation [Wink] is the hesitant self-withholding. The self-withholding creates not only the *emptiness* of privation and austerity but also, along with these, an emptiness as one that is in itself transporting, i.e., transporting into the 'to come' [Künftigkeit] and thereby simultaneously bursting open what has been [Gewesendes]. The latter, by making an impact together with what is to come, constitutes the present [Gegenwart] as a move into [Einrückung] the abandonment that remembers and expects [erinnernd-erharrende].[51]

As with *Ab-grund*, time-space's intimation entails a character of 'hesitancy'. Earlier I defined hesitancy within the register of ground. There, hesitancy describes *Ab-grund*'s liminal status. In other words, *Ab-grund*'s character of hesitancy is its simultaneous inclination to stay away from ground and to ground via its origination of the structures of primordial ground. This is not simply to say that the abyss performs two different actions, but that it is simultaneously inclined in these two ways. This character of *Ab-grund* is also found in the structure of the event more generally. In Chapter 5, we saw that evental differentiation is liminal in character because it simultaneously includes both an aspect determined in the logic of appropriation and expropriation and an aspect exceeding that logic (primal difference).[52] The event has a character of hesitancy because its differential logic is simultaneously inclined in both these ways. The abyss's hesitancy is its simultaneous inclination to determine or intensify itself and refuse itself from determination or to tend towards an intensity of zero. The same thing applies to abyssal difference rendered as time-space. Time-space is hesitant because it is liminal with respect to temporality and spatiality: time-space is the abyss of difference that exceeds the logic of spatiality and temporality, but simultaneously originates and becomes determined in that logic. Hesitancy is a tension held between the dual inclinations of the event.

To see what hesitancy has to do with temporality and spatiality, it will be helpful to jump ahead for a moment. As I will show, temporality is the entirety of the logic of the event, run through in the direction of one of these inclinations, while spatiality is the entirety of the logic of the event run through in the other direction. The 'to come' or futural aspect of temporality is primal difference, insofar as this exceeds the logic of determinateness and intimates its self-distension, that is, originates that logic. 'What has been' or the 'past' aspect of temporality is the logic of determinateness, insofar as this trails behind the 'to come' or abyssal recession of difference. In the concept of hesitancy, the inclination towards the abyss of difference prefigures transporting or the temporalisation of the event, while the inclination towards determinateness prefigures captivation or the spatialisation of the event.

Returning to hesitancy for a moment, if the hesitancy of the event is its dual inclination to determine itself and to withdraw or withhold itself from that determination, Heidegger uses the phrase 'hesitant self-withholding' to designate the *latter* of these inclinations. But the abyss's hesitant self-withholding (the recession of difference from itself) generates the distension constituting the Da or the logic of determinateness. This is the sense of Heidegger's claim that 'the hesitant withholding is the intimation that beckons Da-*sein*'.[53] That is, the abyss withdraws and thereby beckons or calls and originates Da-sein.

As I have discussed in other contexts, one of the primary structures of the Da 'intimated' or generated here is originary 'Leere' or 'emptiness'. In the logic of the event, difference differs from itself and by doing so distends. This distension is the clearing or breaching open of originary openness, 'the first clearing of the open as "emptiness"'.[54] Originary openness is a basic structure of the Da that is diagenically prior to more derivative ontological structures and worlds of beings, which it will help ground. In this sense, originary openness is not populated by anything, it is empty. Originary openness is an originary *emptiness*, not in the sense of an empty vessel, but 'in the sense of a temporal-spatial emptiness, an originary yawning open in hesitant self-withholding'.[55] Here, emptiness should not be confused with the abyss. Since emptiness is a structure of the Da, its origination is a coagulation, intensification, or 'protruding' of the event. Since Da-sein is the event insofar as it determines itself through self-appropriation or, in terms of truth, through the clearing for/of self-concealment, emptiness is in fact a surging forth or self-protrusion of the event. Heidegger's account of the intimation of emptiness is important here because it prefigures his account of spatialisation. The logic of the event running *from* the abyss of primal difference *to* the breaching open of originary emptiness or openness (and the other structures of the Da) is one way of describing the spatialisation of the event. The breaching open of openness is the origination of a distended field or space.

Heidegger's concept of hesitancy prefigures his concepts of transporting or temporalisation and captivation or spatialisation. The evental structure of hesitancy is elaborated in terms of 'Verlassenheit' or 'abandonment'. At the level of time-space, 'abandonment' names a complex structure of the event with two essential dimensions: it 'originarily occurs as remembering and expecting [erinnernd-erwartend]'.[56] An account of these structures of remembering and expecting comprising abandonment will bring us a step closer to Heidegger's account of transporting and captivation.

Remembering and expecting are usually taken to be cognitive behaviours attributed to human beings and other animals. What sense can these terms have in the present context, dealing with features of the event that are ontologically prior to the constitution of any beings? Heidegger clarifies their sense in a parenthetical remark: what remembering remembers is 'a hidden belonging to beyng' and what expecting expects is the 'call of beyng'.[57] Generally speaking, something does not bear the character of abandonment without bearing the trace of what it was abandoned *by*, that is, without bearing a 'remembrance' or inscription referring to what it was abandoned by. Without such a reference to that from which the alien is alienated, it is not alienated. Without that trace, the abandoned would not *be abandoned*, it would just *be*. It is this trace structure that constitutes remembering and expecting.

As I have established, the event's self-determination in the structures of the Da is enabled by the recession of abyssal difference. Additionally, the structures of the Da entail the distortion described by distorted ground and the distorted essence of truth. In that distortion, the structures of the Da obscure parts of other structures of the Da and, most importantly, obscure the abyssal dimension of the event whence they are originated. In this sense, the structures of the Da are characterised by an 'abandonment' by or alienation from beyng. In this setting, if 'remembering' remembers a hidden belonging to beyng, that belonging is the constitutive structural reference of the Da to that whence it is originated: the event's abyss of difference. This belonging is hidden on account of the obscuration involved in distortion. In contrast, if 'expecting' expects the call of beyng, that call is the exact same constitutive structural reference of the Da to the abyss of difference, but with respect to the possibility that what has become alienated can turn back towards the abyss and be articulated in terms of the abyssal logic. Remembering and expecting, taken together, form a temporal loop in the logic of the event. Remembering traces the logic of the event in the sequence of the origination of the Da out of the abyss and into the structures of distortion. On the other hand, expecting traces the logic of the event in the sequence from the Da's structures of distortion into the abyss. This loop is not a duration, but a movement of the genetic 'temporality' of the event. Abandonment can be characterised by remembering and expecting only because the trace of what has abandoned remains essentially determinative for the structure of what has been abandoned.

This brings us to a point where Heidegger's account of the processes of temporalisation and spatialisation can finally be defined. Again, he uses the technical term 'Entrückung' or 'transporting' for the temporalisation of the event. Transporting is the originary essence of temporality. The event's abyssal dimension is the differentiation of difference from itself, such that difference distends and originates the logic of determinateness or structures of the Da (openness and concealment, primordial ground, temporality and spatiality, and the distortion entailed in these). The logic of the event is 'hesitant' insofar as it simultaneously inclines both towards self-intensification in the Da and towards the abyss of primal difference, which has an intensity of zero. The event's hesitancy, moreover, bears the trace structure described by abandonment and its modes of remembering and expecting. Transporting or the temporalisation of the event is the event insofar as it constitutes a genetic sequence or an order of origination and structures originated, that is, an order of grounding and structures grounded. In other words, transporting is the event insofar as the event originates diagenic axes. Here, that which comes first and gives rise to what comes after is the futural dimension of the event, or what Heidegger refers to as the 'to come'. The 'to come' is the abyss of difference differing from itself. In contrast, 'what has been' is that which the abyss has given rise to: the structures of the logic of determinacy and their unfolding in more derivative structures of finitude. Transporting or temporalisation is the logic of the event insofar as it is oriented towards the abyss. In other words, 'transporting' is the event insofar as the structures of the Da are originated ('intimated' or 'beckoned') by the abyss as it withdraws. Temporally speaking, the structures of the Da are the wake of the abyss. Yet by reason of the withdrawal of abyssal difference, the event is simultaneously the origination of the logic of determinateness or 'what has been', and this comprises part of the structure of temporality as well. Taking this into account, transporting must be said to be the structure of the event insofar as it simultaneously develops into what has been and what is to come, while both of these temporal dimensions are oriented by their structural reference to the abyss's withdrawal.

If transporting is the technical term Heidegger uses for temporalisation, 'Berückung' or 'captivation' is what he uses for spatialisation: 'captivation is the spatialisation of the event'.[58] Captivation is the origination of a structural distension. Such distension is the constitution or determination of differentiated structures of the event. I have defined core parts of this process already in terms of the event's origination of 'emptiness' or breaching open of openness, together with self-concealment. Here, difference differs from itself and distends, opening up a field of constitutive referentiality. The same operation is articulated by the origination of a domain of propriety. Moreover, the spatiality originated here includes the differential 'distance' or distension between openness and concealment, the domain of propriety and that of alienation from propriety. Captivation, as the spatialisation of the event, articulates exactly the same logic of the event as temporalisation, but in the opposite direction. Captivation is the event's inclination towards self-determination in the structures of the Da. It is the logic of the event run in a trajectory from the abyss of difference to the logic of determinateness. Captivation names the clearing of the abyss of difference from itself, the distension that generates, and the breaching open of an open realm that this enables.

To draw these core concepts together, in Heidegger's ontology, time-space is the abyssal dimension of the event insofar as this self-temporalises (transporting) and self-spatialises (captivating). Spatialisation and temporalisation are each the entirety of the logic of the event (the logic of determinateness together with the abyss of primal difference), but in inverted orders. Time-space is thus both (1) the shared origin of the temporalisation and spatialisation of the event, and (2) that which constitutes their radical distinction in two different orders.

Notes

1. GA65 33/28.
2. GA9 130/102.
3. GA65 345/273.
4. GA56 383/303.
5. GA65 183/144. Rojcewicz and Vallega-Neu translate the Greek term ὑπόθεσις as 'what is laid down underneath' and ὑποκείμενον as 'what lies underneath'.
6. GA65 §187 outlines these two registers of ground.
7. GA65 307/243.
8. GA65 379/300.
9. WW 177/136 fn. a, and GA65 297/234.
10. GA65 297/234.
11. GA65 380/300, italics removed.
12. GA65 380/300.
13. GA65 379/299.
14. GA65 379/300.
15. GA65 379/299.
16. Ibid.
17. Ibid.
18. GA65 380/300.

19. GA65 380–1/301.
20. 'In withholding itself, the ground preeminently brings into the open, namely into the first opening of *that* emptiness which is thereby a *determinate* one' (GA65 379–80/300, my italics on 'determinate').
21. GA65 379/300.
22. Ibid.
23. GA65 380/300.
24. Ibid.
25. GA65 379–80/300.
26. GA65 380/300, my italics on 'as'.
27. GA65 381/301.
28. GA65 380/300.
29. *HCP* 80.
30. GA65 379/300.
31. Ibid.
32. In *SZ*, for instance, he claims that 'the central problematic of all ontology is rooted in the phenomenon of time' (*SZ* 18/40, italics removed).
33. See especially GA65 §§238–42.
34. GA65 376/297.
35. Ibid.
36. GA65 377/298.
37. GA65 377/297–8.
38. GA65 374/296.
39. GA65 377/298.
40. GA65 372/294.
41. GA65 376/297.
42. GA65 372/294.
43. Ibid.
44. Ibid.
45. Ibid.
46. GA65 371/293.
47. GA65 372/294.
48. GA65 386/305.
49. GA65 386/304–5.
50. GA65 372/294.
51. GA65 383/303.
52. See Chapter 5, section 3.
53. GA65 380/300.
54. Ibid.
55. GA65 380–1/301.
56. GA65 384/303. As a terminological point, Heidegger also sometimes uses 'das Erharren' to designate the 'expecting' dimension of abandonment. GA65 384/303.
57. GA65 384/303.
58. Ibid.

Conclusion

To close, I would like to highlight a few conclusions drawn in this book, rather than summarise its overall argument (for such a summary, I would direct the reader to section 3 of the Introduction).

First, Heidegger's philosophy is organised along complex axes of ground*ing* and ground*ed* terms, the relations of which are both methodologically and ontologically essential to his system. This means the proper method for reconstructing its concepts, accounts, and evolution must work in terms of these axes. This is what diagenic analysis does. The diagenic method allows us to discover and explicate the relations and functions of Heidegger's often obscure concepts and their positions within his overall system, according to the logic of being and thinking that that system works out. It allows us to reconstruct the evolution of his ontology, particularly insofar as it is a reflexive, recursive radical science, not a positive science. In contrast, chronological reconstruction fails on just these counts. It mistakes the chronological time of the author's biography for the logical time of diagenic radical science or, inversely, of onto-genesis. Since the chronological approach cannot provide a radical critique, properly account for the methodologically immanent evolution of Heidegger's concepts, or, upon proper grounds, provide genetic definitions for them, it amounts to *post hoc* analysis, severing concepts from their grounds. This feeds a tendency to parrot Heidegger's unusual terms instead of explain them, and, often, to implicitly substitute an appeal to the authority of the author in place of good justification.

Second, diagenic analysis allows us to discern *two* concepts of event in Heidegger's work, even if he himself was not fully aware of their distinction: the 'historical' and 'ontological' concepts of event. The former names a rupture within the historical framework of metaphysics and its expression in machination, representation, and lived experience. If it were to happen, it would entail a remedy to Dasein's existential alienation (to the degree possible), establish the ground for a transformation of the historical character or style of Da-sein, and initiate the other beginning for thought suggested to be necessary for philosophy and for the practical lives of human beings. The ontological concept of event aims to articulate beyng itself in a way freed of metaphysical errancy. Since we purportedly live and think within the historical framework of metaphysics, the historical concept of event has a temporary methodological priority over the ontological. But since metaphysics cannot provide a sufficient ontology and, instead, there is a diagenic excess of being over metaphysics that makes a rupture in its framework possible, the ontological concept of event – which articulates the structure and nature of that excess – has an ontological priority. In fact, these orders of priority are themselves in play. The methodological priority of the historical event holds only until a sufficiently originary state of grounding is attained: the state in which a well-grounded, non-metaphysical account of beyng is generated that is sufficient for a radical critique of metaphysics. Such a critique must include the ability to give a genetic explanation of metaphysics (even if that explanation is not in fact given). At that state, the difference between methodological and ontological priority collapses: the two merge and the ontological sense of event gains methodological primacy. Philosophical methodology takes on the logic of beyng as event, develops an account of the event from a standpoint immanent to that logic, and establishes the ground for a non-alienated reconceptualisation of the domain of history and its metaphysical epoch.

Third, although historical events can be out of the hands of human beings, the one Heidegger has in mind is something we can endeavour to bring about, contrary to fatalist interpretations of his philosophy. *Er-gründung* or fathoming the ground names this endeavour and, at its heart, works via the conceptually experimental, radical scientific operation of *Grundlegung*, specifically as done in ontology. Bringing about the historical event occurs not by meditating upon the historical, but by generating a non-metaphysical account of beyng, that is, of the ground of metaphysics that metaphysics is unable to think. Heidegger does this via the ontology of truth, for the framework of truth entails both (1) the principle elements defining our intellectual and practical horizons in terms of *Seiendheit*: identity, the reduction of time to presence, subject predication, representation (propositional, cognitive, and conceptual), and so on, and (2) the ontological ground of these elements. As such, 'truth' articulates *both* structures of beyng that are diagenically prior to metaphysics *and* the occlusion of those structures in the framework of metaphysics. By doing the ontology of truth, fathoming the ground provides thought a standpoint within the differential logic of beyng, that is, of the event, thereby undermining metaphysics and establishing the first moment of the historical event. Fathoming the ground tracks the logic of being into the abyss or *Ab-grund* of difference, that is, into the (onto-)logical future. In this sense, the 'other beginning' *is* the future, not the establishment of a new past.

Fourth, since fathoming the ground accesses structures of beyng that are diagenically prior to the apparatus of representation and that form the ground enabling it, it performs the first stage of a radical critique of representation (the second stage being a transformed onto-genetic explanation of representation from out of those grounds). This ground is pre-representational and, ultimately, pre-predicative.

Fifth, contrary to correlationist or anti-realist interpretations of Heidegger, his philosophy supports ontological realism. (It also supports ontic realism, though I haven't explored this in depth here.) This realism is arrived at by (1) diagenic enquiry discovering ontological structures that are independent of human existence (for example, those of the essence of truth), and (2) arguing that a central error of metaphysics and its defining orientation to *Seiendheit* is that it thinks the nature of being on the basis of beings or of the relation of being to beings. This leads to the claim that beyng is independent of beings. This does not entail metaphysical transcendence, but the view that beyng is an immanent ground enabling beings, such that there is a one-directional order of dependence.

Sixth, the most originary concept of the essence of truth in *Beiträge* is differential, not *a-lēthic*. It is arrived at by the conjunction of Heidegger's ontology of difference and his question into the ground of originary ἀλήθεια or openness and λήθη or concealment/withdrawal. Since the question of the essence of truth is the preliminary question via which an account of the event can be given, failing to mark the shift from an *a-lēthic* to a differential concept of the essence of truth results in an account of the event in terms of the *a-lēthic* framework. But this utterly misconstrues the event and, consequently, prevents both (1) the genetic definition of related evental concepts and (2) the possibility of a radical critique of metaphysics, since the genetic explanation of metaphysics is simultaneously precluded.

Seventh, Heidegger's ontology of difference entails a form of 'pure' difference that is diagenically prior to the ontological difference, the manifestation of beings, and the relations between manifest beings, not derived *a posteriori* from them or their relations. One of the most substantial mid-century engagements with Heidegger's philosophy of difference is found in Deleuze's *Différence et répétition*. In the interest of bringing Heidegger's theory of events into closer dialogue with other theories of events, I want to point out the following. In *Différence et répétition*, Deleuze argued that Heidegger made important contributions to the liberation of difference from the framework of identity and representation, and this shows an essential continuity between their respective programmes. Nonetheless, Deleuze seems to suggest that Heidegger's concept of difference – in its early form as the ontological difference and in its late form under the guise of 'das Selbe' or 'the Same' in *Identität und Differenz* – ultimately retained a subjugation to identity. Deleuze, however, did not have access to *Beiträge* or the related private manuscripts. The concept of difference they contain moves beyond that accounted for in *Différence et répétition*'s critique of Heidegger and shows that his ontology is more similar to Deleuze's than the latter recognised. Deleuze argues for a distinctive kind of synthetic transcendental field, which he calls the 'virtual'. This is a differential field that comprises differential structures, which he names virtual 'multiplicities' or 'dialectical Ideas', and their transformations, which he names virtual 'events'. Heidegger's ontological axes of ground describe a similar transcendental field, one that at its most advanced stages in the account of the event is also differential. There, the differential logic of the event is a transcendental logic of beyng. Though there remain important distinctions between Heidegger and Deleuze, this shows a little-explored confluence of their philosophies. It also shows the proper ground for a comparative analysis of Heidegger's theory of events in relation to those of his successors such as Deleuze.

Eighth, in *Beiträge*, beyng as event is the differentiation of 'pure' difference from itself, together with the logic of determinateness this generates. The logic of determinateness is the logic of the event's self-intensification, distension, and elaboration, that is, the origination of the Da expressed in the term 'Da-sein'. Truth, ground, time-space, appropriation, and expropriation articulate the event's logic of determinateness, or, in other words, form the basic logic of the world. Yet the event includes an excess of (primal) difference over the logic of determinateness, which makes the event liminal with respect to determination. As such, beyng as event is irreducible to appropriation, expropriation, or any of the other terms just listed. This also means that Heidegger's ontology entails not only a differential theory of the event and of truth, but of (1) ground and (2) time and space, or, rather, temporalisation and spatialisation, that is, the evental genesis of time and space.

Finally, a few interesting points follow from this, especially in relation to appropriation and expropriation. Appropriation and expropriation name the event's differential origination of structures of propriety and alienation from propriety. The genesis of a structure of propriety is the genesis of a diagenically first 'something' that can sustain any properties or characteristics proper to it at all. In other words, it is the genesis of something that can have a predicate and, thereby, of the framework within which subject predication works. This means the same as to say that the genesis of propriety (and alienation from propriety) is the genesis of identity, albeit in a quasi-stable form. But, the genesis of structures of propriety and alienation from propriety is none other than that of ontological distortion (the 'distorted essence' of beyng or of truth), for the constitution of each entails a structural obfuscation of aspects of the other and of the differential logic of the event whereby it was originated. This means that the genesis of identity is the genesis of distortion and that the logic of identity is the logic of that distortion. This becomes a logic of outright alienation when the differential origin of that distortion, the differential ground of identity, becomes obfuscated. Such obfuscation takes place, for instance, in the Western metaphysical tradition's commitment to the principle of identity as the first principle of thought, to the idea that what *is* is what can be represented in subject predication, and that what happens when something happens – an event – is merely an alteration in the predicates of a subject. In this picture, the alienation characterising the historical framework of metaphysics is rooted in the principle of identity. *As such*, identity *is* alienation. Nonetheless, this alienation is enabled by distortion irreducible from the structure of beyng. Heidegger's ontology of events offers a powerful route for our efforts to remedy alienation, think a pre-representational logic of difference, and grapple with the logic of distortion at the heart of being.

Bibliography

'GA' designations refer to Heidegger's *Gesamtausgabe* volumes.
Multiple works by the same author are referenced alphabetically by title.

Althusser, Louis, 'The Underground Current of the Materialism of the Encounter', trans. G. M. Goshgarian, in *Philosophy of the Encounter: Later Writings, 1978–1987*, ed. Francois Matheron and Oliver Corpet (London: Verso, 2006), 163–207.

Aquinas, Thomas, *Quaestiones disputatae de veritate*, in three two-part volumes, in *Opera omnia iussu Leonis XIII P. M. edita, t. 22.* (Rome: Ad Sanctae Sabinae/Editori di San Tommaso, 1975, 1970, 1972, 1973, 1976).

Aristotle, *Metaphysica*, ed. Werner Jaeger, Oxford Classical Texts (Oxford: Clarendon Press, 1957).

Aristotle, *Metaphysics*, trans. Hippocrates G. Apostle (Grinnell, IA: The Peripatetic Press, 1979).

Aristotle, *Metaphysics*, trans. W. D. Ross, in *The Complete Works of Aristotle*, Volume 2 (Princeton: Princeton University Press, 1984).

Aristotle, *Metaphysics*, trans. Hugh Tredennick (Cambridge, MA: Loeb Classical Library/ Harvard University Press, 1989).

Badiou, Alain, *L'être et l'événement* (Editions du Seuil, 1988). English: *Being and Event*, trans. Oliver Feltham (London: Continuum, 2005).

Bahoh, James, 'Deleuze's Theory of Dialectical Ideas: The Influence of Lautman and Heidegger', *Deleuze and Guattari Studies* 13, no. 1 (2019), 19–53.

Barber, Daniel Colucciello, 'On Post-Heideggerean Difference: Derrida and Deleuze', *Southern Journal of Philosophy* 47, no. 2 (2009), 113–29.

Beistegui, Miguel de, *The New Heidegger* (London: Continuum, 2005).

Beistegui, Miguel de, *Truth and Genesis: Philosophy as Differential Ontology* (Bloomington: Indiana University Press, 2004).

Bernasconi, Robert, *The Question of Language in Heidegger's History of Being* (Atlantic Highlands, NJ: Humanities Press Inc., 1985).

Bowden, Sean, *The Priority of Events: Deleuze's 'Logic of Sense'* (Edinburgh: Edinburgh University Press, 2011).

Braver, Lee, 'Analyzing Heidegger: A History of Analytic Reactions to Heidegger', in *Interpreting Heidegger*, ed. Daniel Dahlstrom (Cambridge: Cambridge University Press, 2011), 235–55.

Braver, Lee, *Groundless Grounds: A Study of Wittgenstein and Heidegger* (Cambridge, MA: The MIT Press, 2012).

Brogan, Walter, 'Da-sein and the Leap of Being', in *Companion to Heidegger's 'Contributions to Philosophy'*, ed. Charles E. Scott, Susan M. Schoenbohm, Daniela Vallega-Neu, and Alejandro Vallega (Bloomington: Indiana University Press, 2001), 171–80.

Capobianco, Richard, 'Coda on Being is (Not) Meaning', Heidegger Circle Forum Post, 30 August 2013.

Capobianco, Richard, *Engaging Heidegger* (Toronto: University of Toronto Press, 2010).

Capobianco, Richard, *Heidegger's Way of Being* (Toronto: University of Toronto Press, 2014).

Carman, Taylor, 'Heidegger's Concept of Presence', *Inquiry* 38, no. 4 (December 1995), 431–53.

Dahlstrom, Daniel, *Heidegger's Concept of Truth* (Cambridge: Cambridge University Press, 2001).

Dastur, Françoise, 'Phenomenology of the Event: Waiting and Surprise', *Hypatia* 15, no. 4 (Fall 2000), 178–89.

Davidson, Donald, *Essays on Actions and Events* (Oxford: Oxford University Press, 2001).

DeLanda, Manuel, *Intensive Science and Virtual Philosophy* (London: Continuum, 2002).

Deleuze, Gilles, *Différence et répétition* (Paris: Presses Universitaires de France, 1993). English: *Difference and Repetition*, trans. Paul Patton (New York: Columbia University Press, 1994).

Deleuze, Gilles, *Kant's Critical Philosophy: The Doctrine of the Faculties* (Minneapolis: University of Minnesota Press, 2003).

Deleuze, Gilles, *Logique du sens* (Paris: Les Éditions de Minuit, 1969). English: *The Logic of Sense*, ed. Constantin V. Boundas and trans. Mark Lester with Charles Stivale (New York: Columbia University Press, 1990).

Derrida, Jacques, *L'écriture et la différence* (Paris: Éditions du Seuil, 1967).

Derrida, Jacques, *Marges de la philosophie* (Paris: Les Éditions de Minuit, 1972).

Dreyfus, Hubert L. and Mark A. Wrathall, eds, *A Companion to Heidegger* (Oxford: Blackwell, 2005).

Dronsfield, Jonathan, 'Between Deleuze and Heidegger There Never Is Any Difference', in *French Interpretations of Heidegger: An Exceptional Reception*, ed. David Pettigrew and François Raffoul (New York: SUNY Press, 2008), 151–66.

Emad, Parvis, *Translation and Interpretation: Learning from 'Beiträge'* (Bucharest: Zeta Books 2012).

Evans, Fred, *The Multivoiced Body: Society and Communication in the Age of Diversity* (New York: Columbia University Press, 2008).

Farin, Ingo and Jeff Malpas, eds, *Reading Heidegger's* Black Notebooks *1931–1941* (Cambridge, MA: The MIT Press, 2016).

Gabriel, Markus, 'Is Heidegger's "Turn" a Realist Project', *Meta: Research in Hermeneutics, Phenomenology, and Political Philosophy*, Special Issue (2014), 44–73. www.metajournal.org

Gabriel, Markus, *Transcendental Ontology: Essays in German Idealism* (London: Continuum, 2011).

Gabriel, Markus and Slavoj Žižek, *Mythology, Madness and Laughter: Subjectivity in German Idealism* (London: Continuum, 2009).

Gilliland, Rex, 'Transformation in Deleuze and Heidegger: Serial and Thematic Repetition', *Philosophy Today* 49 (2005), 138–44.

Guignon, Charles, 'Heidegger's Concept of Freedom, 1927–1930', in *Interpreting Heidegger*, ed. Daniel Dahlstrom (Cambridge: Cambridge University Press, 2011), 79–105.

Heidegger, Martin, [GA65] *Beiträge zur Philosophie (Vom Ereignis)* (Frankfurt am Main: Klostermann, 2003). English: *Contributions to Philosophy: Of the Event*, trans. Richard Rojcewicz and Daniela Vallega-Neu (Bloomington: Indiana University Press, 2012). Alternative translation: *Contributions to Philosophy (From Enowning)*, trans. Parvis Emad and Kenneth Maly (Bloomington: Indiana University Press, 1999).

Heidegger, Martin, [GA66] *Besinnung* (Frankfurt am Main: Klostermann, 1997). English: *Mindfulness*, trans. Parvis Emad and Thomas Kalary (New York: Continuum, 2006).

Heidegger, Martin, [GA79] *Bremer und Freiburger Vorträge*, ed. Petra Jaeger (Frankfurt am Main: Klostermann, 1994). English: *Bremen and Freiburg Lectures: Insight Into That Which Is and Basic Principles of Thinking*, trans. Andrew J. Mitchell (Bloomington: Indiana University Press, 2012).

Heidegger, Martin, [GA71] *Das Ereignis* (Frankfurt am Main: Klostermann, 2009). English: *The Event*, trans. Richard Rojcewicz (Bloomington: Indiana University Press, 2013).

Heidegger, Martin, [GA69] *Die Geschichte des Seyns* (Frankfurt am Main: Klostermann, 1998).

Heidegger, Martin, [GA24] *Die Grundprobleme der Phänomenologie* (Frankfurt am Main: Klostermann, 1997). English: *The Basic Problems of Phenomenology*, revised edition, trans. Albert Hofstadter (Bloomington: Indiana University Press, 1988).

Heidegger, Martin, [GA40] *Einführung in die Metaphysik* (Frankfurt am Main: Klostermann, 1983). English: *Introduction to Metaphysics*, trans. Gregory Fried and Richard Polt (New Haven: Yale University Press, 2000).

Heidegger, Martin, [GA77] *Feldweg-Gespräche* (Frankfurt am Main: Klosterman, 2007). English: *Country Path Conversations*, trans. Bret W. Davis (Bloomington: Indiana University Press, 2010).

Heidegger, Martin, [GA1] *Frühe Schriften* (Frankfurt am Main: Klostermann, 1978). English: *Supplements: From the Earliest Essays to Being and Time and Beyond*, ed. John van Buren (Albany: SUNY Press, 2002).

Heidegger, Martin, [GA53] *Hölderlins Hymne "Der Ister"* (Frankfurt am Main: Klostermann, 1984).

Heidegger, Martin, [GA39] *Hölderlins Hymnen "Germanien" und "Der Rhein"* (Frankfurt am Main: Klostermann, 1980).

Heidegger, Martin, [GA5] *Holzwege* (Frankfurt am Main: Klostermann, 2003). English: *Off the Beaten Track*, ed. and trans. Julian Young and Kenneth Haynes (Cambridge: Cambridge University Press, 2002).

Heidegger, Martin, [GA11] *Identität und Differenz* (Frankfurt am Main: Klostermann, 2006). English translations of the texts in this volume are dispersed in multiple publications. The texts I reference are found in *Identity and Difference*, trans. Joan Stambaugh (Chicago: University of Chicago Press, 1969). My citations to these texts in GA11 include the English page numbers found in the Stambaugh edition.

Heidegger, Martin, [GA3] *Kant und das Problem der Metaphysik* (Frankfurt am Main: Klostermann, 1973). English: *Kant and the Problem of Metaphysics*, fifth edition, enlarged, trans. Richard Taft (Bloomington: Indiana University Press, 1997).

Heidegger, Martin, [GA67] *Metaphysik und Nihilismus* (Frankfurt am Main: Klostermann, 1999).

Heidegger, Martin, *Nietzsche*, ed. David Farrell Krell, 4 volumes (San Francisco: Harper and Row, 1979, 1984, 1987, 1982).

Heidegger, Martin, *Poetry, Language, Thought*, trans. Albert Hofstadter (New York: Perennial Classics, HarperCollins, 2001).

Heidegger, Martin, *Qu'est-ce que la metaphysic?*, trans. Henry Corbin (Paris: Gallimard, 1938).

Heidegger, Martin, [GA42] *Schelling: Vom Wesen der Menschlichen Freiheit* (Frankfurt am Main: Klostermann, 1988). English: *Schelling's Treatise on the Essence of Human Freedom*, trans. Joan Stambaugh (Athens: Ohio University Press, 1985).

Heidegger, Martin, *Sein und Zeit* (Tübingen: Max Niemeyer Verlag, 2006). English: *Being and Time*, trans. John Macquarrie and Edward Robinson (New York: Harper and Row, 1962). Alternative translation: *Being and Time*, trans. Joan Stambaugh, revised and with a foreword by Dennis J. Schmidt (Albany: SUNY Press, 2010).

Heidegger, Martin, *Towards the Definition of Philosophy*, trans. Ted Sadler (London: Continuum, 2000). In German, this is published as part of GA56/57.

Heidegger, Martin, [GA70] *Über den Anfang* (Frankfurt am Main: Klostermann, 2005).

Heidegger, Martin, [GA94] *Überlegungen II–VI (Schwarze Hefte 1931–1938)* (Frankfurt am Main: Klostermann, 2014). English: *Ponderings II–VI: Black Notebooks 1931–1938* (Bloomington and Indianapolis: Indiana University Press, 2016).

Heidegger, Martin, [GA95] *Überlegungen VII–XI (Schwarze Hefte 1938–1939)* (Frankfurt am Main: Klostermann, 2014). English: *Ponderings VII–XI: Black Notebooks 1938–1939* (Bloomington and Indianapolis: Indiana University Press, 2017).

Heidegger, Martin, [GA96] *Überlegungen XII–XV (Schwarze Hefte 1939–1941)* (Frankfurt am Main: Klostermann, 2014). English: *Ponderings XII–XV: Black Notebooks 1939–1941* (Bloomington and Indianapolis: Indiana University Press, 2017).

Heidegger, Martin, [GA7] *Vorträge und Aufsätze* (Frankfurt am Main: Klostermann, 2000).

Heidegger, Martin, [GA8] *Was heisst Denken?* (Frankfurt am Main: Klostermann, 2002). English: *What is Called Thinking?*, trans. J. Glenn Gray (New York: Harper and Row, 1968). Alternative translation: 'What Calls for Thinking?', trans. Fred D. Wieck and J. Glenn Gray, in *Basic Writings*, ed. David Farrell Krell (New York: HarperCollins, 1993), 365–92.

Heidegger, Martin, [GA9] *Wegmarken* (Frankfurt am Main: Klostermann, 2004). English: *Pathmarks*, ed. William McNeill (Cambridge: Cambridge University Press, 1998).

Heidegger, Martin, 'Zeit und Sein', in [GA14] *Zur Sache des Denkens* (Frankfurt am Main: Klostermann, 2007).

Heidegger, Martin, [GA14] *Zur Sache des Denkens* (Frankfurt am Main: Klostermann, 2007). Partial English translation: *On Time and Being*, trans. Joan Stambaugh (Chicago: University of Chicago Press, 2002).

Herrmann, Friedrich-Wilhelm von, *Wege ins Ereignis. Zu Heideggers 'Beiträgen zur Philosopie'* (Frankfurt am Main: Klostermann, 1994).

Hughes, Joe, *Deleuze's* Difference and Repetition (London: Continuum, 2009).

Justaert, Kristien, '"Ereignis" (Heidegger) or "La clameur de l'être" (Deleuze): Topologies for a Theology beyond Representation?', *Philosophy and Theology: Marquette University Quarterly* 19, nos 1–2 (2007), 241–56.

Kant, Immanuel, *Kritik der reinen Vernunft* (Hamburg: Meiner, 1998). English: *Critique of Pure Reason*, trans. Norman Kemp Smith (New York: Palgrave Macmillan, 2003).

Lautman, Albert, *Essai sur l'unité des mathématiques et devers écrits* (Paris: Union general d'éditions, 1977).

Lautman, Albert, *Les mathématiques, les idées et le reel physique* (Paris: J. Vrin, 2006). English: *Mathematics, Ideas, and the Physical Real*, trans. Simon B. Duffy (London: Continuum, 2011).

Leibniz, G. W., 'Discourse on Metaphysics', in *Philosophical Essays*, ed. and trans. Roger Ariew and Daniel Garber (Indianapolis: Hackett, 1989), 35–68.

Livingston, Paul, *The Logic of Being: Realism, Truth, and Time* (Evanston: Northwestern University Press, 2017).

Lucretius, *On the Nature of Things*, trans. W. H. D. Rouse, revised by Martin F. Smith (Cambridge, MA: Harvard University Press, 2002).

Malabou, Catherine, *The Heidegger Change: On the Fantastic in Philosophy* (Albany: SUNY Press, 2011).

McNeill, William, 'On the Essence and Concept of *Ereignis*: From Technē to Technicity', in *After Heidegger?*, ed. Gregory Fried and Richard Polt (London and New York: Rowman and Littlefield, 2018), 251–62.

McNeill, William, *The Glance of the Eye: Heidegger, Aristotle, and the Ends of Theory* (Albany: SUNY Press, 1999).

McNeill, William, 'The Time of *Contributions to Philosophy*', in *Companion to Heidegger's Contributions to Philosophy*, ed. Charles E. Scott, Susan M. Schoenbohm, Daniela

Vallega-Neu, and Alejandro Vallega (Bloomington: Indiana University Press, 2001), 129–49.

Meillassoux, Quentin, *After Finitude: An Essay on the Necessity of Contingency*, trans. Ray Brassier (New York: Continuum, 2008).

Mitchell, Andrew, *The Fourfold: Reading the Late Heidegger* (Evanston: Northwestern University Press, 2015).

Mitchell, Andrew and Peter Trawny, eds, *Heidegger's* Black Notebooks*: Responses to Anti-Semitism* (New York: Columbia University Press, 2017).

Nancy, Jean-Luc, *Being Singular Plural*, trans. Robert D. Richardson and Anne E. O'Byrne (Stanford: Stanford University Press, 2000).

Neu, Daniela, *Die Notwendigkeit der Gründung im Zeitalter der Dekonstruktion* (Berlin: Duncker & Humblot, 1997).

Nietzsche, Friedrich, *The Gay Science*, trans. Walter Kaufmann (New York: Vintage Books, 1974).

Peden, Knox, *Spinoza Contra Phenomenology: French Rationalism from Cavaillès to Deleuze* (Stanford: Stanford University Press, 2014).

Plato, *Republic*, trans. Allan Bloom (New York: Basic Books, 1968).

Plato, *The Collected Works of Plato*, ed. Edith Hamilton and Huntington Cairns (New York: Pantheon Books, 1961).

Polt, Richard, 'Ereignis', in *A Companion to Heidegger*, ed. Hubert L. Dreyfus and Mark A. Wrathall (Oxford: Blackwell, 2005), 375–91.

Polt, Richard, *The Emergency of Being: On Heidegger's Contributions to Philosophy* (Ithaca, NY: Cornell University Press, 2006).

Powell, Jason, *Heidegger's 'Contributions to Philosophy'* (London: Continuum, 2007).

Rae, Gavin, *Ontology in Heidegger and Deleuze: A Comparative Analysis* (New York: Palgrave Macmillan, 2014).

Richardson, William J., *Heidegger: Through Phenomenology to Thought* (New York: Fordham University Press, 2003).

Rockmore, Tom, *On Heidegger's Nazism and Philosophy* (Berkeley and Los Angeles: University of California Press, 1992).

Romano, Claude, *Event and World*, trans. Shane Mackinlay (New York: Fordham University Press, 2009).

Ruin, Hans, 'Contributions to Philosophy', in *A Companion to Heidegger*, ed. Hubert L. Dreyfus and Mark A. Wrathall (Malden: Blackwell, 2005), 358–74.

Saussure, Ferdinand de, *Course in General Linguistics* (Chicago, IL: Open Court, 1997).

Schelling, F. W. J., *Philosophische Untersuchungen über das Wesen der menschlichen Freiheit* (Hamburg: Meiner, 2001). English: *Philosophical Investigations into the Essence of Human Freedom*, trans. Jeff Love and Johannes Schmidt (Albany: SUNY Press, 2006).

Scott, Charles E., Susan M. Schoenbohm, Daniela Vallega-Neu, and Alejandro Vallega, eds, *Companion to Heidegger's Contributions to Philosophy* (Bloomington: Indiana University Press, 2001).

Selcer, Daniel J., 'Heidegger's Leibniz and Abyssal Identity', *Continental Philosophy Review* 36 (2003), 303–24.

Selcer, Daniel, *Philosophy and the Book: Early Modern Figures of Material Inscription* (London: Continuum, 2010).

Sextus Empiricus, *adv. Grammaticos* L. I, c. 13, ed. Fabricius (Leipzig: J. F. Gloedichtius's Sons Fr. Gloeditschii B. Filii, 1718).

Sheehan, Thomas, 'A Paradigm Shift in Heidegger Research', *Continental Philosophy Review* 34 (2001), 183–202.

Sheehan, Thomas, 'Astonishing! Things Make Sense!', *Gatherings: The Heidegger Circle Annual* 1 (2011), 1–25.

Sheehan, Thomas, 'Facticity and *Ereignis*', in *Interpreting Heidegger*, ed. Daniel Dahlstrom (Cambridge: Cambridge University Press, 2011), 42–68.

Sheehan, Thomas, *Making Sense of Heidegger: A Paradigm Shift* (London: Rowman and Littlefield, 2015).

Sheehan, Thomas, 'The Turn', in *Martin Heidegger: Key Concepts*, ed. Bret W. Davis (Durham: Acumen Publishing Limited, 2010), 82–101.

Sholtz, Janae, *The Invention of a People: Heidegger and Deleuze on Art and the Political* (Edinburgh: Edinburgh University Press, 2015).

Sholtz, Janae and Leonard Lawlor, 'Heidegger and Deleuze', in *The Bloomsbury Companion to Heidegger*, ed. François Raffoul and Eric S. Nelson (London: Bloomsbury, 2013), 417–24.

Sokolowski, Robert, *Introduction to Phenomenology* (Cambridge: Cambridge University Press, 2000).

Spinoza, Baruch, *Ethics*, in *The Essential Spinoza*, ed. Michael L. Morgan and trans. Samuel Shirley (Indianapolis: Hackett Publishing Company, 2006), 1–161.

Stambaugh, Joan, *The Finitude of Being* (Albany: SUNY Press, 1992).

'The Ricks Must be Crazy', *Rick and Morty*, television (Cartoon Network, 30 August 2015).

Vallega, Alejandro, *Heidegger and the Issue of Space: Thinking on Exilic Grounds* (University Park: The Pennsylvania State University Press, 2003).

Vallega-Neu, Daniela, '*Ereignis*: The Event of Appropriation', in *Martin Heidegger: Key Concepts*, ed. Bret W. Davis (Durham: Acumen Publishing Limited, 2010), 140–54.

Vallega-Neu, Daniela, *Heidegger's Contributions to Philosophy* (Bloomington: Indiana University Press, 2003).

Vallega-Neu, Daniela, 'Heidegger's Poietic Writings: From *Contributions to Philosophy* to *Das Ereignis*', in *Heidegger and Language*, ed. Jeffrey Powell (Bloomington and Indianapolis: Indiana University Press, 2013).

Vallega-Neu, Daniela, *Heidegger's Poietic Writings: From* Contributions to Philosophy *to* The Event (Bloomington: Indiana University Press, 2018).

Vuillemin, Jules, *L'Héritage Kantien et la révolution copernicienne: Fichte, Cohen, Heidegger* (Paris: Presses Universitaires de France, 1954).

Wood, David, *Time After Time* (Bloomington: Indiana University Press, 2007).

Wrathall, Mark A., *Heidegger and Unconcealment: Truth, Language, and History* (New York: Cambridge University Press, 2011).

Wrathall, Mark A., 'Unconcealment', in *A Companion to Heidegger*, ed. Hubert L. Dreyfus and Mark A. Wrathall (Malden: Blackwell, 2005), 337–57.

Young, Julian, *Heidegger's Philosophy of Art* (Cambridge: Cambridge, 2001).

Ziarek, Krzysztof, 'Giving Its Word: Event (as) Language', in *Heidegger and Language*, ed. Jeffrey Powell (Bloomington and Indianapolis: Indiana University Press, 2013).

Ziarek, Krzysztof, *Language after Heidegger* (Bloomington and Indianapolis: Indiana University Press, 2013).

Index